**Praise for**

"Wow! *Scale* gives you a step-by-step process to grow your business the right way. I've mentored students from some of the best business schools in the nation, including Harvard, USC, and UCLA, and I would give this book to everyone. In fact, I would tell every business owner that they need to read this book. Understanding *Scale* will save you from reviewing twenty-five other business books."

—SANDY GOOCH, cofounder, Mrs. Gooch's
Natural Food Market (later acquired by Whole Foods)

"*Scale* is a masterwork that encapsulates enough practical wisdom to fill several books. The authors had the experience and talent to craft an exquisite cross-section of the why and how of sales, strategy, and operations in a fresh format for founder-builders. They've distilled the essence of complex management situations into practical summaries, with plenty of anecdotes to bring them to life. This book will ignite years of successful growth for any reader who applies what they share."

—ROB KAUTZ, private investor and strategist, former CEO of
Wolfgang Puck Worldwide

"Rapid growth without a good plan can kill a business faster than no growth at all. This book will show you how to grow smart!"

—JOHN JANTSCH, author,
*Duct Tape Marketing* and *Duct Tape Selling*

"David and Jeff, as highly successful business owners of multiple businesses, not only reveal novel ideas that generate huge multiples but also give you tools of *how to think* so you can invent and design actionable processes for *your* business. By focusing on best practices from these top business leaders, you too can generate *maximum* results for your business and your life."

—STEPHANIE HARKNESS, entrepreneur and former chairman
of the National Association of Manufacturers

"With so much global attention on founders and start-ups, this is a refreshing read on innovative approaches to scaling companies and reducing their owner dependency. Scale is a must-read for anyone interested in founders and scaling firms."

—JONATHAN ORTMANS, president, Global Entrepreneurship Week, and senior fellow, Kauffman Foundation

"I've been building businesses for over thirty years and this is the book I wish I'd read years ago. Jeff and David have laid out a concrete framework to scale a company, along with the practical details to create and sustain rapid growth. Every business owner needs to read this book."

—PATTY DEDOMINIC, entrepreneur and past chairman of the Los Angeles Area Chamber of Commerce

"Most owners think that in order to grow and scale a business, they need to work harder and sacrifice their personal lives. Here's a simple road map that will put you on a growth trajectory by working less—a paradox that you'll come to embrace by following this insightful book's path to business success and personal freedom."

—BILLIE DRAGOO, president, National Association of Women Business Owners

"Hoffman and Finkel have hit a grand slam with Scale. Each of the chapters is worth its weight in gold and jam-packed with immediately actionable guidance."

—Jason Jennings, *New York Times* bestselling author, *Think BIG, Act Small* and *The Reinventors*

# BUSINESS OWNER TOOLKIT

Access 36 FREE Business Coaching Tools to grow your business and get your life back

## For a Limited Time Every Reader Gets This $1,375 Business Growth Tool Kit — FREE!

As our way of supporting you to grow your business, we've created a unique online web tool kit to help you apply the ideas you'll learn in this book.

To register, all you need to do is go online to www.ScaleYour BusinessToolKit.com and gain immediate access to this powerful collection of business growth tools. It's designed to help business owners like you apply the *"Scale"* concepts in the book to grow your business and get your life back.

### Here's What You Get as Part of This Valuable *Free* Bonus:

**Over a dozen video training modules** to help make building your business *easier* and *faster*. These include the following five "short courses":

- The *"Grow Your Sales"* Short Course (6 Training Videos and PDF Action Guide)
- The *"Scale Your Operations"* Short Course (3 Training Videos and PDF Action Guide)
- The *"Financial Pillar"* Short Course (6 Training Videos and PDF Action Guide)

(more...)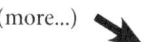

- The *"Strategic Planning"* Short Course (4 Training Videos and PDF Action Guide)
- The *"Time Mastery"* Short Course (3 Training Videos and PDF Action Guide)

You'll also get **free PDF downloads** of the business growth tools we highlighted in the book (including the 4 page *Strategic Planning Document*, the *Sweet Spot Analysis Tool*, and several others).

All this and more are available for a limited time at **www.Scale YourBuinessToolKit.com** (Details in Appendix.)

---

To access these web tools to scale your business and get your life back just go to

**www.ScaleYourBusinessToolKit.com**

# SCALE

# SCALE

Seven Proven Principles to Grow Your Business and Get Your Life Back

## JEFF HOFFMAN
## AND DAVID FINKEL

Copyright © 2025, 2022, 2014 Jeffery Hoffman and David Finkel. All rights reserved.

All rights reserved. No part of the material protected by this copyright may be reproduced or utilized in any form, electronic or mechanical, including photocopying, recording, scanning, or by any information storage and retrieval system, except as permitted under Section 107 or 108 of the 1976 United States Copyright Act, without written permission from the copyright owner.

This publication is designed to provide accurate and authoritative information in regard to the subject matter covered. It is sold with the understanding that the publisher is not engaged in rendering legal, accounting, or other professional service. If legal advice or other expert assistance is required, the service of a competent professional person should be sought.

While the publisher and author have used their best efforts in preparing this book, they make no representations with respect to the accuracy or completeness of the contents of this book and specifically disclaim any implied warranties of merchantability or fitness for a particular purpose. Neither the publisher nor author shall be liable for any loss of profit or any other commercial damages, including but not limited to special, incidental, consequential, or other damages.

The following trademarks are the exclusive property of Maui Millionaires, LLC and are used with permission: Self-Employment Trap™ and Sweet Spot Analysis™. The following trademarks are the exclusive property of Maui Mastermind (NV), LLC and are used with permission: Maui Mastermind® and Level Three Road Map™.

Charts and graphs courtesy of Maui Mastermind®.

Hoffman, Jeff.
   Scale : seven proven principles to grow your business and get your life back / Jeff Hoffman and David Finkel.
      pages cm
      Includes index.
ISBN:
Paperback: 978-1-958545-00-3
Hardcover: 978-1-958545-04-1
   1. Small business—Growth.  2. Corporations—Growth.  3. Strategic planning.
   4. Business planning.  5. Entrepreneurship.  I. Finkel, David.  II. Title.
     HD62.7.H6274 2014     658.4'06—dc23     2014020638

**JEFF:**

To my amazing family, who have endured and supported me throughout the high-speed roller-coaster journey I dragged them on by choosing to be an entrepreneur

**DAVID:**

To my wife, Heather, and my sons Adam, Matthew, and Joshua—thank you for making my life so much richer

# CONTENTS

Introduction     1

**PART I**

**Building on a Solid Foundation**     7

**PRINCIPLE ONE**
Build a Business, Not a Job     9

**PRINCIPLE TWO**
Build on the Scalable Base of Systems, Team,
and Internal Controls     23

**PRINCIPLE THREE**
Understand Why Your Customers *Really*
Do Business with You     37

**PART II**

**Focusing on Fewer, Better Things**     61

**PRINCIPLE FOUR**
Create the *Right* Strategic Plan     63

**PRINCIPLE FIVE**
Learn to Read the World So You Build for
Tomorrow's Marketplace     95

## PART III

**Obstacles to Scaling (and How to Overcome Them)**   107

### PRINCIPLE SIX
Remove the Predictable Obstacles to Growth—
Pillar by Pillar   109

### YOUR SALES/MARKETING PILLAR
Build Scalable Lead-Generation and Conversion
Systems   119

### YOUR OPERATIONS PILLAR
Three Breakthrough Ideas to Scale Your Capacity   147

### YOUR FINANCE PILLAR
CFO Secrets to Manage Cash Flow, Improve
Margins, and Fund Growth   171

### YOUR TEAM PILLAR
Attracting, Retaining, and Unleashing Talent   197

### YOUR EXECUTIVE LEADERSHIP PILLAR
Alignment, Accountability, and Leading Your
Leadership Team   209

## PART IV

**You DO Have the Time**   227

### PRINCIPLE SEVEN
You *Do* Have the Time to Scale Your Company   229

### PUTTING IT ALL INTO ACTION   251

Acknowledgments   259

Appendix: The Sccale Tool Kit – Your FREE $1,375 Gift
from the Authors   261

About the Authors   263

Index   267

A Final Message for Business Owners Who Want to
Get Their Lives Back Faster   277

# INTRODUCTION

In 1992, a 22-year-old undergrad dropped out of college to launch his own business. He wanted to be his own boss and decided to build a company selling health products. His sisters told him he was a "*$%*&^@" idiot, and his befuddled parents asked him softly if he wouldn't rather finish his degree first. But he was committed to make this, his first real attempt at formally building a business, a massive success. He bought the wholesale rights to a line of health products and invested his life savings ($3,200) in stocking inventory and setting up a small office, then spent long hours marketing the line, personally posting thousands of flyers and making hundreds of sales calls.

Eight months later, the business had failed; his family graciously never said "*I told you so.*" But the story doesn't end there. The good ones never do.

After taking some time to lick his wounds and salve his bruised ego, our now 25-year-old recent college grad made another go in a totally different business. His earlier failure had taught him some crucial lessons (including a sorely needed dose of humility). Cataloging his talents and interests, he decided on a new industry—info-marketing. He made a list of the top ten business leaders in this industry and approached each one, asking for the opportunity to interview them about how they had built such successful companies, and asking for any advice they could give to someone just starting out. Initially, these big players ignored him, but he was persistent, hounding them until he finally got eight of the ten to meet with him. In their interviews, these leaders spoke candidly about the lessons they had gleaned after decades in the business world, climbing the same peaks our young businessman wanted to scale. He took their advice to heart, following up on skills and topics they said he would have to understand to be successful. He read dozens of business books and made a study of how to successfully build a business.

Eight years later, he was an "overnight" success, the owner of one of the top real estate training companies in the United States, having trained more than 50,000 investors who went on to buy and sell over $1 billion of properties. With no debt or outside investors, his company generated over $3 million of annual operating profit and was valued at $10 million to $16 million. After he sold this company, he went on to found and build half a dozen other successful companies, each time leveraging the lessons and experiences from his earlier businesses.

In 2009 a mutual friend introduced him to a business superstar—a guy who had helped launch and grow one of the fastest-scaling companies of all time, Priceline.com, which had grown from $0 in sales to over $1 billion *in less than four years*. When the two of them met in Atlanta, they talked for hours, realizing they had a lot in common—especially their shared passion for mentoring and coaching other business owners. One had built several multimillion-dollar companies and personally trained more than 100,000 business owners; the other helped build a multi*billion*-dollar company that revolutionized an industry. But they both loved coaching and mentoring business owners to scale their companies.

You may have already guessed that the college dropout turned successful entrepreneur was David, and the Priceline.com superstar was Jeff. Like David, Jeff launched his first start-up, a software company, while still in college. Unlike David, Jeff and his team nailed it with their first company, which they later sold to American Express for millions. Priceline.com was actually Jeff's fifth start-up, and after the company went public and Jeff transitioned out of the business, he went on to be the CEO of uBid.com and RedTag.com. He even launched a very successful entertainment company, Black Sky Entertainment, which went on to generate over $100 million in sales.

We've both lived the life of serial entrepreneurs, not just launching companies, but leading them through those all-important middle years when a business must either stay stuck as an extension of the founder, or scale and grow independent of the owner. Over the years, we've grown our friendship and shared the stage teaching at various business conferences. During that time, we came to realize that we shared a complementary skill set and approach to growing companies. And we also learned that we had shared experiences of those scary, absorbing, and exciting years when these businesses began to grow at triple-digit rates or faster. We joked that at times it felt like we were on the back of a rodeo bull, holding on with all our might, praying for that eight-second buzzer to sound. The thing we discovered is that whereas in the rodeo those eight seconds are literal, in your business the buzzer doesn't go off for *years*.

We also realized that we shared a frustration with the existing business books that addressed scaling a company. Too many told readers what to do, but didn't have the details on *how* to do the what to do. That's why we decided to pool our years of experiences to write this book. We wanted to put in one place a structured, systematic approach not just to create growth, but, more important, to show you how to survive and enjoy that growth by leveraging the systems, team, and internal controls necessary to sustain that development over the long term. Following this methodology, not only do you get growth in sales and profits, but you'll also enjoy increased freedom as the business owner. You can build a company that is stable, vibrant, valuable, *and* a joy to own. This book contains the guiding principles and the concrete formulas you can apply to consistently create the dual results of business growth and personal freedom.

We are primarily serial entrepreneurs, not authors. We love building businesses, and have been fortunate to enjoy some big successes, and to have survived the stupid, messy mistakes that, looking back, were both predictable and avoidable. While we wouldn't trade our paths, we wanted to catalog and share our real-world lessons about how to do it better, smarter, and faster. This is the book we *wished* we had read when we were struggling to grow our earlier businesses.

Everything you read here has been tested and validated. It is proven to work; we've used it to build more than a dozen successful companies with combined sales in the billions. More important, over the past ten years, we've taught these ideas to more than 100,000 business owners around the world, and the results they've gotten have proved the concepts, strategies, and tools are transferable and get results. We wrote it so that you can read any chapter, put down the book, and immediately apply several of the key ideas the very next day in your business—generating immediate results.

The ultimate goal for a business owner is to build a company that he or she can one day sell, continue to scale, or even own passively. Most business owners reach for growth by working harder and personally trying to produce more. This is a flawed model that at best will lead to only moderate growth. At worst, this strategy can literally put your entire company at risk.

Instead, we will introduce you to the Level Three Road Map, a comprehensive model for building and scaling your business. Essentially the Level Three Road Map will help you go from a Level One business (a start-up), through Level Two (an owner-reliant company), to Level Three (a rapid growth or "exit stage" company).

The bottom line is that scaling your company and reaching the ambitious goals that you really want requires that you move beyond an "owner-reliant" business to one that is systems driven, with a solid management team and intelligent business controls in place—a Level Three business.

## Overview of the Book

First and foremost, this is a book about rapid growth, and how you can build a scalable business that not only consistently grows, but also sustains that growth over time. What you'll come to learn is that a direct by-product of building your business the right way is that you'll get your life back. It is a broken model that says you must work 80-hour weeks and sacrifice everything to grow your company.

You don't have to choose between your business and your life. Rather, if you do it right, you get your business *and* your life. In fact, we strongly believe that the only way to build a truly scalable business is by radically reducing its reliance on you, the owner, and supporting that rapid growth through systems, team, and internal business controls.

Part one of the book focuses on building a solid foundation. You'll learn the essence of the Level Three Road Map. This structured formula to scale your company not only will help you create and sustain rapid growth, but at the same time will help you dramatically reduce the company's reliance on you. It closes with a simple tool to help you clarify your business context—the market you serve, the competition you face, and the position you want to claim in the market. We'll approach all three of these key dimensions of your business context in a radically different way than it's likely you have ever done before.

In part two, you'll identify the fastest leverage points to grow your company and how to turn those leverage points into a winning business strategy. What's more, we'll give you our step-by-step process to create a clear, actionable, one-page plan for executing your strategy on a rolling, 90-day basis. You'll also learn how to read the rapidly changing world around you in order to continually keep your business fresh and relevant to the marketplace.

In part three, we'll walk you through how to overcome the predictable obstacles to scaling, pillar by pillar. From lead generation to lead conversion, operations, finance, HR, and leadership, we'll give you proven solutions to dozens of the toughest challenges you'll face as you scale your company. You'll learn how to build "expert systems" to pull out the key know-how that currently is locked in the heads of a few, expensive employees and replicate that expertise in scalable systems; systematically grow your sales;

manage your cash flow; fund your growth; and create a culture of accountability inside your company.

In part four, you'll find out how to leverage your time to scale your company. We'll give you a brand-new model to think about time, and six simple time mastery strategies that will help you upgrade eight hours a week of time you are *already* working for higher and better uses to grow your company. We'll also give you a clear plan to implement the ideas from the book in a manageable way.

Whether you're a small, 3-person retailer doing $350,000 a year in sales, or a 22-person service business with annual sales of $2.5 million a year, or even a 255-person manufacturing company with $26 million a year in sales, this book will give you clear, actionable insights to grow and scale your company. Not only will the systems we share help you sustain long-term success, but you'll also see fast results.

The road map we've laid out for you to follow will enable you to scale your company the way you've always dreamed you could. We hope you'll reach out to us after you read this book, and share your own stories of success. (Our contact information is at the end of the book.)

---

### FREE Scale Tool Kit for Business Owners ($1,375 Value)

Because we know how important *executing* on these ideas is to help you enjoy the growth and freedom you want, we created a special website with a complete tool kit to help you apply what you'll learn in this book and get faster results. This free value add for readers like you includes downloadable **PDF** versions of the strategy and system-creation tools you'll be introduced to in this book, along with dozens of valuable video training sessions and other tools to help you build an owner independent company and get your life back.

To get immediate access these tools, just visit www.ScaleYourBusinessToolKit.com. (See the appendix for full details.)

# PART I

# Building on a Solid Foundation

Sometimes it feels more like my business owns me than me owning my business. I'm reasonably intelligent and self-motivated. I'm willing to put in the work to grow it, I just need the right road map to show me the best path to grow my company and get my life back.

—Comment by anonymous business owner at recent conference

# PRINCIPLE ONE

## BUILD A BUSINESS, NOT A JOB

To the outside world, Tom was success. He was running a successful wholesaling business in Florida earning a 7-figure income, but the 80-hour work weeks were getting to be too much. He had two young kids at home whom he wasn't seeing enough, and he felt torn between the demands of the business and being present with the important people in his life.

And if Tom was tired, so was his wife, Lee. She was tired of Tom missing out on family dinners, not being more involved in family activities, and of watching Tom's long hours impact his health.

Tom and Lee knew they needed to find a way to get out from under the crushing pressures of running the business day-to-day, but they didn't know how. Nor did they want to lose the momentum in the business. They felt the same way so many of us do—trapped by our business, like Atlas, holding the world on our shoulders, afraid to take a step back to reevaluate our position for fear that the whole thing could come crashing down around us. We dream of a way to grow our businesses without sacrificing our lives. But for Tom and Lee, as for a lot of us, it just wasn't obvious *how* to do this.

So Lee went online to research potential solutions. That's when she learned about a business workshop we were hosting in Arizona to raise money for several nonprofit charities.[1] The goal of this workshop was to teach business owners how to design their businesses both for growth and for reducing their reliance on the owner. Lee wanted to encourage Tom to continue to grow the business but to do so in a way that allowed him to spend more time with the family and didn't take such a harsh toll on his health. She bought him a ticket to the event and arranged his travel.

That workshop taught Tom many of the same tools, strategies, and principles that you'll be learning in this book. When Tom returned home, he immediately began implementing what he had learned and watched as his business blossomed. He also saw his family and his personal life bloom as well, since he finally learned how to manage them both together. Our goal in this book is to help you achieve that same balance of business growth and personal freedom.

Prior to the workshop, Tom thought his business needed him to oversee each and every detail. He believed he had to be there every moment of the day to drive his team forward to produce results. We introduced him to a new approach to scaling his company, one that he could implement in his business in bite-sized chunks that fit in around his responsibilities running the day-to-day. Quarter by quarter, he watched his business grow and its dependencies on him shrink. Seven years later, not only had he scaled his $5 million a year wholesaling business into a $23 million per year venture, but he had reduced his hours in the business to under twenty per week.

We share Tom's story with you not because he is special (he is a very nice guy with a lovely family, but he doesn't walk

---

[1] That event Tom attended raised over $250,000 for several charities, including the Justa Center in Phoenix. One of the best parts of building a successful business is the causes and groups you can support.

on water), but because he is likely a lot like you. You're driven to succeed but feel stuck as to the best way forward. You carry the weight of your business on your shoulders without complaint and are the linchpin that holds everything together. While you work hard to grow your business, what you may not have realized is that one of the most powerful chains holding you back from succeeding on the scale you want is the way you've designed your business in the first place. Your business's heavy reliance on you, which may have been necessary when you first launched your business, has become a major weakness.

Why is it that some owners can move from one successful company to another, seemingly with a golden touch? Because they have learned to master the critical methodology of building a successful business. It's like the football coach who keeps winning everywhere he goes. He wins not because of the team he has at each new organization, but because he has a *system* for building winning football programs. While every business is different, just like every team, it's our belief that the commonalities of building a successful business far outweigh their specialized differences. What's more, you likely already know enough of the specialized idiosyncrasies for your industry. If you just mapped them onto a better model of building a business, you'd soon enjoy a radically enhanced success with your business.

Still, there are going to be many owners who say, "But my business is different. It's special." What they never realize is that by asserting their business's specialness, they've locked themselves into being involved in every detail of that business. Their belief that their business can't be weaned off its reliance on them since it is so specialized, complicated, or unique is one of the most expensive limiting beliefs they could ever own. It literally costs them millions of dollars of lost growth. What's more, it also costs them their freedom as they become trapped in the very business they once launched to help them become free. If you think your business is unlike any other company out there, you miss the chance to learn from what other successful companies and business owners have spent years learning and proving. Imagine a football team that had a chance to be coached by the winningest football coach of all time, but instead says, "We don't want your help because you coached other teams, not ours."

So why would a business owner turn his back on a proven methodology to sustainably grow his company, and instead lock himself into an expensive cycle of solo trial and error? Generally, it's because he equates reducing his business's reliance on him with a loss of control. He fears that by his letting go of the "control," major disasters will strike and the business will be irreparably harmed. The irony is that the more the owner feels like he is in "control," the more he isn't. Although the superficial reins of power may be his, at the core he doesn't own the business—the business owns him.

Take Sandy's example. She owned a very successful company that worked for large corporations planning and executing major promotional events and campaigns. When two of her key employees had family emergencies, she was the one who had to step in and fill in all the gaps. A third key employee went away on a previously planned vacation right in the middle of that business storm, leaving Sandy the sole manager left behind to deal with the stress and strain of the massively understaffed company.

It probably won't surprise you that when we asked Sandy what she would do if faced with the same family emergencies as these two key employees, Sandy said she would find a way to work *and* handle the emergency. As for what she would have done if she had been the one with the vacation planned for this time, well, she didn't even hesitate—she'd cancel the vacation to deal with the business crisis. When you centralize all the control on you, your business doesn't have the depth and strength to operate without you there. You've built a business—and backed yourself into a corner.

## The "Hit by a Bus" Test

We want to ask you an extremely important question, one that very few business owners ever allow themselves to consider because often the answer is too painful to contemplate:

If you were hit by a bus tomorrow (or otherwise incapacitated), what would happen to your business?

We surveyed more than 1,000 business owners over the past five years, and our findings revealed that if the average business owner became incapacitated and couldn't work, their business would fail in less than 30 days. Thirty days! Think about what this would mean for their families, employees, and customers. You put in all those years of blood, sweat, and tears to build something that could literally end in an instant.

Even if you are blessed with the health and good fortune never to be hurt or unable to work, that doesn't mean you're home free. The unfortunate reality is that most business owners build a job for themselves, not a business. The businesses they are creating are dependent on their showing up to run them, day in, day out. They have built what we call owner-reliant businesses, with long hours, no real freedom, and no defined exit strategy

Even "successful" businesses have to deal with this challenge. In fact, many owners of successful companies are so busy doing the day-to-day *job* of their business that they don't have the time or energy left to grow and develop it as a business. Here you are, having done all the hard work of growing sales and production, yet you're likely still so consumed by managing the day-to-day operations that you don't get to truly enjoy all the fruits of your labors. If you're not present each day, your business suffers, in many cases grinding to a halt.

Are you really free if—even as the "business owner"—you don't control your time and what you do with it? Isn't that the entire reason you became a business owner, to control your own schedule and enjoy the time and freedom to do what you wanted, when you wanted? Of course it is.

Furthermore, you simply cannot safely scale your company if you are the critical lodestone for your business. In order to scale your company you will need to build a business, not a job.

## Escaping the Self-Employment Trap

All businesses start at Level One (start-ups), feeling their way forward to launch their new venture. Those that survive reach Level Two (owner reliant). It's here that most companies get stuck. A Level Two business is a business that works, but only because you, the business owner, are there every day to make it work. *You* make most of the decisions. *You* generate most of the business. *You* meet with all the key clients and perform most of the important work of the business. *You* stay in full control. Sure, you have people to help, but they're there to do just that—help—not to lead or take ownership of central parts of your business. The core knowledge of how to manage and direct the business is locked up in your head, and if something should happen to you, your business would crumble. Even if you manage to somehow escape for a short vacation, you probably sneak your iPad or smart phone with you on the trip and check email when your family isn't looking.

The painful reality is that most Level Two business owners get caught in the Self-Employment Trap. They're so busy doing the "job" of their business that they can't step back and focus on growing their business. What's more, because of the way they are building their business, the more success they have, the more trapped they become inside their company.

So what's the way out of the Self-Employment Trap? You've got to work less and get your *business* to produce more. Remember, the more you do, the more you have to keep doing. The more you get your business to do, the more time you have to grow and build your business. This means building your business with the end in mind, the end being the day when it is no longer reliant on you the owner. We call this type of business a Level Three business.

In the early years of your business, you're naturally the main engine driving your business forward. You'll wear all the hats at various times, and you'll have few formal structures and systems within your organization upon which you can truly rely. But as the business matures, you become more confident you'll generate consistent sales and ensure that your business stays profitable. At this point, you've got a Level Two business.

As you enter Level Two, you'll face a crucial decision point at which you can settle for owning a Level Two company or instead choose to raise your business to be a strong and independent entity that benefits from your involvement but is ultimately independent of it.

This isn't something that "hard work" alone is going to solve. Blindly working hard is part of the problem. The more your growth is based on your personal production, the more dependent your business becomes on you for that production. You've got to make sure that even in the midst of meeting the daily demands of your business, you take some of your energy and invest in the systems, team, and internal controls that will allow you to scale your business beyond just you.

## The Paradox of Freedom

We first spoke with Mark Huha during a busy summer when he attended a workshop we hosted. He and his wife, Diana, owned a successful $750,000-per-year service business in Oceanside, California. For close to 15 years Mark had worked hard growing the company, commonly putting in 70-hour weeks. He was fast burning out.

We worked with Mark and Diana to apply the same ideas you're learning about in this book to their company. They got clear on their business strategy. They focused on fewer, better activities and cut out the lower-value distractions. They worked with their team to introduce systems and controls into their daily operations, which freed Mark up to focus on generating more sales. This in turn allowed them to bring on more team members, who now were immediately enfolded in a systems-driven culture of accountability and contribution. This sparked another dramatic jump in their business. And each quarter, Mark, Diana, and their key team members stepped away from their business for an offsite planning session to evaluate their progress, brainstorm ideas, and map out the coming quarter.

How did all this pan out for Mark and Diana's business? In a conversation we had with him in 24 months later, Mark shared, "We've grown by over 44 percent in the past two years to sales of over $1.1 million. This is literally ten times faster growth than in the prior 15 years we've had the business. But the thing that amazes me is how well my team is using and building our systems to create results. I've cut my hours back to under 35 hours per week and the business is doing better than ever."

We share this example with you to illustrate a point: Working harder isn't the answer; it's often a big part of the problem. To most owners, working harder equates with personally producing more for their companies. But the more they immerse themselves in the day-to-day operations, trying to produce more, the more they become the limiting factor for the business. The world doesn't pay you for the hours you put in; it pays you for the value you create.

Putting in lots of extra hours may indeed spark a short spurt of growth, but eventually this caps out because you simply can't work any harder, nor can you personally produce any more. This is why the first principle of scaling your company is to understand that the less you do, and the more you get your business to do, the faster the business will grow. Equally important, the easier it will be to sustain that growth over the long term.

There is a time and a place when the hard work and the dedicated, passionate hours of the owner can drive the business forward, but it is just that—a time and a place. The goal of owning a business is not to be needed, but in fact the opposite: to build a business that doesn't need you. When you reach the day when you can be away from the business for a period of time and no one calls or emails asking for your help, you've achieved your goal and have built the well-oiled, efficient machine that can continue to scale organically.

## The Level Three Road Map

Successful companies go through predictable stages of development. We've refined our observations of hundreds of successful companies—our own and others—into a concrete model that we call the Level Three Road Map. The Level Three Road Map (Figure 1.1) is the defined pathway through the complete life cycle of your business from launch to exit. It takes you through three distinct levels, from the chaos of the start-up, through the owner-reliant years, to the exit-stage phase. Remember, the finish line is not to just be profitable; the real finish line is to build a truly scalable business that creates massive value in the marketplace *without* needing you to be there every day to run it. Our goal in this book is to get you and your business to Level Three.

**FIGURE 1.1:** THE LEVEL THREE ROAD MAP

**Level Three**
SELL · SCALE · OWN PASSIVELY!

**Level Two**
**Advanced Stage**
Becoming systems reliant.
Establishing your management team.

**Middle Stage**
Building your core.
Escaping the Self-Employment Trap.™

**Early Stage**
Securing early clients.
Reaching profitability.

**Level One**
Creating your business plan.
Making sure your business is viable.

Copyright © Maui Mastermind®

## Level One: Pre-Launch Start-up

*Focus: Planning your business, raising capital, and getting initial market feedback to see if it's viable.*

At Level One, you're designing and planning your start-up. You're gathering your initial team, raising any required start-up capital, and executing your launch plan. Your focus at Level One is to plan your new business and get immediate market feedback to learn if your concept and model are economically viable.

Typical Level One business owners are filled with a mixture of doubts and dreams, fears and ambitions. They work long hours, scrambling to turn their business idea into a tangible, practical, cash-flowing enterprise. And they do all of this with no certainty that the business will be profitable, let alone sustainable.

## Level Two Early Stage: Post-Launch Start-up

*Focus: Making those early sales and learning to produce and fulfill on its core product or service so that the business reaches profitability.*

Fresh in the marketplace, an Early Stage Level Two business has just started actively marketing and selling its products or services. This is the time to learn your business and market, and if needed, discover and fix any fatal flaws in your business model or how your targeted customers perceive the value you're creating.

Your early focus while launching a business isn't on building the perfect product or service, but rather on figuring out how you can get people to buy. Too many entrepreneurs get caught in the trap of making the perfect widget, but never actually sell enough of that widget to ensure a profit. Of course you need to deliver on your promises, but you can iterate and improve your product or service as you go. Without sales, you have no business.

At this stage, you'll be wearing just about every hat in the business. That's OK for now, but as you move toward Middle Stage Level Two, you'll need to find ways to leverage your personal production for the business by hiring staff and building the basic business systems and controls you need.

An Early Stage Level Two business is working to generate sales, establish a market position, and become a sustainable business.

## Level Two Middle Stage: The Owner-Reliant Business

*Focus: Stabilizing your core and beginning to remove "you" from the center of the business.*

Once your business is profitable and you are confident that it is going to survive, it is time to build your business's four core systems:

1. Lead Generation: your system for finding prospects.
2. Lead Conversion: your system for closing sales.
3. Production and Delivery: your system for producing and fulfilling your core product or service.
4. Collections: your system for collecting on what you are owed.

These four systems—for finding leads, closing sales, producing your product or service, and collecting on your receivables—are the four core systems of every business.

Most businesses get stuck in Middle Stage Level Two. Why? Because the owners build their businesses for control based primarily on their personal production. They are the ones who make the key decisions, close the big sales, and manage much of the day-to-day operations. Sadly, these typical Middle Stage Level Two business owners stay stuck at the tactical level of doing the *job* of the business instead of creating the time and space to step back and *build the business as a business*.

Middle Stage Level Two requires building your core systems, team, and controls, while balancing your business's need for you to continue to lead its daily operation. This is a delicate balance between operating the business in the here and now, and building the structure you'll need to grow beyond your current situation.

Once you have established your solid base, you'll progress to Advanced Stage Level Two.

## Level Two Advanced Stage: The Rapid-Growth Company

*Focus: Scaling your business in earnest.*

At Advanced Stage Level Two, you'll begin the important work of refining your systems, building your management team, and scaling your business in earnest. This is the "Rapid Growth" stage of your business.

In this stage you'll also begin to build out the auxiliary systems you need in other parts of your company, from hiring to training to marketing to managing and more. You'll see that your revenue is exploding and often you'll feel like your business is bursting at the seams as you struggle to keep up with the growth.

A key shift at this stage is to enroll your team in building the systems, controls, and scalable solutions your business needs *alongside* you. Where a Middle Stage Level Two business owner commonly sees her team as a way to leverage her own personal production, an Advanced Stage Level Two business owner sees her team as partners in taking the business to the next level. This essential shift is what allows businesses to successfully make the leap to Level Three.

## Level Three: The Exit-Stage Company

*Focus: Choosing and executing on your "exit strategy"—to sell, scale, or own passively.*

A Level Three business is systems reliant, with a winning management team in place, and strong internal controls that allow the business to run smoothly and effectively independent of any one person. At this point, you truly have built a business, not a self-employed job. The business runs smoothly and your clients look to the business, not the owner, to fulfill on its promises.

Now it is time to determine and execute your exit strategy. This may or may not mean actually selling your business. In fact, many Level Three business owners choose to stay actively engaged. What's the critical distinction? Continued involvement is a personal *choice*, not a business *requirement*. You get to make that decision and choose any of these three main exit strategies:

1. You can sell the business and move on to your next great adventure.
2. You can scale the business to the big time.
3. You can passively own the business, with a greatly diminished role for yourself in its daily operation, generally fewer than five hours a week.

## A Short Quiz to Determine Where You Are on the Level Three Road Map

Now that we've gone through the complete life cycle of a business from Level One to Level Three, at what level and stage is your business right now? To identify where you fall on this path, circle the statement below that presently best describes your business:

**Level One:** You're still working on your business plan, raising your start-up funding, and preparing to launch your new business.

**Early Stage Level Two:** Your business is in its infancy, scrambling to make those early sales and fulfill customer promises.

**Middle Stage Level Two:** Your business is sustainable, but only if you're present to work for it. You're the main producer and director around whom your company revolves.

**Advanced Stage Level Two:** Your business is growing fast, with employee leaders in two or more of your five core pillars (Sales/Marketing, Operations, Finance, Team, and Executive Leadership). You're in the process of refining your business systems and building your management team.

**Level Three:** Your business is firing on all cylinders with employee leaders in at least four of your five core pillars. Your business is systems-reliant and ready for you to choose your exit strategy—to sell, scale, or own passively.

---

**SCALING PRINCIPLE ONE:
BUILD A BUSINESS, NOT A JOB.**

---

# PRINCIPLE TWO

## BUILD ON THE SCALABLE BASE OF SYSTEMS, TEAM, AND INTERNAL CONTROLS

Imagine you're about to sit down on a stool. You'd want that stool to be a sturdy, stable seat. If it had only two legs or, even worse, one leg, you'd be worried about that stool toppling over.

Most business owners build their companies on a one-legged stool, with that one leg being "team." Now if everything stays in balance and alignment you can sit on that one-legged stool, but it is a wobbly place to sit. When you scale based solely on hiring "key" people, you just create a new problem for yourself. You move the critical dependency from your shoulders to those of your key hires. What happens if you have an employee issue? What happens if a critical team member's spouse is relocated, or someone gets hurt? If the only leg of your stool is "My people will handle it," your stool will topple over the moment your people are not, for whatever reason, there to handle it.

Scaling Principle Two is about building on the stable, scalable, three-legged base of systems, team, and internal controls. Sure, you'll still want great talent on your team, but you'll also create stability and scalability by empowering your team with the structure (i.e., systems and controls) they need to produce more, better, and faster for your company. Scaling on the stable base of systems, team, and controls means that your business can handle the loss of a key team member. Plus, by having the other two legs of systems and controls, it's much easier to find, hire, and onboard new team members because you have a structure into which to integrate them.

Let's briefly define exactly what we mean when we use the terms "systems" and "controls." They are the key ingredients in designing a business that is both capable of scaling and no longer dependent on you alone to achieve that scale.

## Systems: The Backbone of Your Level Three Business

Systems are the reliable processes and procedures that enable your business to consistently produce excellent results for your clients or customers. They are the documented best practices and tools that increase your company's efficiency, reduce costly mistakes, and make your business more scalable.

Systems include the checklists your operations manager follows when working with a new client, the orientation process you use to onboard all new hires, the sequential process for producing your core product or service, and the automatic email sequence that goes out to each new prospect. Basically, business systems include any essential company know-how that you have captured in a tangible format as opposed to information locked in the brain of an individual team member.

Done right, systems make life easier for your team and success more predictable for your business. Sometimes when we introduce systems to a company, employees worry that they are "replacing themselves." Well-built systems don't replace people. Rather, they empower your team to consistently create more value.

## The Two Layers to Every Successful Business System

Every successful business system has two layers: the process layer and the format layer.

**The process layer** consists of the step-by-step process or procedure you've created to complete any given task or process. Your system should accurately capture the steps of the process so that when you follow it, you consistently get the desired result. It does you no good to formalize poor processes; you want your systems to document your winning moves, making it easier for your company to replicate and scale those successes.

But having a solid process isn't enough. You have to package that process in ways that your team will actually use. This is where the second layer of your system comes into play.

**The format layer** deals with how you package and present your system to your team. Systems should be easy to use, transparent so that team members intuitively understand how to use them, and automated to an extent that much of the work happens via technology instead of manual work.

How do you know if your system has a good, usable format? Ask yourself one simple, unambiguous question: *Is your team using it?* The real test of a system's utility is whether your team embraces it, ignores it, or, even more tellingly, creates an ad hoc shortcut for the task.

Your team members want to do a good job. If your business systems are simple, intuitive, and effective, they will use them. If they're confusing, complicated, or cumbersome, they'll ignore your systems, even creating their own "cheat sheet" hybrid versions instead. These homespun, individual hybrids normally aren't scalable; in fact, they usually only work for that one team member and only as long as the volume of your business stays relatively level. Plus, even if these private shortcuts work, rarely are they ever captured in a way that the rest of your business can use.

To get the format layer right, watch the way your team members use, or don't use, your systems. Don't argue, preach, or cajole—simply observe their interaction with your systems. Take their behavior as critical feedback to refine and improve your systems, whether it reveals that you need to simply adjust the design of your format, or that you need to revamp the process in order to streamline the steps or more reliably produce the desired result. Remember, systems are meant to leverage, empower, and simplify the lives of your employees, so don't fall in love with any specific system. Rather, fall in love with the result it's intended to generate.

---

**FIGURE 2.1:** 32 EFFECTIVE FORMATS TO PACKAGE YOUR SYSTEMS

---

Different formats to package your systems work better for different situations and roles. Here is a quick list of 32 potential formats for packaging your systems to make them easier and more effective for team members to use:

- Checklists
- Scripts
- Worksheets
- Custom forms
- Written guidelines
- Step-by-step instructions
- Software that automates a process
- Merge documents with precompleted data-entry fields
- Databases of key information
- Pricing lists
- Templates and samples
- Written policies
- Common Q&A sheets
- Written "warnings" for an area, providing how to deal with predictable problems
- Spreadsheets with built-in formulas
- Camera-ready artwork
- Filing system (paper or electronic)
- Preapproved vendors lists
- Standardized equipment and parts
- Online communication tools for effectively sharing information (discussion forums, wikis, whiteboards, social networks, etc.)
- Delivery timetables

- Job or role descriptions
- Instructional videos
- Illustrative picture or diagram
- Budget templates
- Automated data backups
- Project management software with reusable project pathways
- Reporting templates
- Organizational charts
- Preapproved forms and contracts
- A timeline or master calendar
- Complete enterprise management software

## The Biggest Myth of Building Business Systems

Does all of this talk about building systems inspire you to step away from your business for a few months to write out all your systems into a complete policies and procedures manual?

**CAUTION!** Don't do it. This is a recipe for disaster. Even if you were to write up all your systems into one long manual, you'd end up with a static and dated policies and procedures manual that no one would actually use. (Between 2009 and 2022 we surveyed more than 1,000 businesspeople, and fewer than 3 percent reported ever using a policies and procedures manual to do their job after the first 30 days on the job.) What's worse is that the moment you write a policies and procedures manual, it is already out of date. For your business systems to work, they must be firmly rooted in reality. The best way to create them is bit by bit as you grow your company.

What's needed is a living, breathing *discipline* inside your company of creating, refining, following, and, when need be, replacing systems.

In chapter 8, we'll share with you three powerful concepts to help you systematize your business, but what matters now is understanding that building your business systems is an ongoing process, not a onetime project. Early on, the systems you start with are going to be rudimentary and incomplete. That's OK; over time, you'll upgrade and flesh out your business systems so that they are a powerful leg in the stable base of your company. This leads us to the next leg of your stable base—team.

## Team: Leveraging the Talent, Time, and Attention of Other People

With all this talk of the importance of systems, and the vulnerability of a "one-legged stool," we don't want you to think that your team doesn't matter. Of course your team matters—they matter a lot. In fact, we're going to spend all of chapter 10 sharing with you our bottom-line best ideas on attracting, retaining, and unleashing the talent you need to win the game of business. But know that having a solid team isn't by itself enough to allow you to sustainably scale your company to Level Three.

You'll also need to define a palpable culture within your organization that bonds your team to one another and to the company. It will help ensure that you hire the kind of people who will work well together and truly execute your vision. What's more, building and maintaining a solid culture helps your team solve problems and deal with novel situations that your systems don't cover. Your company culture is a subtle and powerful force that helps shape your team's behavior and support scaling.

## Controls: Specialized Systems That Protect Your Company

Controls are the intelligent processes, procedures, and safeguards that protect your company from uninformed, inappropriate, or just plain careless decisions or actions by any team member. To scale your company, you want your team to have the authority to get tasks done without running everything past you. To do so, you want to make sure there are safeguards in place to protect the business and give your team the feedback it needs to make adjustments and stay on course.

Take, for example, a financial control. To reduce the potential for embezzlement, you could have one person make deposits and a second, unrelated person reconcile your bank statements. Or you might formalize how you give team members levels of decision-making authority that align with their experience and the degree of consequence if they decide poorly. Perhaps you will institute daily and weekly reporting of key indicators that help your team monitor their own performance and proactively respond to changes in your business. These are all examples of business controls.

Remember, every business control is also a "system"—it's just a special kind of system that is designed to safeguard your company. In the next section we want to highlight a crucial distinction about how emphasizing the implementation of sound business controls is not the same thing as you personally trying to maintain control over all aspects of your business.

## A Common Question That Could Lead You Astray

During a small-group coaching session for our clients, Cheryl asked an interesting question about growing her business. Cheryl owned a successful owner-reliant Middle Stage Level Two glass installation company with two locations and a steady stream of clients. Like most business owners, Cheryl was dealing with the challenges of delegation. She was jaded by her past experiences of delegating to her staff only to later learn that they ignored the company's systems and missed important details. The more this happened, the more Cheryl micromanaged her team when handing them responsibilities. She mitigated this problem when her business grew from one to two locations by working harder and closely managing her team. But she knew that it would be impossible to grow to three or four locations without getting her team to produce more. She simply didn't have the capacity to manage the staff at these other locations that closely. So in our session, Cheryl shared her primary concern:

"How do I delegate more and more of my day-to-day responsibilities to other people on my team and still maintain control of my business?"

In this simple question lies one of the greatest business dilemmas you'll ever face. On one hand, you need to leverage your team to get more done by delegating. On the other hand, you want to maintain control of your business to avoid negative consequences if team members drop the ball or do things the wrong way.

The solution to this problem isn't choosing either of these: delegating or controlling. Instead, we have to reformulate the question. As it is stated, the question presupposes that you, the business owner, *should* maintain personal control of your business. That creates a false dilemma, and if you fall prey to it, you'll lose both your freedom and your control over your business. The key is to let the business control itself. Talented people following efficient processes with controls and systems behind them will achieve far more than your business will ever achieve if you are the main point of control.

It's not a choice between "delegate and lose control" or "hang on to things and keep the control." Deciding between those two choices is counterproductive. If you're committed to building a Level Three business, you must learn the distinction between *control* and *controls*. The former will keep your business stuck in Level Two; the latter is key to scaling your business to Level Three. Here's the difference.

**CONTROL IS A LEVEL TWO REACTION:**

- It's fear based.
- It's autocratic.

- It means you're gathering more and more of it for *yourself* versus the business.
- It says, "Check with me" and "I'll make that decision each time it comes up" and "Don't take the next step until I look it over."

**CONTROLS (WITH AN *S*) ARE A
LEVEL THREE RESPONSE:**

- They're proactive.
- They're enterprise driven (building controls for your *business*, not for you, the owner).
- They're tools that allow everyone in your business to see the status of a given process, check on results, and self-correct as needed.
- They say, "Check the dashboard" and "Follow our internal process" and "How do we implement a systems-based control here?"

Cheryl's initial question—"How do I delegate more and more of my day-to-day responsibilities to other people on my team and still maintain control of my business?"—was understandable. Prior to reading this book, you may have asked the same question. But now that we have a clearer understanding of control, let's reformulate her question to a more empowering alternative:

"How can I design my company with intelligent controls that safeguard the business as we scale?"

## The Three Kinds of Business Controls

There are essentially three kinds of business controls.

1. **Visual controls.** These include checklists, dashboards, scorecards, budgets, etc. They let you *see* that the right things

are happening; if not, they raise a flag that alerts you to fix the situation. The best visual controls empower the person doing the task with real-time feedback to do his job better.

Visual controls aren't just about giving management better control, but ideally give your team autonomous control to do a better job without needing as much oversight. And at the same time, they create a clear accountability structure so that if things aren't going well, management knows about it early enough to work with a team member to improve the situation and get things back on track. We are constantly surprised at how few businesses use the low-cost and highly effective tool of visual controls. A simple real-time dashboard can enable your employees to evaluate and correct their own performance without waiting in line to talk to you and get your feedback.

2. **Procedural controls.** These include things like your standard review process for all new hires, a rule ensuring that two unrelated parties internally check or be involved in the flow of money, and a clear process for escalating customer service issues to get the problem resolved in a smart way. Procedural controls establish a known pathway to a consistently secure result. They are especially important in institutionalizing key learnings so that your entire team follows your best practices. The consistency you get from procedural controls also helps build your company brand by ensuring that customers know what to expect from your business in various situations, and comforts you with the knowledge that in these situations, your team will know how the business wants them to respond.

3. **Embedded controls.** Embedded controls work automatically in the background without someone's having to remember to do something to use them. They make the default behavior

the right behavior. These include things like standardized contracts, automated data backups, and automatic tracking and reporting of your sales team's call metrics directly out of a database.

With all this talk of controls, we need to emphasize a critical point. Building strong internal controls is not about you, the business owner, being in control, but rather about enhancing and giving control to your *business*. The best controls make the default behavior the right behavior. And they empower your team to get better results with less effort by giving them immediate feedback and a more defined playing field. You don't want your controls to be a police officer hiding in a speed trap to catch and ticket an unwary team member. Rather, you want your controls to be more like a speedometer or cruise control system that helps individual team members autonomously do better work.

The best controls also empower your managers and leaders with immediately clear and actionable information on how to coach and redirect their team, by letting them know what's going on in an area at any given moment.

Collectively, your systems, team, and controls are what allow you to scale your company.

---

FIGURE 2.2: 21 EXAMPLES OF BUSINESS CONTROLS

---

### Sales/Marketing

- Written list of preapproved concessions or negotiating parameters
- Approvals process for all sales exceptions
- Standardized sales paperwork and contracts
- Sales scripting
- Limited/segmented access to company database of prospects and clients
- Master marketing calendar
- Lead-generation scoreboard
- Automated marketing email sequences
- Standardized sales collateral

### Operations

- Operating budgets
- Production schedule/timeline
- Customer surveys
- Preapproved vendor list
- Competitive bidding process for all contracts over a certain dollar level
- Quality review checklist

### Financial

- Cash registers
- Formal employee expensing system
- Formal refund policy
- Written customer credit policy
- A/R write-off approval process
- Prenumbered invoices (with controlled access)

# Refining Your Systems and Controls as You Grow

Looking back at the three-legged stool analogy we shared at the beginning of this chapter, it's tempting to think that you can just build that stool once and use it as is forever. But your business and the markets you serve aren't static; they are in a constant state of flux. This means that over time you'll need to refine and even redesign your systems and controls too. In fact, the more you grow, the more that growth will require you to evolve your systems.

Have you ever watched the television show *This Old House?* Imagine you were a guest on the show, working on a 75-year-old house with its original electrical wiring and plumbing. What would happen if you plugged a full complement of modern electrical appliances into the outdated electrical system? You'd blow the fuses, not to mention create the potential for an electrical fire to break out. Similarly, what would happen to your plumbing if you went from a well-water system to tapping into the higher pressure of city water? Can you say rain gear?

Likewise, rapid growth makes increasing demands on the outdated systems in your business. The systems that worked for a

$500,000-a-year business are no longer sufficient to cope with a $5 million business, and not even close to being adequate for a $50 million business. At first, the additional sales will cause a few "leaks," but before long, your business will have burst pipes and water everywhere. This is why you need to approach your systems and controls as a work in progress, never a finished, static thing. As you grow your business, your systems and controls must grow with you.

> **SCALING PRINCIPLE TWO:**
> **BUILD ON THE STABLE BASE OF SYSTEMS, TEAM, AND INTERNAL CONTROLS.**

# PRINCIPLE THREE

## UNDERSTAND WHY YOUR CUSTOMERS *REALLY* DO BUSINESS WITH YOU

Ray ran a business that sold sand. That's it—sand. He had a big industrial lot and trucks came in all day to load up on sand and pay him. He had started out small, and while growth was slow, it was steady. He was happy but busy, sourcing sand, managing delivery trucks and logistics, negotiating payment terms, dealing with weather issues and raw material shortages, and battling new competitors when they came into the market and undersold him. Even though he could never really just sit back and rest, he made good money and built a loyal customer base.

One day, though, Ray finally maxed out his market. His growth had plateaued; most of the trucks within reasonable driving distance were already his customers. "Now what?" thought Ray. He felt stuck. Why keep working this hard without the hope of further growth?

Ray called us for help. He said he was out of ideas and couldn't see any way to continue to grow. He was so busy running his business that he didn't really even see his customers anymore; they were just trucks and transactions. Ray's real problem was that he had stopped seeing beyond his daily operations, blinding him to the potential growth opportunities.

We came out to visit Ray and decided to run a little experiment. When trucks came to get their sand loaded, we sat with the drivers and asked them many questions about *their* business, not Ray's. It turns out that over 90 percent of Ray's customers weren't just buying sand to buy sand; they were using the sand to build bridges. Ray knew nothing about the bridge-building business, except that obviously it required sand. From there, we dug deeper and started asking Ray's customers to tell us all about the bridge-building business. When Ray realized the true goal of his business was to help his customers build bridges, not sell them sand, he quickly created and launched other products and services he could offer his customers in addition to selling them sand. For example, Ray's customers mixed his sand with concrete and poured the mix into wooden forms to shape and set it. Ray started to sell those wooden forms to his sand-buying customers. Today, Ray's business is five times the size it used to be, and growing strong.

Knowing about your customers' businesses helps you put your business in context. This is why Scaling Principle Three is to understand the *real* reason your customers do business with you. Why do they need and want your product or service in the first place? How does it help them solve a painful problem or in some way add real value to their lives? Why do they buy from you rather than one of your competitors? Why do they continue doing business with you over the long haul? The combined answers to these questions frame out your business context.

Let's say you and a friend just arrived in a new city and were making plans to see the sights. Your friend picked up a pad of paper and started listing all the places he or she wanted to go over the three days of your visit. So far so good—brainstorming ideas is a good start. But at this point your friend simply tears off the page with the list, grabs a coat, and heads for the door. "Wait!" you say. "We need to take a look at a map to see the layout of the city and figure out which sites are near each other and which are far apart. And if we can't get to all of them we should prioritize the list so we hit the top sites first in case we want to change plans later."

Most business owners are like this friend—charging off to "do" their business without ever pausing to step back and get a sense of the "map" of the world in which their business operates. They are so consumed by the day-to-day that they don't stop and think about the broader business context in which their business operates.

Understanding your business context—the map of the market in which you sell, produce, fulfill, and grow your business—is crucial in building a scalable business. In this chapter, we'll guide you through a simple process to clearly lay out the three dimensions of your business context—your customers, your competition, and your positioning. When we're done, you'll have a clear, concrete picture of your target market, including the critical "Marketing Markers" that will help you qualify and screen for your best buyers. You'll also get a simple chart, the Competitive Matrix, to determine how you stack up against your competition in eight key criteria, so that you can narrow your focus to the one or two elements that you need to leverage to effectively compete. And finally, we'll give you two powerful tools to help you intentionally craft your market position and brand that work in the stressed-out and resource-strapped world of small business.

Let's get started with the first dimension of your business context—your customers.

## Your Customers—Whom You Serve and What They Really Want

As crazy as it seems, most business owners never concretely clarify whom they serve and what this target market *really* wants. The average owner is so busy marketing, selling, producing, and fulfilling that they never step back and think through precisely whom they serve, much less the deep aspirations, fears, hopes, dreams, and frustrations of this target market. This makes about as much sense as the salesperson who spends all day going door-to-door selling pool care products—in an apartment complex! When you ask him why he'd waste his time selling a product that clearly this group of people is unlikely to buy, he says, "The doors are so close together that I can call on five times as many people than if I go to the neighborhood you suggest."

Can you tell us who the ideal target market for your product or service is? Within that target market, who are your best prospects? Too many businesses take a broad approach to marketing and claim that "everyone" in their target market can use their product or service. This is ineffective. Instead, think of your marketing the way the world's most successful companies do: as a series of concentric circles. In the middle of the target, the center of the bull's-eye, are the people who are most likely to use your product now and have the highest closing ratio. If you approach these people, you'll have the shortest sales cycle. Identifying those "fastest to close" customers in your target market is critical to achieving momentum in growing your sales.

Here is a list of prompts to help you clarify who your target market and ideal customer are by determining what key elements your best customers have in common. While not every question will apply to your business, most will. We encourage you to pause with each item and jot quick notes as you go.

The list of prompts will differ if you sell business to business or business to consumer, so choose the applicable list. Follow the cascading series of questions to determine the key elements that ultimately identify who your best buyers likely are, and the target market you're going to go after (and which tempting markets are distractions you'll avoid for now).

## Clarify Your Target Market

**List the key elements that your best buyers have in common:**

**IF BUSINESS TO BUSINESS:**

- Industry(-ies)
- Size of customer
- Geographic location of business
- Title of decision maker
- Titles of key influencers in decision process
- Where the decision maker and key influencers spend time (physical locations, online websites, periodicals, events, etc.)
- With whom the decision maker and key influencers already have trusted relationships

**IF BUSINESS TO CONSUMER:**

- Age
- Gender
- Income level
- Marital status
- Educational level
- Where they live, work, and spend time (passions, affiliations, social networks, media favorites, etc.)
- Who commonly recommends or advises them on purchase decisions for your type of product or service

**Your Top Five Marketing Markers:** Given all you've reviewed about your target market, which five qualifications are your best clues that you've found a great prospect? Which five elements most reliably predict you've found a likely buyer? These clues are your "Marketing Markers." Your goal is to get better at quickly spotting those prospects who are most likely to buy your product or service. You'll use these markers to focus your sales and marketing efforts on your best leads. For example, perhaps you should be focusing on companies with 50 to 100 employees, or steel fabrication companies with sales over

$10 million. Or perhaps you should focus on homeowners who recently moved into one of three ZIP codes, or families with children under the age of 12.

**Who Your Target Market Isn't:** What are the three to five markets that, while tempting, for the time being you are clearly identifying as NOT your current target market? It's important to know these markets in order to help your sales/marketing team focus on your target market and not be distracted and pulled off track by pursuing these other markets. You'll want to revisit your assumptions and decisions on your target market annually, but in your day-to-day marketing, making this decision will help you invest your limited resources where they'll do the greatest good.

---

Here is an example of the power of defining your Marketing Markers, not just to help you target your markets, but also to help you qualify your sales prospects.

Several years after his helping build Priceline.com, Jeff was running an online liquidation service for manufacturers and retailers called uBid.com. At the beginning, Jeff helped his sales team put together their sales presentation and went on the road with them to meet with prospects. At the first meeting, they went through all 20 slides with their prospect. At the end of their presentation, she said she would think about their offering and get back to them. At the next sales pitch, with another company, they were only on slide two of the presentation when the prospect said, "I'll take it!"

You don't want to do a bunch of long sales presentations, hoping that your prospect will call you back. What you want is more prospects who say yes on the second slide. To figure out what differentiated their prospects, Jeff and his team created a detailed profile that described all they knew about their customers, and assigned points to the answers to each main question. They asked: Was the customer already looking for a solution to this problem? Did the customer already have money approved to pay for a product or solution? Was the person in the room an actual decision maker? And so on. Sure enough, when Jeff and his team put their early prospects into the profile, the second prospect they had visited (who bought after the second slide) scored an 89 on the 100-point profile, and the first customer only a 37.

The lesson is this: You can identify the prospects you should be pursuing by building a profile of your true target customer. Who is most likely to need your product, understand your sales pitch, and pull out their checkbook *now*? Before you go on any sales calls, run potential customers and market segments through this filter and go after only the ones who score high enough to meet your minimum criteria. We call this a "best-first search." If you had a crystal ball, you would go to the best customers first and not waste your time on customers who take forever to convince. Our tool can work like this crystal ball, by narrowing your focus to those customers most likely to buy your product or service.

The Marketing Markers you identified a moment ago are the center circle of your prospect target. You'll use these elements to both target your marketing efforts *and* be more strategic about where you invest your finite sales energy.

Now that you know who you serve, we need to dive deep into what these prospects *really* want. In order to succeed, you need to understand the hopes and aspirations, fears and frustrations, needs and desires that drive and move your target market.

In the early days at Priceline.com, Jeff asked some of his colleagues what business they thought the company was in. Most answered, "We sell airline tickets." But the truth was that none of their customers woke up in the morning wanting to buy an airline ticket and sit on a plane. No, what they really wanted was to be able to afford a way to go to their sister's wedding. They *had* to buy an airline ticket, but they *wanted* to go to a wedding.

Do you think you'd run your business differently if you thought your job was getting people to their sister's wedding as opposed to just selling people airline tickets? This insight sparked one of Priceline.com's most effective early marketing campaigns, where they bought blank pages in major U.S. magazines and asked customers to send their own pictures and tell their own stories about using Priceline.com. Knowing that Priceline.com helped others like them afford to go on a trip or get to an event they couldn't have attended otherwise really resonated with Priceline's target market.

Ask yourself: Why do my customers *really* come to me? What do they worry about when they wake up in the morning? Figure that out and you will be able to market to them much more effectively.

In Figure 3.1, we share a simple tool to help you map out the deep psychological and emotional needs of your target market. To see how this all plays out in real life, we've filled out the answers for these questions for David's company, Maui Mastermind.

**FIGURE 3.1:** CASE STUDY: MAUI MASTERMIND

### Case Study: Maui Mastermind Business Coaching Services

**Target Market:** Business owners of companies with sales of $1-50 million per year who want help growing their business and reducing its reliance on them, the owner.

**Their Strongest Desires & Aspirations**
- Freedom – especially TIME freedom.
- To make a difference with their business. To serve and contribute.
- To create – have a drive to turn their business ideas into a concrete reality.
- Family – time and opportunities with those they love most.
- Connection – to feel part of an upgraded peer group of business owners rather than a lone wolf.
- Certainty – to feel confident that they're on the right path with their business, that if they follow the coaching, they'll get great results.

**Their Biggest Frustrations & Pain Points**
- Feel trapped in their businesses.
- Feel pressure and anxiety. Routinely say, "It's all on my shoulders!"
- Lack of time – never enough time to get it all done.
- Employees – they quit, flake, mess up, and it's hard to find the good ones.
- Feel overwhelmed – too much to do; don't know where to start.
- Feel stuck and are unsure of the best way forward to grow the business.

**Their Biggest Fears**
- Failing in the business.
- Losing control; feeling helpless.
- Being overextended with the business (financially).
- Growing too big – the business will take over their lives.
- That they'll do all the work and it still won't work.

**Their Greatest Opportunities**
- Scaling and growing their companies.
- Applying the Sweet Spot concept to push back their #1 limiting factor.
- Reducing their business's reliance on them.
- Focusing on fewer, better things as a company.
- Actually executing on all they know to do.

Copyright © Maui Mastermind®

You can download a blank PDF version of this tool for free at **www.ScaleYourBusinessToolKit.com**. Take 15 minutes to fill out your answers for your business. Once you've got your answers down, share this tool with your team. Ask them to answer these same questions. Come up with a one-page "company" version that you share and reinforce throughout your organization. This is one of your key marketing controls.

Clarifying who your target market is and what they really want will help you identify and search out your best prospects, strengthen and focus your marketing message, and qualify and prioritize the leads you generate so you invest your best sales energy on your most qualified prospects. With this concrete picture of your best buyers in hand, it's now time to move to the second dimension of your business context—your competitors.

## Your Competitors

While the most important place to start is with your customers, it is essential that you take stock of your competitors too. Whom do you compete against? What are their strengths and weaknesses? How can you best position yourself and your products and services relative to them? Answering these questions will highlight strategic opportunities for you to seize.

Take the example of how Zappos.com used its competition's weaknesses to differentiate its business and grow tremendously as a result. Zappos realized that the traditional model of customer service was to handle as many customer service calls in the call center as quickly as possible. Call center agents were measured by how many calls they processed per hour, which meant getting the customer off the phone as fast as possible, leaving many customers feeling rushed and unfulfilled. Unlike its competitors, Zappos instructed its customer service agents to focus on the happiness of the customer, not minutes on the clock. Its customer service agents were to spend as much time with any one caller as necessary to ensure the caller felt great at the end of their conversation. As a result, word spread quickly that Zappos cared about its customers. Its competitors' weakness became Zappos's biggest strength, and powerfully differentiated it from all its competitors.

You have three types of competitors, two of whom you likely haven't given much thought to. We'll explore all three types of competitors, then look at a simple tool that will help you compare your company—side by side—with your top competitors.

## Your Direct Competitors

Generally, when you think of competition, your direct competitors come to mind first. Direct competitors are those companies that are actively in the same market you are in, selling a comparable product or service. For example, Sasha Ablitt owns a dry-cleaning business in Santa Barbara, California, that she has built into the most successful dry cleaner in the area. Her direct competitors include more than a dozen other dry cleaners in her area.

Identify your top three direct competitors. What are their top strengths, weaknesses, pricing structure, and market share? This is the minimum information you need to get a good handle on who your direct competitors are and how you can effectively compete against them.

## Your Indirect Competitors

How else does your target market satisfy their needs with respect to the problem your product or service solves other than with your or your direct competitors' solution? We call these competing solutions your "indirect" competitors. Going back to Sasha's dry-cleaning business, her *indirect* competitors include people doing their own hand wash and new washing machines with specialized cycles for delicate clothing.

Or take Jennifer Lyle, owner of Software Testing Solutions, Inc. Jennifer's company sells a software tool that automates how a hospital blood bank tests and validates its testing process. Her *indirect* competitors are hospitals manually conducting the testing validation themselves or outside consultants that hospitals hire to come in and manually validate their testing process.

To figure out who your indirect competitors are, ask yourself who or what your target market turns to—other than you or your direct competitors—in order to solve the core challenge your product or service solves.

The mental exercise of determining who your indirect competitors are is a critical one. All too often we see businesses direct their limited marketing resources (i.e., time and money) to luring customers away from their direct competitors, when sometimes it's much cheaper to acquire a customer that no one currently has. Sasha, for example, can focus her energy on getting the woman who does her own hand wash at home as her next customer, as opposed to targeting the customer who is currently loyal to the dry cleaner down the street.

Who or what are your two main indirect competitors? What are the biggest advantages for someone using these indirect competitors? What are their most glaring deficiencies or weaknesses? What is the best way you can position your company, product, or service relative to them to outshine them?

## Disruptive Competitors

Step back from your business for a moment. In your worst nightmares, who or what could totally change the way the game is played in your industry? Think of what Apple did to the music industry with iTunes, what Amazon did to brick-and-mortar retailers, or what FedEx did to the U.S. Postal Service.

Many businesses fail to spot a disruptive competitor in their industry because they put blinders on and choose not to see it. They have so much invested in the status quo that it warps their perceptions and thinking process. In chapter 5, we'll share with you a process to protect yourself from being blindsided by disruptive competitors by learning to systematically read the world around you. A big part of identifying disruptive competitors is watching for trends and new technologies that aren't even being used in your industry—yet.

For example, with Sasha's dry-cleaning business, potential disruptive competitors could be fabric manufacturers who create a memory fabric that allows people to machine-wash dress clothing, which then pops back into its pressed shape. Or an ionization machine from a different industry that could be applied to dry cleaning that totally eliminates the need for solvents or chemicals.

Now it's your turn. Who do you think your two biggest potential disruptive competitors could be? What might it look like if they made a move into your niche? What steps you could take now to preempt or undercut these moves? It doesn't matter that you have the perfect answers to these questions; for now, it is enough that you train yourself to consistently ask the questions.

## Building Your Competitive Matrix

We've got one last step—to map out, in one simple chart, how you stack up against your competition. We call it your Competitive Matrix (Figure 3.2). This chart asks you to fill in your top three direct competitors, your top two indirect competitors, and your two scariest potential disruptive competitors. Then, rate your business and that of your competitors on the eight variables (e.g., price, value, service, etc.) listed on a scale of 1 to 5, with 5 being the highest score possible. For example, if your company is very attractive on price to your target market, then rate yourself a 4 or 5. If your brand is very weak (not well known in the market, has a poor reputation, etc.), then you might rate it a 1 or 2, and so on. When completed, this matrix will offer a clear side-by-side comparison between you and your competition.

FIGURE 3.2

| Competitive Matrix | | | | | | | | Score 1-5 (5 = Very Strong) |
|---|---|---|---|---|---|---|---|---|
| | Price | Value | Service | Quality | Innovation | Brand | Marketing | Salesmanship |
| Our Company | | | | | | | | |
| Direct | | | | | | | | |
| 1. | | | | | | | | |
| 2. | | | | | | | | |
| 3. | | | | | | | | |
| Indirect | | | | | | | | |
| 1. | | | | | | | | |
| 2. | | | | | | | | |
| Potentially Disruptive | | | | | | | | |
| 1. | | | | | | | | |
| 2. | | | | | | | | |

Copyright © Maui Mastermind®

At this point, what matters is understanding where you stand relative to your competitors, not that you outshine each of them on every variable (which usually isn't possible anyway). If you know that competitor A is significantly less expensive, then competing on price would likely be a mistake. Instead, you may decide to compete on service, quality, or brand. This is why we are asking you to lay out a visual view of the competitive playing field. You can use this information to pick the one variable that not only matters to a large enough subset of your target market, but is also the one in which you can trounce your competitors. Having laid out your Competitive Matrix, it's time to turn to the final dimension of your business context—your positioning.

• • •

# Your Positioning

Your market position is made up of two closely related elements: your chosen "parking space" and your brand. Your parking space is the intentional way you have positioned your company (or its products or services). It is the frame of reference through which you want your market to see you. Your brand, on the other hand, is the emotional shortcut you've helped your market develop that links your company, products, or services to a specific emotional response. Your brand becomes a filter that colors how your market interprets each of its interactions with you.

Both your parking space and your brand are two pieces of the same puzzle, and are critical for your business to successfully scale. Let's look at them in detail.

## The Parking Space Theory of Positioning

The easiest way to think about strategically positioning your company is using a simple analogy we call the "Parking Space Theory of Positioning." Imagine driving into a parking lot, looking for a space to park your car. What would you look for? An open space, of course! Theoretically, you could move a car out of an existing space so you could park your car there, but that would require quite a bit of muscle power to do.

The same concept applies when you are looking for the right space in which to position your business in the marketplace. You should look for an open parking space. The right parking space for your company lies at the intersection of three factors: your company's biggest strengths (your parking space must rely on what you do really well); your market's deepest desires around your type of product or service (it must be something that your market values); and the open spaces your competitors don't already own in the mind of your market (it is very expensive to move another company out of a space if they truly already own it).

Your "parking space" is the heart of how you position your company, and its products and services, to be seen by your target market. It represents the *single* thing you want to be known for—more than anything else. Here are several examples with well-known companies and products:

- Walmart ("Lowest prices" parking space)
- Bayer Aspirin ("Gentlest aspirin on your stomach" parking space)
- Volvo ("The Safest" parking space)
- Prego Spaghetti Sauce ("Thickest spaghetti sauce" parking space)
- Zappos ("Best customer service" parking space)
- Amazon ("Easiest place to buy online" parking space)
- Priceline.com ("Lowest-priced discount travel" parking space)

Why is it so important that you be known for a single thing? After all, you may say you are both the low-cost provider and have the best service in your market—oh, and your product is the best quality too. Why can't you be known as the "lowest price, best service, highest quality" provider? As soon as we spell it out like that, it becomes obvious how watered down and confusing this will likely prove to your market. It's hard enough to own any *one thing* in the minds of your market, let alone two or three things. Yet if we look at marketing materials for a group of small businesses (e.g., websites, sales brochures, advertising, sales scripting, etc.), many are pushing multiple positions at the same time. And their materials probably don't look all that different from their competitors'. Sound familiar?

One of the things we tell the businesses we work with is that in order to achieve exponential success, you need to win a gold medal in something. You need to find a category in which you can truly win—so that you can stand out in your marketplace. Picking your parking space carefully is a critical long-term decision.

Here is a short series of questions to help you triangulate and pick the best parking space for your business:

1. What are your company's top three to five strengths that create value in the market? These should be things that set you apart, or potentially *could* set you apart from your competition. Does your cost structure allow you to price more attractively than your competitors? Is the technical expertise of your client support team or credibility of your company unique in your market? Just because a parking space is empty doesn't mean it's necessarily a good choice for you and your company. You have to be able to truly deliver on the promise of that space.

2. What are the top three to five things that a sizable chunk of your target market values highly with respect to your type of product or service? What are the key factors that your market wants in your product or service that would trigger them to buy? Is it the speed of delivery? Flexible payment options or financing to make it more affordable? Ease of use?

3. Which parking spaces (best price, best quality, best service, easiest to use, most environmentally friendly, etc.) are empty and not already "owned" by one of your competitors? If you aren't sure if someone owns a specific parking space in the minds of your market, likely no one does. A simple test to determine this is to ask ten prospects in your target market which company (or product or service) comes immediately to mind when they think about _____ (fill in the blank with the parking space you're curious to see if someone owns). If all ten prospects say the same company delivers the best prices on dry cleaning, for example, then that parking space has a competitor parked in it. If they each have a different answer, or better yet, no single company comes to mind for them, then likely no one is parked in that space and it is potentially open for you to claim.

Now that you've listed the three sides to the parking space triangle, determine which parking space you can claim that leverages one of your business's key strengths, delivers a benefit that your market values highly, and is not already occupied by a competitor.

The goal behind this parking space exercise is to carve out the one singular space where you can beat your competition by doing something you are very good at for a set of customers who will love you for doing it and pay you well.

Now it's time to turn our attention to a closely related subject—branding.

## Branding in the Real World

Your brand is simply the emotional associations and gut-level "sense" of how your company, product, or service is intuitively perceived by your market. If your "parking space" is about choosing the one single element you want to relentlessly burn into the minds of your market so that they'll automatically associate your company with that space, then your brand is the broader emotional response that instantly springs to mind when someone in your market imagines what it will be like to interact or work with your company.

The easiest way to make branding real is to determine what we call your top three "brand emotions." We'll walk through exactly what this means in just a moment, but first let's quickly turn to the biggest branding mistakes we've watched small and midsize businesses make.

#### THE THREE BIGGEST BRANDING MISTAKES

1. They've never given any real thought to their brand or market positioning. They have no real strategic understanding of how they are perceived or how they ideally *want* to be perceived.

2. They regularly do things that contradict or water down their brand because they are not congruent with their desired brand.
3. If they have given thought to the brand they want to embody, they lack a clear, practical understanding of how to take this idea and translate it into how they do business. Their branding all feels theoretical and academic.

Your brand is the sum total of the emotional, mental, and experiential associations your marketplace has to your company and offerings. The reason brands work is that they help people quickly make meaning out of the world. The value of your brand is in direct relationship to how valuable the market judges your promise, and how much people trust your company to keep its "brand promise," the informal contract you've made with the market to offer a reliable and consistent experience when interacting with or buying from your company.

To make this concept actionable and intuitive in your business, think about your brand promise as a set of three core emotions that you want your market to experience after every interaction they have with your business. We call these three core emotions your "brand emotions." Here are a few examples of various well-known companies and their brand emotions.

**APPLE:**

1. Sheer pleasure. ("It is a joy to handle and touch these devices.")
2. Cool. ("When I own and pull out my iPhone, I feel cool and hip.")
3. Smooth and easy. ("They just work and are so intuitive to use.")

**VIRGIN:**

1. Well served. ("They really do take care of my needs.")
2. Great value. ("I know I got a great deal.")
3. Fun. ("Interacting with Virgin is fun.")

**LEXUS:**

1. Luxurious. ("It just feels so rich to be riding in this car.")
2. Status. ("I feel more important when people see me in this car.")
3. Trust. ("I know I can rely on the car and the dealer to serve my needs.")

What about your business? What are the top three brand emotions that you want your market to experience after every interaction with you?

Now comes the breakthrough part—making your brand emotions real in your market.

## How People Make Meaning of the World

The world is a whirling storm of complex forces and experiences that can quickly overwhelm a person. It seems like everyone, everywhere, is trying to get our attention and sell us something. To deal with this complexity and make sense of all the noise, we find shortcuts to simplify and structure our experiences that help us to navigate and thrive. People evaluate a business's performance on its brand promise by applying a powerful quirk of human nature called *inductive perception.*

Inductive perception is a thinking shortcut where a person takes a relatively small sample size of experience and makes that small experience stand for the broader whole. This meaning then becomes a filter that progressively grows more and more pronounced—and through which that person views all his or her interactions with you and your company. For example, let's say one of your company's brand emotions was "trusted." Imagine your salesperson set a 2 P.M. appointment to call on a prospect. If your salesperson is 20 minutes late, what will your prospect likely make that mean? If your salesperson is 5 minutes early, how will your prospect interpret that?

Let's expand this exercise to say that, during the first sales call, your salesperson carefully takes notes, and at the end clarifies the two items she has promised to follow up on and send over to the prospect. How would the prospect perceive it if, later that day, he got an email that said, "Hi, John. I wanted to follow up and get you both items I promised to send by close of business. They are attached to this message. . . ." Can you see how the prospect will start to generalize that your company is one that he can trust?

Understanding that people take symbolic slivers of their experience and inductively expand what they mean by generalizing outward, you can intentionally design your market's interactions with your business to increase the odds that they'll feel your brand emotions. The more consistently you help your client or market feel your brand emotions after they interact with you, the stronger your brand is with those people. Now, how to do that in the real world?

Go back to your brand emotions. Think of simple things you can do to design your client experience so that your client is more likely to feel one or more of your brand emotions. For example, if you owned a Lexus dealership, you could look for simple ways to enhance a customer's sense of status the moment they walked on the lot. You could have them call all staff on the lot by their first name, while your staff would still address the customer as Mr. or Ms. (putting the customer up on a pedestal emotionally). If they needed to get their car fixed, you could help them arrange a "service appointment." You could sponsor high-end arts events and invite your customers. You could even give customers a visible luxury gift like a watch or fancy key chain, to extend the feeling of high status into their lives outside of their car.

During his time with Priceline.com, Jeff worked with an experimental service called Priceline Yard Sale, an attempt to bring its unique "name your own price" model to yard sale items. Early on in this project, Jeff and his development team realized that they wanted their customers to get as close as possible to the excitement of winning the lottery or a big roll of the dice in Las Vegas. Knowing that one of their key brand emotions was "excitement" (as in, "I won!"), they intentionally made subtle shifts in how their site worked. For example, they didn't say, "Thank you for your purchase" (yawn); instead they said, "Congratulations! You won the item you bid on!" And rather than just have a mundane image pop up while a visitor's bid was processed, they intentionally showed a slot machine with numbers spinning on the three dials, landing on 7-7-7 when the response came back that his bid was accepted. These subtle design elements made a big impact on customers' tell-a-friend viral marketing ratio, and helped Priceline firmly establish this key element of its brand.

David's company, Maui Mastermind, recently redesigned its core business coaching platform to help reinforce one of its brand emotions—"confidence." That redesign included building a simple accountability structure into the company's coaching app. The owner visually *knows* when her team is meeting deliverables or not and the app delivers weekly progress reports from everyone on her team. Clients can now also actually *see* the progress they are making on a quarter-by-quarter basis relative to their strategic action plan and the other key metrics inside their company. The end result was an upgraded ability to give clients the confidence (brand emotion) of knowing they are on the right road to reaching their business goals.

Select one of your brand emotions and brainstorm possible ideas—large and small—that you could concretely design into your customer experience to *prompt* them to feel that brand emotion. Now go on to the second and then third of your brand emotions and ask yourself the same question. When you're done, choose from the ideas you've come up with to implement in your business. (In the next chapter, we'll share with you a powerful strategic tool called the "Sweet Spot Analysis" that you can use to pick the best of your ideas to implement.)

## The Two Most Important "Reality Checks" for Your Brand

Now we come to the final two reality checks to your company's brand. First, just because you say it's so, doesn't make it so. Your *clients* ultimately determine your company brand by an accumulative process. Once you've been labeled by the market, it's very hard to stray too far from it. You can tweak it, twist it, and bend it, but rarely break it. You're almost better starting fresh and creating a new brand.

If you are being brutally honest right now, how does your market currently see your company brand?

Second, your brand emotions must be meaningful and real inside your company or they won't last. Smoke and mirrors are great in a stage production but do not last long in the market. You've got to get the substance of your brand emotions into the way your company sees itself and its mission. Your team needs to understand how it is *everyone's* job to reinforce your brand emotions any way they can. For your brand emotions to be real for the long term, your entire team has to live your brand every day, in every way. That means being consistent in every touch point and every interaction with a client, whether it's a phone call, in-person conversation, email, or advertisement. A brand can really only achieve its goal when it's consistently applied by everyone at your company, in everything they do.

Unfortunately for too many companies, "brand" is just an external marketing message and, internally, merely a poster on the wall. The world's best companies actually do live their brand every day, in everything they do. Remember Zappos? They made the huge decision to build their brand around one powerful brand emotion: delivering happiness. And they're extremely committed to following through on making sure you leave happy when you interact with them.

Jeff was delivering a keynote address at a large business conference and wanted to give the audience a vivid example of what it meant to live your brand promise. He asked the conference staff to bring a speaker phone up onstage. There, live and unscripted, he dialed the Zappos customer service line. When the customer service agent answered, Jeff told her he was shopping for a barbecue grill. She politely informed him that Zappos sells men's and women's shoes and accessories. Jeff replied that he didn't need any of those things, but a new barbecue grill would make him quite happy. To the amazement of the audience, the customer service agent asked him a bunch of questions about the grill he was looking for, went online and researched his specs, and then emailed Jeff links to grills that might serve his needs! She then reminded him that if he ever needed shoes and accessories, he knew whom to call. This is an incredible example of being true to your brand.

## It All Starts with Your Customer

The place to start is with your customer. Let your customer's needs, desires, fears, and aspirations deeply impact how you run your business. Once you have a clear understanding of whom you are serving and why they choose to do business with you, review your competition. Take the strategic insights found by looking at your Competitive Matrix and use them to help you sharpen your positioning. While you may never nail your parking space and branding as effectively as Zappos does, you can make real improvements that will help you sustain your growth. Your brand isn't just about helping your customers feel a certain way about your company. When your brand is vibrant and real inside your company, it can powerfully shape how your employees see themselves and your business.

> **SCALING PRINCIPLE THREE:**
> **UNDERSTAND WHY YOUR CUSTOMERS *REALLY***
> **DO BUSINESS WITH YOU.**

# PART II

# Focusing on Fewer, Better Things

Courage rather than analysis dictates the truly important rules for identifying priorities: Pick the future against the past; focus on opportunities rather than on problems; choose your own direction, rather than climb on the bandwagon; and aim high, aim for something that will make a difference, rather than for something that is "safe" and easy to do.

—Peter Drucker

# PRINCIPLE FOUR

## CREATE THE *RIGHT* STRATEGIC PLAN

When Jeff was CEO of uBid.com, the team developed a technology engine that could track incoming inventory, manage the dynamic pricing of that inventory, set up and run online auctions for that inventory, and handle all the shipping and logistics to deliver and report on sold inventory. It was an impressive set of assets. But the company wasn't growing. It was positioned as a more trustworthy alternative to eBay, but it was difficult for David to go out and pick a fight with Goliath. eBay had a massive marketing budget and huge brand recognition with consumers; people weren't going to easily leave it.

What was uBid.com to do? First, they asked themselves if their strategic positioning was correct. Turns out, it wasn't. They were pointed at the wrong market, living in eBay's shadow. Acknowledging that their current strategy simply wasn't working, they stepped back and reassessed their strategy.

They concluded that with their assets (product, people, relationships, etc.), they were better suited to pursue the excess inventory market, not the consumer-direct market. Under their new strategy, they offered themselves as a solution to major manufacturers and retailers, filling a need that was underserved. In this new strategic position, they could beat their competitors, unlike when they were challenging eBay. The company signed a series of new contracts with major customers who now knew exactly what value the company could provide to them. They carved out a well-defined niche in which they were positioned to win, and as a result, uBid's stock quintupled in value.

Now that you understand your business context (your market, your competitors, and your positioning, as we discussed in Principle Three), Scaling Principle Four says it's time to determine your strategy to grow and reduce that strategy into a series of rolling, one-page, quarterly action plans that help you execute and get results. In this chapter we'll walk you through a concrete, structured process to do exactly this.

Your strategic plan is the road map that directs your company's focus to the fewer, better things that will allow you to dominate your market niche and create explosive growth. It prompts you to look at the big picture. What really matters? Where are you committed to going? How can you meaningfully and accurately track your progress? Your strategic plan also helps you prioritize and intelligently allocate your company's resources to their best advantage. Finally, your strategic plan helps align your team on the big picture so they can better manage their responsibilities and contribute more to the real needs of the business.

Conventional wisdom says your strategic plan is where you write down your answers; that it is a fixed-in-stone plan to accomplish your key business goals. In theory this sounds great, even alluring—a simple document that contains the secret plan to marshal your resources and smoothly attain your goals. Alas, that's just not how things work in the real world of business.

If a combined 50 years of running companies has taught us anything, it is this: Your strategic plan is not a place for fixed answers, but rather it is a trusted process comprising provocative questions you systematically ask yourself as you iterate your way to success. It is not a onetime exercise but a recurring activity you engage in with your business's best minds to continually learn, evolve, refine, and, at times, radically re-create your business.

Many companies write a strategic plan at the end of each year to serve as their map for the next year. While this is indeed a valuable intellectual exercise, the next time they see that plan is one year later. Imagine a football coach putting together a game plan for Sunday's big game. At halftime they are down 28–0. Would the coach say, "Well, since we write out the plan for each game in advance, we'll stick with the old plan for the next half. We can talk about changes next week"? Of course not. The best coaches make adjustments to their plans at halftime. They change their defense or adjust their offense in response to real-world results. Your business should do the same thing. Schedule your own halftime, go back to the locker room, revisit your plan, and make ongoing adjustments based on the market feedback.

Our model of strategic planning is iterative. We encourage you to frame powerful questions, explore potential answers, test those answers in the market, and willingly (dare we say eagerly) challenge those trial answers every quarter.

As you iterate your way to success, you must find a working balance between change and momentum. Change says, "Hey, let's question our focus and radically redesign our approach." Change is essential to keep your business fresh and relevant in the marketplace. It allows you to nimbly seize opportunities. But change also stresses out your team and puts increased demands on your limited resources. It often causes you to scrap existing systems, products, and infrastructure as they become dated, even obsolete. Going from a static idea to a moving, producing idea in the market demands extra energy (read: time, effort, and money). Meanwhile, momentum says, "I'm working. Feed me! Support my success and build on my breakthroughs." It leverages your known winners and doubles down on your strongest successes by scaling and optimizing what has been proven to work in the market. But momentum can be lazy, complacent, and naïvely oblivious to market shifts that can pull the rug out from under it.

Clearly, you need both to successfully grow your company. You need change to secure your future and best position your resources to go after opportunities; you need momentum to give you time to build on successes and develop the infrastructure that allows you to scale. The two often come into conflict and cause tensions in a company.

How do you maintain this dynamic balance? While there is no perfect, permanent answer to this question, we do have a working solution that has produced amazing results for our businesses, and for tens of thousands of business owners we've shared it with. Once a year (we suggest December or early January), go off-site with your executive team for a one-to-two-day strategic planning retreat. Your assignment is to take a critical look at your long-term plan and examine the state of your business with the following questions: What are the current market conditions? What trends are coming our way? What is our business context? Are our key objectives still the right ones? Is our strategy to get us there still working? Once you know the state of your business and market, make any big-picture corrections needed.

Every quarter, we recommend taking your executive team off-site for a half- to full-day session to revisit this plan and concretely map out the next 90 days. You'll lay out your top three strategic priorities for the coming quarter, and write up a simple one-page plan of action specifying exactly what you must do that quarter to grow and develop your business. At the end of the quarter, you'll repeat the process. At the end of the year, you'll step back and do a fresh pass on your big-picture, long-term plan for your company.

The reason why this process works so well is because it prompts you to look freshly at your business every quarter while also allowing you and your team to dive deep into the execution and actually accomplish meaningful progress on clearly prioritized focus areas of maximal importance to your business. Without this clear framework, too many owners change their focus so often that their teams are left dizzy, feeling the vertigo of too much change, and frustrated because, just when they seem to be on the verge of really getting something big done, the owner shifted the playing field yet again, forcing them to abandon projects prior to completion and wasting hours of their effort. The business owner who finds himself changing things on his team monthly (or even weekly!) may just be addicted to the adrenaline of change or the illusion that this enhances his control. Generally, stepping back once a quarter to determine your priorities and resource allocation is your best bet.

An important part of finding the balance between change and momentum is the concept of "opportunity cost." In addition to constantly reexamining the work you are currently doing in your company, you also need to look at what work you could pursue if you changed your focus. Some businesses get so much momentum going that it would be like stepping in front of a speeding train to change direction in any way now—but those same businesses could potentially be speeding past new opportunities that could make the difference between short-term survival and long-term success. The concept of opportunity cost prompts you to ask, *If we weren't doing the things we are doing right now, are there other goals or activities that we would be free to pursue that are more valuable?* If not, then keep on truckin'! If yes, you'll need to examine how to pursue these more lucrative opportunities.

Done well, these quarterly 90-day sprints reward your business with the biggest benefits of regular opportunities to change and adapt, *and* also the results you get from the momentum of disciplined execution on known priorities quarter by quarter.

We've developed a six-part process to craft your big-picture strategic plan and turn that plan into a one-page quarterly action plan. Let's dive in.

• • •

PART ONE:

# Three Questions to Start Your Big-Picture Planning Process

Take out your notes from chapter 3 clarifying your business context (your market, your competition, and your position). Working from those, here are the next three questions for you to answer about your current position that will help you define the highest-level view of what you are in business to do and why it matters. Take 10 to 30 minutes to thoughtfully answer these three fundamental questions.

### Question One: Why is your company in business?

This first question cuts to the heart of why you are in business in the first place. Often it helps to approach this from two perspectives: externally (your customers) and internally (your team).

**Externally:** What is it that your customers *really* buy from you?

For example, with Jeff's former company Priceline.com, its reason for being was to help Jenny get to her sister's wedding at a price she could afford. With David's company Maui Mastermind, his clients may be superficially buying business coaching services, but what they are really purchasing is a business they love owning. When someone orders from Amazon.com, they might be buying a widget, but what they are really getting is the simplicity and ease of buying from a trusted marketplace that offers just about every type of product available online.

**Internally:** Besides just the money, what inspires you to show up to work each day?

At Jeff's current company, ColorJar, their internal "why" is to help companies maximize the success of a new product launch. They see themselves as mission control of the moon launch; when that Go button is pressed to launch, they know they have done all that is possible to make sure everything has been prepared, tested, and will work flawlessly. Their internal "why" shapes how they see themselves. Sure, they are in business to make a profit, but what really inspires them is to design, orchestrate, and run a perfect product launch for their clients.

What are your company's external and internal reasons for being in business?

### Question Two: What is your Singular Goal?

What is the one goal that you are mobilizing all your company's resources to accomplish over the next three to five years? This is your Singular Goal. Another way of coming up with your company's Singular Goal is to ask, "What business are we committed to build over the next three to five years?" Approach your answer two ways: quantitatively and qualitatively.

**Quantitatively:** What does your future business look like in terms of things you can measure and count? What are your annual sales? Your annual number of transactions? Your market share? Your average sales per customer? Your gross profit margin? Your operating profit margin? Your retention rate of clients? Your sales per employee? Pick three to five of the most important *quantitative* ways to describe your future business.

**Qualitatively:** What does your business look like in other ways that you can't easily measure or count, but that still matter greatly? Who are your key customers? What is your brand? What is your market reputation? Who do you have on your team helping lead the business? Which markets do you serve? What key products or services do you offer? What impact do you have on the lives of your customers? What is your future role as the business owner? Pick three to five of the most important *qualitative* ways to describe your future business.

After you've combined both the top quantitative and qualitative descriptions of your future business into one single target, whittle away at this picture until you are left with a tight, clear statement that can guide your company's focus over the next several years. Here's an example of what a Singular Goal might look like:

*By December 31, 2020, we've built Growth, Inc., into a thriving Level Three business with $24 million in annual sales and a 20 percent operating profit margin. We have deeply penetrated four distinct verticals, with no single vertical or customer representing over 30 percent of our business. We continue to grow at 25 percent a year or more.*

Of course, your Singular Goal depends on your industry, business model, and goals. The key is that you want to end up with a concentrated statement that describes the one target all of your team is focusing on helping the business reach.

By the way, because you took 5 to 15 minutes to clarify the business you are working to build both quantitatively and qualitatively, you have just completed one more key component to help you reach that goal—you have drafted your enterprise-level scoreboard. (And you thought you were just dreaming on paper!) You now have a clear list of the key variables that describe your key business objective. These are the variables that you'll measure at least quarterly.[2] For example, looking at the sample Singular Goal we shared, you can see that for Growth, Inc., their enterprise-level scoreboard would track: gross sales, operating profit margin, number of verticals they have penetrated and how deeply, percent of total sales each customer and vertical represent, and the company's annual growth rate.

### Question Three: What's in it for you and your team?

If you accomplish your business's Singular Goal and build the business you've described, what's in it for you and your team? In other words, what would accomplishing this goal do for each of you? Obviously the financial rewards come easily to mind, but don't stop there. What opportunities would accomplishing your Singular Goal create for your team? What kind of impact would

---

[2] You can download a free four-page PDF version of our Strategic Planning Tool discussed in this chapter at **www.ScaleYourBusinessToolKit.com**. See appendix for full details.

you have in the lives of your customers and how would that directly impact you and your team? What kinds of cool new projects would it open up for you? What you're trying to do with this line of questioning is concretely link the rewards and meaning of reaching your business's Singular Goal with your and your team's deeper drives and motivations.

This is a great topic to bring up at a team meeting. Again, make sure you go beyond just the financial rewards to the other nonfinancial benefits that energize and inspire everyone in the company. If one of the keys to successfully growing your business is having a great team of highly motivated people, then the key to motivating those people is to make sure that you as a business owner know what your employees want out of their careers at your company as well.

PART TWO:

# Uncover Your Business's Top Leverage Points

If part one of the planning process had to do with clarifying the big-picture view of your business, then part two focuses on spotting the biggest leverage points inside your business to help you accomplish your top goals. A leverage point is a place in your business where a small amount of effort yields a magnified return, and identifying them is one of the keys to scaling your business.

## Conduct a "S-O-O-T Review"

A S-O-O-T (Strengths-Obstacles-Opportunities-Threats) Review is a structured way to see where your business stands today. It helps you lay out the key landmarks from which to craft your company's strategy to scale. Here are the four components to review about your company:

**Strengths:** Any strategy that you eventually choose must rely on your strengths. Keeping your company's Singular Goal clearly in mind, what are its top five strengths to accomplish this goal?

**Obstacles:** Each key obstacle is a clue as to what next steps you need to take in your business. What are the five biggest obstacles that you see currently blocking your company from achieving its Singular Goal? When you look at them from this frame, obstacles become stepping stones to help you cross the gap from where you are to where you want to go.

**Opportunities:** Opportunities are where you win the game of business. What are the three biggest opportunities your company could pursue that could potentially help you achieve this goal? One guiding strategic principle is to put your best people and resources on seizing your biggest opportunities rather than fixing your squeakiest wheel.

**FIGURE 4.1:** CONDUCT YOUR S-O-O-T REVIEW

| Five Top Business Strengths | Five Biggest Business Obstacles |
|---|---|
| 1. _____ | 1. _____ |
| 2. _____ | 2. _____ |
| 3. _____ | 3. _____ |
| 4. _____ | 4. _____ |
| 5. _____ | 5. _____ |
| **Three Greatest Business Opportunities** | **Three Greatest Business Threats** |
| 1. _____ | 1. _____ |
| 2. _____ | 2. _____ |
| 3. _____ | 3. _____ |

Copyright © Maui Mastermind®

**Threats:** What are the three biggest threats that could massively harm your business? Look at those things that, if they fell wrong, could literally put you out of business: a harmful market trend, a disruptive competitor, government regulation, or even the loss of a key customer or supplier. Your goal is to take simple, proactive steps now to mitigate these dangers later. There will likely come a day when you'll either say, "Why didn't I do something about this earlier when I had the luxury of time?" or "I'm so glad I prepared for this contingency."

## Find Your "Sweet Spot"

Your business's biggest Limiting Factor is the single biggest constraint currently limiting your growth. It's the *one* ingredient that, if only you had more of it, would allow your business to grow instantly. The more precisely you can identify your Limiting Factor, the easier it is to effectively push it back. For example, if you say your Limiting Factor is "lack of sales," you might come up with a dozen ideas to increase sales.

But before you solve this, dig deeper and see if you can pin your Limiting Factor down more precisely. Is it the need for more leads on the front end? Perhaps your business has enough leads but instead lacks the sales capacity to effectively follow up on all the leads you are already generating? Or is it that you have plenty of sales staff, but lack a proven sales process so your sales team's conversion is too low? As you can imagine, depending on your answer here, you'll need to take an entirely different approach to solve that Limiting Factor. That's why it is so critical that you narrow down your Limiting Factor to the most accurate kernel you can.

While every business has multiple limiting factors, each has *one* Limiting Factor (capital L; capital F) that does the most to limit its growth in the here and now. Pushing back your biggest Limiting Factor is a major leverage point to grow your company. One key way to grow your business is to identify and push back your current Limiting Factor quarter by quarter. In the context of creating a true Level Three business, you need to build the systems, team, and controls to help you push back your Limiting Factor *long-term*. Doing this usually exposes a new Limiting Factor you'll need to work with. It's like lying in bed on a cold night with a blanket that just isn't big enough. You pull it up to your chin because your chest is cold, and in doing so, leave your feet exposed to the cold. You curl up your feet under the cover and the blanket untucks from your back. Every time you push back your Limiting Factor so it is no longer your biggest constraint, you expose a new Limiting Factor to work on. Good! This is how you grow your business in a leveraged way—by focusing each quarter on pushing back your current Limiting Factor.

Once you've pinpointed your company's current Limiting Factor, it's time to pick the highest-leverage tactics to push this Limiting Factor back. We developed the three-part **Sweet Spot Analysis Tool** to help you do just that.

First, brainstorm a list of all the potential ideas you have to push back your Limiting Factor. Don't settle for five or six ideas, push yourself to come up with at least 10, ideally 15 to 20, ideas. For example, if your Limiting Factor is a lack of sales capacity to follow up effectively on the leads you currently generate, your list of ideas could include: a better lead-qualification system to prioritize your sales efforts, hiring more salespeople, or creating a sales video to do some of the selling for you. The key is to push yourself to come up with as many ideas as you can that could potentially help you push back your Limiting Factor. The best way to come up with a few great ideas is to first come up with a potential list of *a lot* of ideas.

Next, run your brainstormed list of potential tactics through two filters: the "Low-Hanging Fruit" filter and the "Home Run" filter. A **Low-Hanging Fruit** is a no-brainer opportunity that you're almost certain will work. While it may or may not have a big impact, it is fairly straightforward to implement and you have a very high level of confidence that it will work. A **Home**

**Run**, on the other hand, is an opportunity that if you hit it well and all goes just right, has a *huge* payoff for your business. Go through each brainstormed idea on the list and ask, *Is this tactic a Low-Hanging Fruit?* If it is, mark it with "LH" for Low-Hanging Fruit. Then in a second, separate pass, go through your list of brainstormed ideas and ask of each item in turn, *Is this tactic a Home Run?* If it is, mark it with "HR" for Home Run.

What you're looking for are those tactics that are *both* Low-Hanging Fruit and Home Runs; these are your Sweet Spot ideas, the highest-leverage choices to push back your Limiting Factor. Low-Hanging Fruit are easy to implement with high odds of success, and Home Runs offer big impact if they work. These Sweet Spots are the best tactics to focus your company's resources on first.

Finally, now that you've identified your Sweet Spot tactics, turn them into a mini–action plan of who does what by when. (See Figure 4.2 for a sample Sweet Spot Analysis.)

## Put Your Key Strategic Decisions on Trial

It's been said that the enemy of the best is not the worst, it's the good that wastes resources and distracts you from investing your resources in the best. This directly applies in your business as you likely are frittering away your resources (such as staff time, focus, money, and customer attention) on too many choices.

This is again the concept of opportunity cost. The things you are working on are "good," but there may be "great" things that would yield a better return if you focused your resources there instead. This is why we are coaching you to put your key strategic decisions on trial every six months. While not every choice is critical for every business, generally three to five of them strongly influence your company's growth. Pick the three to five strategic decisions that matter most to your company, and put them on trial twice a year. Here are the seven strategic decisions you can examine:

FIGURE 4.2: THE SWEET SPOT ANALYSIS TOOL

## Sweet Spot Analysis™ Tool

**Low-Hanging Fruit:** Solution that would be easy to implement with a high chance of success.

**Home Run:** Solution that, if it worked, would have a BIG impact.

**Sweet Spot:** Solutions that are both Low-Hanging Fruit AND Home Runs.

**Our single biggest Limiting Factor is...**

Lack of sales capacity

| What are 10+ ideas to push this Limiting Factor back? | LH | HR | Mini Action Plan | Who | By When |
|---|---|---|---|---|---|
| 1. Hire more salespeople. | ☑ | ☑ | Solution 1: Hire more salespeople. | | |
| 2. Sell to groups vs. 1:1. | ☐ | ☐ | ☐ Clarify ideal salesperson profile. | Tim | 1/21 |
| 3. Outsource part of sales. | ☐ | ☑ | ☐ Rewrite ad and place. | Tim | 2/1 |
| 4. Train our techs to sell. | ☑ | ☑ | ☐ Hire 2-3 new associates. | Tim | 3/1 |
| 5. Create a sales video. | ☐ | ☐ | ☐ Orient and train. | Tim | 3/30 |
| 6. Sell via website. | ☐ | ☐ | Solution 2: Train techs to sell. | | |
| 7. Sell annual contracts. | ☑ | ☐ | ☐ Pick 4 techs to train. | Lee | 1/31 |
| 8. Charge for sales appointment (no longer do free evaluation). | ☐ | ☑ | ☐ Create 2 sales tools for them. | Lee | 2/15 |
| 9. Create prospect scoring system. | ☑ | ☑ | ☐ Train them (role-play). | Lee | 2/28 |
| 10. Shorten sales cycle. | ☐ | ☑ | ☐ Evaluate and refine. | Lee | 3/15 |
| 11. Create incentive prospect loses if sale not closed in 30 days. | ☑ | ☐ | Solution 3: Prospect scoring system. | | |
| 12. Create sales events to get multiple prospects in office at one time. | ☐ | ☐ | ☐ Create baseline scoring system. | Ellen | 1/21 |
| | | | ☐ Test against last 6 months of leads. | Ellen | 2/15 |
| | | | ☐ Refine scoring system. | Ellen | 2/28 |
| | | | ☐ Implement with sales team. | Ellen | 3/15 |

Copyright © Maui Mastermind®

1. **Choice of target market.** Who will you focus on selling to and who will you ignore? Which markets are the easiest for you to dominate? Cost the most to reach? Are the most profitable for you? Taking all this into consideration, which clients

should you fire? Phase out? Refuse to take on? Aggressively court? Who should your customers *really* be if you want to reach your business's Singular Goal?

2. **Choice of product or service.** Which products or services will you develop and promote? Which of your products have the best margins? The strongest competitive advantages? Are the easiest for you to scale? Which products or services should you eliminate? Phase out? Aggressively promote?

3. **Choice of business model.** How will you profitably charge for the value you bring to the market, and who will be paying for that value? Will customers buy a product or rent a hosted solution? Will you sell direct to your market or through a wholesale model? Will you use physical locations, mobile locations, conferences, or sell online? If you didn't have your current investment in how you do things and were starting over today totally fresh, what business model for your company would most excite you?

4. **Choice of pricing.** How will you price your product or service? In relationship to your costs? Your competitors? The cost of your customer's pain? Should you price with one large payment due up front or with an ongoing subscription fee paid monthly? Or offer long-term financing to your customers? If you have a limited supply of your product or service and strong demand, how do you use pricing to control demand? It's all too common for business owners to have legacy pricing or pricing models left over from when they first opened their business. Back then, you often had lower costs since you were operating on a shoestring, and priced relative to your competition with the goal of being lower cost than they were. Well, that might have served you once upon a time, but does it still? If you were starting fresh with how you price and the payment options you offer clients, what would you choose?

5. **Choice of marketing channel or sales model.** What is the main means by which you market and sell your product or service? Do you use an inside tele-sales force or a field sales team? Do you use strategic partners who already have existing relationships with your target market as your main means to sell, or do you build your own marketing list? What marketing or sales channels are working well for you that you should scale? Which are ineffective and should be cut or phased out?

6. **Choice of positioning and branding.** What "parking spot" have you chosen for your company? What is your essential brand promise and your top three brand emotions? Is this choice of position and branding consistent with how you are perceived by your market? Is it consistent with your real strengths? If you were a third-party consultant looking at your business, what choice of positioning and branding would you recommend the company go after and why?

7. **Choice of product pathway.** How will your customer likely move through your suite of products or services? Which will be your "gateway" purchase? What is the desired flow of purchases they will make to optimally benefit from your product or service? How does this optimal purchase pathway relate to how you currently do business? What changes or adjustments do you need to make?

All too often business owners get so caught up in the day-to-day adrenaline of running their business that they forget to step back and ask the hard, strategic questions that would have such a dramatic impact on their business. Take Thomas Jordan, the owner of a successful mobile bottling company.

Jordan's company, Peregrine Mobile Bottling, mainly served wineries in Northern California and Oregon. The business was doing well, but he wanted a clearer path forward to continue his growth and knew he needed a better strategy to scale. With a little prompting from us, he stepped back and put his key strategic decisions on trial, especially his choices of market and service offering. Although the fifty-five-foot production trailer that he and his team brought on-site to bottle for his customers was technologically head and shoulders better than his competitors', on many jobs, he wasn't able to price in this greater value because of the customers he was serving.

Thomas recognized that he needed to focus on the niches that would pay a premium for the higher quality and other advantages his equipment offered that his direct competitors simply couldn't match. He chose to focus on the higher-end wineries that valued his company's greater precision and quality. He also went after wineries that produced semisparkling wines because he was the only mobile bottler in the market who could provide this value-add in his services. By leveraging his technological advantage to focus on semisparkling wine producers, Thomas was able to grow his business by over 35 percent in less than 12 months. By putting two of his strategic decisions on trial, he found that his best growth strategy became obvious.

PART THREE:

# Choosing Your Business Strategy

Now that you have clarified the bigger picture, explored the biggest leverage points inside your company, and put your key strategic decisions on trial, it is time to pick the strategy that will help you best harness one or more of these leverage points to accomplish your big-picture goals.

Here is a six-question sequence you can use to craft the best strategy for your business:

1. **What criteria would a successful strategy have to satisfy?** In other words, what would a winning strategy need to do for you in order for it to work? For Thomas, a winning strategy

would have to help him command a premium price by working with customers who valued his higher quality and technological capabilities, dominate a niche market that was large enough for him to grow 200 percent over a three-year period, and differentiate his value offering relative to any alternatives the market had.

2. **What possible strategies could you choose that would likely meet all or most of the above criteria?** Brainstorm a list of all the potential choices you have. Thomas's potential strategies included aggressively courting semisparkling wine producers and hard cider producers.

    Which of the potential strategies seems best suited to give you what you want while relying primarily on your current strengths? Remember that you are trying to win a gold medal in something, so always focus on the things that you and your company do exceptionally well. For Thomas, his strength was his technical advantage to not only bottle liquids, but also control the carbonation during the process.

3. **In order for this strategy to be successful, what assumptions would have to prove true?** For Thomas, this included the assumption that consumers wanted semisparkling wines, and that he could manufacture these wines at attractive prices for the wineries that were his customers.

4. **How could you measure or observe this strategy in action to see if it is in fact working?** What should you pay attention to that would provide objective data about whether your assumptions are true and the strategy is in fact working? Create a dashboard internally for your assumptions so that you can closely monitor whether or not they are proving true, or if adjustments need to be made. Thomas researched wine sales data to verify the upward trend in consumption and sales of semisparkling wines. He also test-marketed his carbonation

bottling services to his customers, measuring the price premium he was able to command.

5. **How would you know that your strategy wasn't working, and at what point should you stop and choose another strategy?** What is the stop-loss point that signals you've reached your threshold for investing in this strategy? It's important to determine in advance what success would look like, and also what failure would look like, so you don't keep investing time and money once you've hit your stop-loss threshold.

6. **If you should hit that stop-loss point, what is your rollback plan?** What is your plan B and even plan C to handle the contingency of your chosen strategy not working?

Here is another case study of how this question cascade can help you find your winning business strategy. Genevieve was the founder of the online babysitting and pet-sitting service Sittercity.com. She originally started the company to help solve a problem that she herself was facing—finding reliable sitters that were prescreened and responsible hires. She originally marketed direct to consumers, and the business worked, growing well over the first seven years. Then growth slowed to a halt. Her company had reached a plateau that she didn't know how to break through.

Rather than just keep pushing harder with her existing strategy, or even picking a new one, Genevieve followed the process we just shared with you. She laid out the criteria that a winning strategy would have to produce for her. The strategy needed to give her a way to market one-to-many versus one-to-one, so she could sell one larger group or association on her service and they would promote the service to all of their members; the groups or associations she worked with would have to have a large membership base to promote her service to; those members would have to be people with kids and/or pets; the members would need to be people who traveled a lot.

When she brainstormed all the potential strategies that could match her criteria, she kept coming back to the idea of marketing to the U.S. Department of Defense. Its employees were relatively young, many with kids and pets at home. Plus they regularly had to travel, both on short and long trips. Approaching the Department of Defense was a scary move for Genevieve as she had never sold to the military before, but she knew it was worth trying. She contacted the Department of Defense offering to provide a solution to one of its employees' problems—how to care for their children or pets when they traveled. In essence, Genevieve said, "Hey, check me and my company out thoroughly. Then and only then let your employees know about our website. Your employees will get a discount on our services and you'll have happier employees." The strategy worked and worked big. Once she was reviewed and approved, the Department of Defense promoted her site to close to a million of its employees!

In her past, Genevieve would have dismissed this strategy because it intimidated her. But when she went through the structured questions you just learned, she realized that pursuing the Department of Defense really did potentially meet all her key criteria. It paid off handsomely too. She doubled her business over a 24-month period and Sittercity.com has continued to grow.

Genevieve and Thomas are great examples of this seven-step process in action. You can see by these structured questions that we approach crafting your strategy with the real bias of iterating and testing to find the winning strategy. Once you've found your proven winner, we believe strongly in the power of doubling down and pressing that winning strategy forward. The key is that rarely will you know which strategy is the winning one right from the start. Smart entrepreneurs accept that they don't have all the answers and take smart, small steps that yield great results, if they work. And if they don't work, these missteps are survivable and yield great insights to help owners more effectively take their next steps.[3]

Yes, this approach takes a little bit more time—emphasis on "little bit"—but it dramatically increases your chances of success. It protects you from blindly choosing a strategy and jumping in with all you have before you have proven it will work. It prods you to challenge your status quo and think through your strategy freshly. And it keeps you from stubbornly sticking with a failing strategy far past the point where you should have known it was a bust. All of this from a simple six-step process that takes less than 30 minutes of time to think through? We think that's a great return on investment.

PART FOUR:

# Applying Reverse Leverage by Saying No

There are two layers to any strategy. The first layer is your choice of big-picture path to accomplish your key objectives and goals. This could be the choice of a new product to develop and launch, the selection of two markets to clearly focus on, the creation of a new pricing structure to sell your service under, or even a combination of several of these elements. This is the "theoretical" part of creating your strategy.

There is a second, deep layer to strategy—the practical, "on the ground" reality of how your company's daily decisions about where it focuses resources cumulatively define what your strategy actually is in the real world. You might say your strategy is X, but if day-to-day you don't back that up by actually investing your key

---

[3] There are two fantastic books that helped us put to words what our combined decades of practical experience as entrepreneurs taught us on this subject. They are *Just Start* (Schlesinger et al.) and *How Will You Measure Your Life?* (Christensen et al.). In fact, on **www.ScaleYourBusinessToolKit.com** we've posted what we consider to be the ten must-read books for all business owners.

resources (e.g., employee time, customer attention, money, equipment, capacity, etc.) in this area, then this reality isn't your strategy. Your *real* strategy is the one that gets the resources, regardless of what you *say* your strategy is.

If we were there with you in your business as informal observers and advisers, what would we actually *see* your business investing resources in? Whatever your business consistently invests its best resources in defines what your real strategy is. This can be a painful realization when you finally see how much of your resources are being wasted and that your beautiful strategy has no legs. Further, despite what your strategy is, or whatever the posters on your walls say, your team will always respond to the things that you yourself seem focused on. They will spend their best efforts on the things you actually judge them on, not the theoretical plan you created at the beginning of the year. Deploy your best resources to do the things that can actually help you win.

We once worked with a company that had developed a product that could reliably deliver important messages *securely* to key personnel, and then report back on their engagement around that message, telling the sender if they read it and acted on it. Their official company strategy said they were marketing this tool as an HR solution for delivering highly sensitive communications that needed to be responded to. When we visited the company, however, we saw that their marketing and sales teams weren't actually doing this. Instead, they were spending the majority of their time and money creating collateral material to show why people should use their product instead of email. Their sales team was attending conferences in the email industry. In essence, the marketing and sales teams were acting as if the strategy was to sell to the IT departments of large companies, not through the HR door.

We pointed out to them that if their goal was to get engagement from HR departments, then their people should be spending all their time and effort visiting HR departments. They took our feedback and acted on it, reassigning their best resources to focus on the direct tasks of working with HR managers instead of the indirect tasks of trying to get in through the IT departments. The result of this realignment with their stated strategy was immediate. Within a six-month period they increased sales by over 80 percent.

The idea of "reverse leverage" is to say no to something ordinary so you can free up resources for better, more potent things. Considering your chosen business strategy, what activities or initiatives should your business reduce, discontinue, phase out, or avoid altogether? Actually list these activities or behaviors on a "Stop Doing" list. Every quarter, revisit this list, adding new items that might otherwise tempt you to squander your limited company resources.

PART FIVE:

## Your Capabilities—Thinking Ahead About What Ingredients You'll Need to Achieve Your Business's Singular Goal

You've likely heard the expression that the best time to plant a shade tree is 50 years ago. Looking back, what capabilities do you wish you would have cultivated as a business five years ago? Although we can't give you a way to go back in time to have done just that, we can prompt you to make sure that five years from today, you answer that same question very differently.

Ask yourself: Over the next three to five years, what capabilities will my company need to cultivate, acquire, or tap into to achieve its Singular Goal? These capabilities could include the competencies and strengths, the staff, the products or services, the resources, the systems and controls, and the strategic elements necessary for your business to achieve its top long-term goals.

Let's pretend you were an injection-molding plastics manufacturer in the United States in early 2000. You would have seen more and more of your customers ordering from competitors in

China and India, driving down prices, shrinking margins, and commoditizing the products you sell. What would you do?

This was exactly the situation in which Stephanie Harkness, owner of Pacific Plastics and Engineering, found herself. She and her husband Jack had spent more than ten years in the business, building their company into a real success, but all of that was threatened by the increased presence of overseas competitors. She realized that her company needed to develop the capacity to compete on price for large orders, which meant that it needed an overseas production partner. In her case, Stephanie decided to co-venture on a facility in India. Now, when her company approached customers, it had the ability to offer both faster turnaround from its United States–based facility and also lower-cost production offshore, if that is what the customer wanted. It was a clear growth move.

Stephanie also knew that her exit strategy—selling the business—called for her company to establish itself as a leader in a lucrative niche that was of much higher value than the traditional injection-molding plastics work they had done in the past. She determined that this niche was the world of medical-device manufacturing. This was not a market they were able to step into overnight; it took several years to develop the skills, experience, and accreditation that allowed them to add this value offering to their mix. Once they did, however, the impact was massive. When Stephanie and Jack went to sell their company, they commanded a huge premium (three times more than their competitors') because of how valuable these enhanced capabilities were to their market.

It's important to think about trends and new developments in this process. For example, digital media was a new technology that seemed to have no home when it first came out, so many companies ignored it, including those in the music industry. If they had wondered more about possible uses of this new technology, they might have predicted the MP3 and digital music formats and started retooling their businesses in advance.

Now it's your turn. Take five minutes to look at your capabilities relative to your Singular Goal. What are the positives, the needed capabilities you have currently that are strengths of your company? What are the negatives, the capabilities you don't currently have but will need if you are somehow going to reach your Singular Goal? What steps can you take this quarter to enhance your capabilities so that you'll be better positioned as a company to achieve your Singular Goal?

## The Power of a Rolling, One-Page Quarterly Action Plan

At this point, you've looked at your company from the highest level. You know why you're in business, whom you serve, what they really want from you, and what your company's top objectives are. You've also identified the key leverage points and big-picture strategy you'll use to reach your business goals. So how do you make all of this actually work in the real world?

The key to executing on your strategy to accomplish your business goals lies in the quarter. The quarter is the perfect unit of time to bridge your big-picture goals, which likely have a two- to five-year timeline or longer, and your weekly planning and daily action. It's long enough that you can get meaningful units of work done that collectively bring you closer to your long-term goals, but short enough so that you can frequently course-correct and hold your focus.

We want to walk you through a simple system to create your one-page quarterly action plan. Yes, you read right: one page! You're busy, overwhelmed with competing demands for your time and attention—and so is your team. Your one-page quarterly action plan accepts this reality and lets you have a clear, visual anchor to hold your company's focus true for 90-day sprints. A one-page plan forces you to distill your key action items into a short list of prioritized demands that you can see in one whole place with a single glance.

**FIGURE 4.3:** SAMPLE 1-PAGE QUARTERLY ACTION PLAN

# Sample Quarterly Strategic Action Plan

| Focus Area One:<br>Increasing production capacity<br><br>**Criteria of Success:**<br>• Written process for how we produce our core service.<br>• Conducted a Sweet Spot Analysis to increase our production capacity by 15+%.<br>• KPI: Revenue generated per service team production days. | Action Steps/Milestones | Who | By When |
|---|---|---|---|
| | ☐ Map out our current "production" system. Identify biggest current constraints. Conduct Sweet Spot Analysis to best increase production capacity. | Carlos | 1-15-xx |
| | ☐ Review Sweet Spot ideas and pick the winners. Create implementation plan. | Carlos | 1-31-xx |
| | ☐ Formal check-in #1: Insights? What's working? What adjustments need to be made? Update plan. | Carlos | 2-21-xx |
| | ☐ Formal check-in #2: Insights? What's working? What adjustments need to be made? Update plan. | Carlos | 3-15-xx |
| | ☐ Review status at end of quarter—capture lessons and plan to refine production system into Version 2.0 next quarter. | Carlos | 3-30-xx |

| Focus Area Two:<br>Hire a great director of marketing<br><br>**Criteria of Success:**<br>• Have clear, written role and candidate descriptions.<br>• Reduce candidate profile to the 5 "must haves" and hire to those specific items.<br>• Have written onboarding plan to successfully integrate our new hire.<br>• Formally debrief at end and improve our hiring process for future. | Action Steps/Milestones | Who | By When |
|---|---|---|---|
| | ☐ Create a written job description and candidate profile. Reduce to the 5 "must haves" for this role. Review both with key stakeholders. | Tina | 1-15-xx |
| | ☐ Create our written recruitment game plan. | Tina | 1-21-xx |
| | ☐ Launch recruitment efforts. | Tina | 1-31-xx |
| | ☐ Run our selection process and get to our finalist candidates. | Tina | 3-7-xx |
| | ☐ Create our written onboarding plan for this hire. | Tina | 3-15-xx |
| | ☐ Hire our winning candidate and run our onboarding process. | Tina | 3-30-xx |
| | ☐ Formally debrief process: What worked best? What can we do to improve our hiring process for future? Update hiring process based on learnings. | Tina | 3-30-xx |

| Focus Area Three:<br>Increase client retention<br><br>**Criteria of Success:**<br>• Complete retention analysis and explicitly identify the 1–2 biggest "drop points."<br>• Retention "Tiger Team" to conduct Sweet Spot Analysis and implement ideas to increase retention.<br>• Formally debrief at end and create Q2 plan to continue improving retention rate.<br>• KPI: Retention score. | Action Steps/Milestones | Who | By When |
|---|---|---|---|
| | ☐ Analyze current retention stats and drop points. Share results with retention Tiger Team. | Marcus | 1-15-xx |
| | ☐ Conduct Sweet Spot Analysis to increase retention rate. Pick 1 or 2 winners and create implementation plan for quarter. | Marcus | 1-21-xx |
| | ☐ Formal check-in #1: Insights? What's working? What adjustments need to be made? Update plan. | Marcus | 1-31-xx |
| | ☐ Formal check-in #2: Insights? What's working? What adjustments need to be made? Update plan. | Marcus | 3-7-xx |
| | ☐ Share results with leadership team along with formal retention game plan for next quarter. | Marcus | 3-15-xx |

Copyright © Maui Mastermind®

Here is our three-step process to craft your one-page quarterly action plan.

## Step One: Pick Your Top Three "Focus Areas" for the Quarter

Every quarter you'll sit down and decide on what the top three Focus Areas for your business are for that quarter. You may decide that your Focus Areas are increasing your lead flow, improving your sales conversion system, speeding up your collections cycle, or making a specific key hire. Your Focus Areas are the three most important areas for your business to spotlight during the coming quarter. Sure, you'll still have to "take care of business," dealing with your normal operational needs to push the business forward, but your Focus Areas will pinpoint where you will invest a portion of your *best* resources that quarter because you know that these areas are what will really help you scale and develop your business.

Why do we limit your company to three Focus Areas? Why not four or seven? Because too many top priorities means you have no top priorities. Ninety days comes fast, and if you spread your company too thin, you'll find that you partially do more things instead of fully doing a few key chunks that actually produce value for your company. Not only is this a waste of resources, but it is incredibly frustrating for your team, who crave clear priorities and strategic direction. If you want, choose two or only one Focus Area for the quarter. Just make sure you cap your choices at three.

What should you choose for your Focus Areas? Below is a simple cheat sheet to help you determine what Focus Areas to pick for your business for the coming quarter.

**Focus Area One: Pushing back your current Limiting Factor.** Your first Focus Area should be something that directly helps you push back your number-one Limiting Factor for your business. By definition, your Limiting Factor is the single biggest current constriction to growth, and hence it is a great leverage point. If you take concrete steps each quarter to push back your current number-one Limiting Factor, you'll be putting your resources where they will do great good in growing your business.

**Focus Area Two: Seizing one of your biggest opportunities.** Your second Focus Area should be about seizing one of your company's biggest opportunities. You win the game of business by effectively leveraging big opportunities, not by inching your way along accepting the status quo. That is why each quarter you should choose one of your biggest opportunities to invest some of your best resources in. Often some of the best opportunities will take more than one quarter to seize, and as such you may find yourself working on this Focus Area for several quarters.

**Focus Area Three: Mitigate one of your gravest threats.** As you uncovered in your S-O-O-T Review, every business faces threats that could deeply harm or even kill it. That's why for your third Focus Area, we recommend looking at your short list of the top threats facing your business, and picking one of those threats to mitigate this quarter. Maybe you can't eliminate it completely in one quarter, but you can take definite steps to reduce your business's exposure to this danger.

## Step Two: Clarify the Criteria of Success for Each of Your Three Focus Areas

Now that you've picked your three Focus Areas for the quarter, it is time to clarify your criteria of success for each. What would you need to accomplish this quarter in order to feel successful in this Focus Area? Be ruthlessly realistic about what is possible for you to accomplish in 90 days. Generally we suggest you try to pick criteria of success that you have control over (or at the very least over which you have a great deal of influence). It's important to look for criteria that are as objectively and quantitatively measurable as possible. When criteria are too subjective, you may reach the end of the quarter without agreeing on whether or not you succeeded.

Also, we suggest that for every Focus Area you pick one "Key Performance Indicator" (KPI) to track. If you look to this KPI to determine your performance, you'll know if your company is on track to succeed in this Focus Area (more on KPIs in chapter 11). In laying out the criteria of success for each Focus Area, not only are you defining what success will look like in this 90-day sprint, but you now have a clear yardstick against which to measure progress as you go. Plus, laying out your criteria of success for each Focus Area *before* you map out your action steps provides clear clues to what you'll actually need to do over the quarter. Most of your action steps are evident in your criteria of success.

## Step Three: Lay Out Your Key Action Steps and Milestones for This Quarter

Now is the time to lay out the key action steps and milestones you need to take or reach to accomplish your criteria of success for each Focus Area over the coming quarter. In order to keep your plan to one page, you'll likely break each Focus Area down into five to seven action steps and milestones. While your plan must be detailed enough to guide your actions, it must not be so detailed that you feel overwhelmed or lose yourself in the minutiae.

If your quarterly plan creeps into 2, or 3, or 12 pages, you just won't use it. We know this. When you have a one-page plan, you can easily keep a printout of it on your desk. You'll refer to it each week to see what key steps you need to take that week to progress your business. And your team will digest and use the plan too. Of course, you can go into greater detail on one of your Focus Areas to help you plan better, but do that in a separate document and not your one-page plan.

For each action step, pick a specific team member to be ultimately responsible for executing the step by a definite date. While you can have multiple people contribute to a specific step or steps, you need to pick one person who is tasked with the responsibility and authority to get that step done and done well. We say that this person "owns" the task. This sense of ownership is critical to your success. It's hard to hold anyone accountable for missed milestones when it wasn't clear who was really responsible in the first place. With this structure, the owner doesn't have to do all of the work herself—she just needs to be responsible for making sure that it gets done in the best way possible within the company.

Congratulations! You now have your first quarterly action plan. Here's a quick recap of our strategic planning framework.

> **Annually: Full Big-Picture Strategic Review.** Is the destination still the same? Is your overall strategy working? What major adjustments need to be made? How is the world changing around you?
>
> **Quarterly: Strategic Execution.** How effectively are you executing on your strategy? Is it still the best strategy to follow? What has changed in the world around you? What fewer, better things do you need to focus on this quarter to grow and develop your business? What tactical changes need to be made to best execute your strategy?
>
> **Weekly: Accountability on Deliverables.** What three items are most important for you and your team to do this week? Did you get your items done for last week? What did you learn? Are you still on plan? What tactical adjustments need to be made? (We'll have quite a bit more to say starting on page 209 about creating the best accountability structure to get results.)

Together, your big-picture strategy, quarterly one-page action plan, and weekly execution will give you and your team a powerful and comprehensive framework to scale your company. In the next chapter, we'll share with you one more critical component (learning to read the world) to make sure your strategic planning doesn't become complacent or anemic.

> **SCALING PRINCIPLE FOUR:**
> **CREATE THE RIGHT STRATEGIC PLAN AND REDUCE THAT PLAN INTO A SERIES OF ROLLING, ONE-PAGE QUARTERLY ACTION PLANS THAT HELP YOU EXECUTE AND GET RESULTS.**

# PRINCIPLE FIVE

## LEARN TO READ THE WORLD SO YOU BUILD FOR TOMORROW'S MARKETPLACE

In August 2000, Jeff was working as the CEO of an entertainment start-up. He was trying to make a remake of the hit movie *Grease* with pop sensation 'N Sync in the starring role. He knew the band and was spending the day with them while they did a promotional event at the flagship store of one of the largest music retailers in the world. While his friendship with the band didn't make him one ounce cooler, it did give him a unique view into the inner workings of the music industry.

Because of the immense popularity of the band at that time, the CEO and several other top executives of the music company were in the store for the event. Watching people come in and out of the massive store to buy music, Jeff turned to the company's CEO and key leaders and asked why they thought people shopped in their stores.

"To buy CDs," they told him. When Jeff replied, "I don't think so. Nobody here or anywhere wants to buy a CD," they looked at him like he was nuts. They responded indignantly, "Do you have any idea how many millions of CDs we sell a year?"

Jeff pushed further. "Nobody in the world wakes up in the morning thinking to themselves, 'Wow, I wish I was holding a round piece of plastic with a hole in it right now.' They wake up in the morning thinking, 'I want to hear that new song right now!' They *have* to buy a CD, but what they *want* is to listen to a song right now!"

Walking away in disgust at Jeff's apparent stupidity, the CEO said to him, "What's the difference?"

The difference is this: If the music industry had understood that it existed not to sell records or CDs but to offer the fastest, easiest way to let you hear the song you wanted to hear, they would have invented the iPod and iTunes. Instead, they got steamrolled by Apple, a company *not even in the music industry*!

Now Apple makes billions of dollars selling music online, while record companies and music stores have suffered years of massively declining sales. And that major music retailer? They are no longer in business, having filed for bankruptcy the first time in 2004, and finally closed their doors for good in December 2006, six years after Jeff's visit to the store. All because the music industry let its vested interests blind it from seeing what its customers really wanted and the ways in which the world was changing. What they didn't do was constantly scan the world around them to see what was coming next and make the hard choices to reinvent themselves before someone else came along and pulled the rug out from under their feet.

They kept saying, "We're doing fine," right up until the day they went over the fiscal cliff. Those words, "We're doing fine," may just be the three most dangerous words that any business owner can say. In a rapidly changing world, the status quo never stays static for long.

If you think the upheaval of the music industry was a fluke, think again. Remember Arthur Andersen? How about Swissair? Or Circuit City? Or Hollywood Video? For years each of these companies was "doing fine," feeling like they could do no wrong. That is, until they day they went out of business or into bankruptcy.

We are not trying to scare you, but we do want to strongly remind you that your business cannot rest on its laurels. Scaling Principle Five says that you must learn to read the world so that you stay relevant and build your business for tomorrow's marketplace, not yesterday's reality. If you don't, your business will become marginalized and dated. That's why it is so important that you learn to read the world, to connect the dots between trends and ideas from various parts of the world to your business. This ensures that you are building your business with an eye on the future.

In the 1930s in St. Louis, Missouri, Grand National Bank added a new innovation to banking—the drive-up teller. For the first time ever, bank customers could make deposits or withdraw money from the comfort of their car. It took over a decade for In-N-Out Burger founder Harry Snyder to connect the dots and apply this innovation to restaurants when he opened his first In-N-Out restaurant with a drive-through lane in 1948. Can you imagine a fast food restaurant today without drive-through windows? This was an idea that was invented in one industry (banking) and took over a decade to be applied to another industry (restaurants).

When was the last time you left your industry for a day to go explore another, seemingly unrelated one? Have you *ever* done that? Probably not. Most people don't. It may never have seemed necessary or important for you as a restaurateur to look for ideas at your local bank, or your local medical doctor, or your local car dealer. Likely you felt the problems you faced in your industry were unique. But the world is a smaller place today, and trends tend to move freely across industries and geographic boundaries. If you don't broaden your world to let strange ideas connect, you just might be missing out on your next big innovation—and as a result, you could get left behind by your competition.

In this chapter we are going to share with you a proven two-step process you can use to read the world around you, and to use those insights in growing your company.

## Step One: Stimulate Yourself with New Inputs

As humans, our default setting is to fall into habitual patterns. We drive the same way to work each day. We visit the same websites, read the same magazines, and listen to the same podcasts each month. It's almost as if we go on autopilot as we live much of our lives.

But creative breakthroughs don't come from following routine. They come from seeing the world in a new way. This is why the first step in this process is to regularly explore the world, letting your natural curiosity pull you along. One of the best ways to be creative is to let outside stimuli help you make a strange connection between two seemingly unrelated ideas. This is what comedians do that startles and delights us as they point out the outrageous craziness in our daily lives. This is what business innovators do too; they let an idea from one part of their world collide with a problem or opportunity they are facing in another area, and then they connect the dots.

So the first step in this innovation process is to consciously make time to stream new ideas and inputs through your life to spark magic.

Set aside 30 minutes a week to:

- **Flip through a magazine that you'd normally never pick up.** Read with a fat sharpie (or Apple Pencil) in hand and circle, underline, and annotate as you go.
- **Watch a webinar for a totally unrelated industry.**
- **Visit a business that you've never seen before** and ask a ton of questions about why they do what they do.
- **Google a topic that you've never Googled before** and follow the links down the rabbit hole to see where it takes you.
- **Play the "Mash Up" game.** Ask yourself what it would look like if you took two or more unrelated ideas that you saw and applied them to your business.

- **Spend a few hours with a group of people who are from a radically different age, culture, or industry from yours.** Ask them questions about their world (we'll cover several great questions to ask them later in this chapter) and take notes on their answers. You can do this by paying your teenage daughter and four of her friends $20 each to give you an hour of their time. Or you can attend a trade show for another industry and interview three of the people there for their answers. (If you're over 40, we strongly recommend you start by interviewing a group of 16- to 22-year-olds. You'll be blown away by how differently they see the world.)

The goal of this step is to let two things happen. First, to let the magic of randomness mix things up so that when you follow your habitual thinking patterns, you're starting from a different place and working with a slightly different set of initial conditions. You'll be amazed at how radically this can lead you to new conclusions. The second goal of your regular 30-minute explorations is to let new ideas collide, knowing that out of some of those collisions new breakthrough ideas are born.

Keep a journal of the ideas you come across that you find intriguing or moving or frustrating or exciting. David keeps his "reading the world" ideas in photo album on his iPhone and iPad. He takes screenshots and marks them up as he reads magazines, websites, business books, and blogs. This way the photos are always with him so we can flip through them later to stimulate his creative thinking. Jeff does the same thing. Every time he reads or hears something interesting, he makes a note using Notepad on his phone or computer. A few times a week, he looks at all those interesting data points to see if he can connect all the dots to create something new, a new product or way of thinking that might not even have been possible yesterday.

Consider each new thing you learn as another puzzle piece in the game of business, and constantly shuffle the puzzle pieces around on the table to see what you can make of them.

This isn't a big or tedious research project. Just jot down simple one-line bullet points, or quickly cut and paste interesting photos or headlines. The idea is to start a blender of new thoughts and ideas whirling in your head, and to let those ideas mix and recombine.

## Step Two: Engage in Structured Innovation Sessions Every Quarter

We suggest that as part of your quarterly strategic planning process, you and your executive team (if you have one; solo if you don't) take 45 minutes to creatively reimagine the world and brainstorm ideas by answering the following six provocative questions.

*Question One: "What can I do today that I couldn't do yesterday?"*

(E.g., *share a video with the world from my cell phone; have 2,000 people join me for a webinar; video conference with five of my team members for effectively no cost; access hosted solution software for nominal fees where once I would have had to pay thousands or millions to develop the tool on my own;* etc.) The goal of this question is to make sure you constantly reassess the landscape of possibilities. The world changes so fast now that every morning when you wake up, something has changed that may create a brand-new opportunity for your business.

*Question Two: "What things do I observe in the world that..."*

**Startle and Surprise Me:** (E.g., *how ubiquitous smart phones have become—I feel lost when mine isn't at hand or when it's out of power; how when a question in conversation comes up that we don't know the answer to, someone just Googles the answer on the spot; how little direct mail I get in the mail anymore;* etc.) Identifying the things in the world that surprise you prompts you to integrate relevant changes into your business.

**Delight and Intrigue Me:** (E.g., *how Wikipedia makes finding an answer so easy; how convenient it is to order off Amazon.com; how I can be a voyeur in the lives of old acquaintances on Facebook without even talking with them; how much I live my life to a soundtrack of my choosing;* etc.) Think of ways to apply these intriguing new tools to the work you do for your customers.

**Terrify Me:** (E.g., *how short people's attention spans are now; how overwhelmed with choices I feel; how powerfully the media plays up fear, making the world appear so unsafe and dangerous; how intermixed the economy is and how things that I have no control over can wreck my business;* etc.) This exercise can help you spot threats from outside your industry or your normal range of competitors that you might otherwise have never seen coming.

**Question Three: How has the way people are buying things in the world changed (especially outside of my industry)?**

(E.g., *how we consume bite by bite with micropayments; how we comparison shop online, using aggregated websites and comparison engines to find products that we may not have known existed; how we listen to what other people say about the product via customer reviews, and how we no longer rely on the seller or advertising to educate ourselves; how we use new forms of payment that didn't exist a few years ago;* etc.)

**Question Four: What is changing in the lives of our customers (whether it has anything to do with our company or not)?**

(E.g., *they are getting older as a whole [on average five to ten years older]; they are spending two hours a day on social media; regulatory restrictions are making their lives much tougher and increasing the time they must spend per site on compliance; they are struggling to find the right workforce domestically;* etc.)

*Question Five: "Wouldn't it be cool if . . ." (Come up with at least ten endings to this statement.)*

(E.g., *wouldn't it be cool if we had a waiting list for our service that was booked six months out; wouldn't it be cool if I could eliminate all spam from my inbox; wouldn't it be cool if customers paid us to give them a sales quote; wouldn't it be cool if we had an app that thousands of our customers used that taught us exactly what they loved and used with our product; wouldn't it be cool if I could be onstage playing with a rock band;* etc.)

All five of these questions are designed to help you spark new ideas, to effectively see the world differently than you normally would. Why? Because we filter our own ideas with our preconceptions of what will work and what won't—and we base that on what worked in the past, not what might work in the future. We need to open our minds and toss out some crazy ideas in order to find true innovations. By themselves, these ideas may not be concrete enough for you to take action on. But when you mix a little creativity with an idea you brainstormed, you can come up with some pretty cool stuff. For example, take that last idea, "Wouldn't it be cool if I could be onstage playing with a rock band?" Think of the ways you could apply this to a business. If you were a concert promoter, could you have a journalist or blogger embedded onstage writing about the experience and sharing that experience in real time? Or maybe you could get a celebrity friend of the band with a big following to do it? Could you hold a contest to give three fans the chance to join the band and let the band's fan base choose the winners online?

What if you didn't have a concert promotion business and instead own a dry-cleaning business (about as far from the cool of a rock band as we can think of at the moment)? Could you have a local reporter spend a day behind the scenes and write about what it really takes to deliver your beautifully cleaned and pressed clothes? Or could you follow the day in the life of a rock band's stage clothing in your video blog with a final press release afterward? (Oh, and don't forget the huge signed poster of the band thanking your cleaners to hang in your store.) Or maybe you do it from the frame of a local business tycoon. (Can you see the suit sitting at the closing of some big deal?) Even if none of these ideas are what you choose, they still move your thinking to new territory, and all the rest of your strategy session will be infused with a new energy.

**Question Six: Imagine you were starting to build your business from scratch all over again today. What business would you ideally build? What would it look like? Why?**

Pretending that your business didn't exist at all and you were starting from scratch today allows you to get creative about your business without worrying about all the existing worries, challenges, givens, and investments that you normally take for granted.

An amazing example of this is when Apple decided to "cannibalize" its own product line. Apple was making lots of money selling iPods. But they saw that one day someone would be able to add music players to phones. Instead of waiting for someone else to kill its iPod business and then struggling to find a revenue stream to replace it, Apple launched its next growth engine right away by developing iPhones that had music players on them, so customers no longer needed to purchase its previous product. It was a bold and painful move in the present that created a huge future for Apple.

Now that you've stretched the way you normally look at the world and your business, it's time to look for ways to apply your insights to your business. What insights came up through this process that you can no longer afford to ignore? The question is no longer whether or not you can afford to do R&D and risk some potentially unsuccessful experiments. The question is, can you afford *not* to?

Instead of starting from your existing products and company, or even what other companies in your industry do, pretend none of it exists. When most companies try to innovate, they look at their existing business, products, and industry, and try to find a way to make it better. If you have been in the health care business for 20 years, you won't achieve a breakthrough by staring at 20 years of health care products and services. Instead, you'll make small linear improvements and create health care 21.0.

In order to really stretch your thinking when it comes to your company, imagine what you would do if you were starting your company from scratch *right now*, using everything you've learned, and all the new technologies and techniques that were not available when you first founded your company. Go a step further—pretend there are absolutely no rules, no regulations, no requirements—even the laws of physics could be broken! Don't edit your ideas by what's possible or practical; imagine anything is possible and there are no constraints. Go wild and think of ideas with the abandon of a seven-year-old child! When you start with the way you would build your company if there were no rules, and then edit it back to reality, you wind up way farther ahead than if you start with your existing business and try to improve it.

Here's a real example from one of the regular innovation sessions that Jeff's company, Colorjar, runs. His team was focused on a client working to innovate in the fast-food industry. The goal was to improve the speed at which you get your lunch in the drive-through lane. Instead of going inside a McDonald's to look at ways to improve the existing systems, his team pretended they were designing a new drive-through lane that would exist in a world with no gravity—literally! With these constraints eliminated, how would an ideal ordering system work? One of the Colorjar team members suggested that customers could text their order to McDonald's, then, without ever stopping the car, unroll their windows as they pulled through the drive-in lane. Restaurant employees would use the same cannons used to fire T-shirts into the crowd at concerts to fire lunches into the moving cars. Crazy, yes, and very unlikely to happen tomorrow. But that wide-open thinking was the starting point, and designing back from this idea led Jeff's team to come up with a new idea for speeding up drive-throughs: installing an electric eye in the drive-through parking lot that could see your car coming, check your order history, prepare your order, and bill you electronically. Not as much fun as shooting lunch from a cannon, but a really cool idea that went straight to prototype. Regularly re-imagine your business using this type of blue-sky methodology so you keep your company fresh and relevant. In a rapidly changing world, it's the only way to keep your business safe.

Continue to read the world and gather cool, interesting, terrifying, intriguing data points for your next innovation session. The journey never ends.

What does thinking big inspire you to build or do? What is the first step and when will you complete it by? Do something. Even a small experiment with a new way of doing something or a new product is better than doing nothing at all. Take that first bold step, and see where it leads you. A journey into imagination sometimes yields powerful and unexpected results. Reading the world is a new discipline that will pay dividends over the long term.

---

**SCALING PRINCIPLE FIVE:**
**LEARN TO READ THE WORLD SO THAT YOU STAY RELEVANT AND BUILD YOUR BUSINESS FOR TOMORROW'S MARKETPLACE, NOT YESTERDAY'S REALITY.**

# PART III

# Obstacles to Scaling (and How to Overcome Them)

Obstacles are a blessing. They give you sturdy stepping-stones to cross the gap from where you are to where you want to go.

# PRINCIPLE SIX

**REMOVE THE PREDICTABLE OBSTACLES TO GROWTH—
PILLAR BY PILLAR**

At its core, every business has five functional areas that carry the load and provide a stable base upon which to scale and grow: Sales/Marketing, Operations, Finance, Team, and Executive Leadership. In the next five chapters, we'll share with you dozens of concrete strategies and tools to help you systematically remove the predictable obstacles to growth, pillar by pillar.

Before we go into each pillar in detail, however, we want to give you a high-level view of these five pillars of your business, and then ask you to evaluate your business's performance in each of them using a tool we call the Five-Pillar Audit, which we've included at the end of this chapter (see Figure 6.1).

## Pillar 1: Sales/Marketing

No leads, no sales. No sales, no business. It's that simple. The Sales/Marketing pillar finds clients, makes sales, and generates revenue. It's the part of your business that makes it rain cash.

Sales is everything you do to make your offers as effective as possible and to close selling opportunities. Your offers can be delivered in a variety of ways—from trained sales reps in a call center, to a sales force in the field, to direct response sales letters or print ads, to interactive websites, to retail locations.

Marketing is everything you do to get one of your offers in front of the right prospective buyers under the best possible conditions. Marketing crafts your company's identity and positions it in the hearts and minds of your marketplace so you consistently generate the volume of sales leads you need. You want leads that are primed and ready for your selling systems to convert into thrilled clients or repurchasers.

Too many entrepreneurs focus on this pillar only because they have to, not because they want to. They feel intimidated by the idea of selling. But understand this: When your business is in Early and Middle Stage Level Two, it's crucial for you as the company founder to focus a majority of your energy on generating profitable sales. If you don't, your new business won't survive, let alone thrive. Only as you grow your business can you relieve yourself of the responsibilities of this pillar. In the early days of your business, you focus on making sure sales happen, which means meeting with clients and closing deals yourself. Later, however, you must shift your focus to creating repeatable and scalable sales and marketing *systems* that don't depend on your involvement.

Every pillar has clear component responsibilities it must take care of for the business to succeed. While we'll go into depth on every pillar's core functions in the next five chapters, we want to give you a quick summary of what these responsibilities are as we highlight each pillar.

**THE SIX KEY RESPONSIBILITIES OF
YOUR SALES/MARKETING PILLAR**

1. Defining your target market and knowing what it really wants
2. Clarifying your offer(s) and creating sales collateral

3. Lead generation and lead management
4. Lead conversion and sales system
5. Sales and marketing strategy and planning
6. Branding and positioning

## Pillar 2: Operations

Your Operations pillar is the part of your business that creates the products or delivers the services your business offers, fulfilling on the promises made by Sales/Marketing. Your Operations pillar also performs the general and administrative back-end functions of your business.

No company will thrive without having a well-organized, strong Operations pillar. Sure, you can generate sales, but unless you're able to fulfill on the promises you've made, your business won't last.

As crazy as it may sound, there are many cases of businesses that were killed by success. Their front-end sales/marketing pillar was so successful that their back-end operations pillar couldn't keep pace. This caused an extreme disconnect between the promises these companies made their customers and the execution in fulfilling those promises. The results were predictable—angry customers and enough bad press to put these companies six feet underground.

A very visible example of this was the online retailer eToys.com. They had a great marketing program and sold thousands of toys for the 2000 holiday season. But their operations department was less than a well-oiled machine, and many families got their holiday presents delivered in January, after Christmas. The company's lack of operational efficiency led to bad press, many lawsuits, and ultimately the death of the company.

• • •

**THE SIX KEY RESPONSIBILITIES OF
YOUR OPERATIONS PILLAR**

1. General administration
2. Key company infrastructure (e.g., facilities, equipment, websites, etc.)
3. Production and quality control
4. Fulfillment and delivery
5. Customer service
6. Purchasing/cost controls

## Pillar 3: Finance

The Finance pillar of your business encompasses all the essential functions of collecting, tracking, distributing, and reporting the flow of money in and out of your business. It includes your billing procedures, collection practices, and accounts payable processes. It also includes all financial reporting from balance sheets to profit and loss statements, and the managing of cash flow. As your business matures, it will also include the management of risk, the sourcing of capital, and the forecasting to help your management team make better business decisions.

**THE SIX KEY RESPONSIBILITIES OF
YOUR FINANCE PILLAR**

1. Bookkeeping and financial reporting
2. Collections (AR)
3. Bill paying (AP)
4. Budgeting, planning, risk management
5. Cash flow management
6. Tax planning/filing

## Pillar 4: Team

Your Team pillar establishes how you hire, orient, train, assess, compensate, and if necessary, let go of, your staff. It deals with your policies and procedures for team members and the legal requirements of working with employees.

To grow most businesses, you'll need talented team members to both spark and support that growth. Whether it's adding sales team members to increase sales, engineers to design products, or accounting staff to keep track of the money, your company's greatest source of leverage is its ability to attract, hire, integrate, and empower talented, committed people to play on your team.

Scaling your company and growing your freedom depends on your ability to find, hire, and retain talented people to help you build the systems and controls your business needs to scale.

**THE SIX KEY RESPONSIBILITIES OF YOUR TEAM PILLAR**

1. Hiring and new team-member orientation
2. Regular staff evaluation, coaching, and training
3. Compensation and benefits administration
4. Compliance procedures for all applicable labor laws
5. Troubleshooting and personality challenges
6. Exit process for both friendly partings and expedited exits (firings)

## Pillar 5: Executive Leadership

The final pillar of your business is Executive Leadership—the area that leads your leaders and sets the big-picture direction for your company. It's also likely the final area for you to personally let go of. Remember, many Level Three business owners *choose* to stay in their businesses as CEOs and continue working. The key distinction is that this is a choice, not a requirement for their companies' survival. Successful business owners groom their successors and ready their organizations to successfully transition leadership when the time is right. They intentionally nurture the culture that helps their team successfully operate the business even when the founder is not there in the room.

On a macro level, your job as leader is establishing what your business stands for and how it sees itself; that is, where it focuses its resources and what its key goals and priorities are, and the values through which it makes its daily decisions. Leaders create the narrative through which all stakeholders interpret the business and their relationship to it. As you grow your business, it becomes increasingly important that you shape the stories and traditions that will become part of your company's heritage. These hold your business on course even when you're no longer present each day to drive it.

On a micro level, you want to create a business in which all team members understand their roles, know what they're responsible for, how success in their role will be measured, and how leaders and team members will provide feedback as they go.

Your most important role as a leader is building a workplace where the most talented people want to come to work and stay. When people who could work anywhere want to work for you, that's when you know you got it right.

**THE FOUR KEY RESPONSIBILITIES OF**
**YOUR EXECUTIVE LEADERSHIP PILLAR**

1. Strategic planning (company as a whole)
2. Leadership development/continuity planning
3. Company culture and traditions
4. Communication company-wide

It's time to map your baseline of precisely where your company currently stands in each of the five pillars. The Five-Pillar

Audit tool below will give you a quantitative breakdown of how your business is doing. Take five minutes and complete it now.

---
**FIGURE 6.1:** THE FIVE-PILLAR AUDIT
---

Rate your five business pillars in each of the six subareas listed on a scale from 1 to 10, with 1 being lowest and 10 being highest. For example, under "lead generation," if you think your business does a fantastic job at consistently generating new leads, give yourself a 9 or 10. If your business struggles to find new leads, barely generating enough to keep it afloat, give yourself a 2 or 3. Total your score for each pillar (possible high score of 60 for each pillar) and then total your score for the entire audit. When you're done with this audit, we'll walk you through your score and what it means for your business.

### SALES AND MARKETING PILLAR:

Lead generation  _____

Lead conversion  _____

Client repeat business  _____

Client "upgrade" business  _____

Revenue growth (Short term)  _____

Revenue growth (Long term)  _____

Subtotal  _____

### OPERATIONS PILLAR:

General administrative function  _____

Performance of client work or fulfillment of client orders  _____

Client's rating of your company's performance  _____

Cost controls for operation of your business  _____

Business infrastructure (website, physical location, equipment, etc.)  _____

*Operations Pillar (cont.)*

Scalability of your core product or service _____

Subtotal _____

## TEAM PILLAR:

Communication systems for team to work together _____

Having the right team in the right positions _____

Systems for bringing on new team members _____

Systems for training and reviewing team members _____

Compensation and benefits administration _____

Compliance procedures with all applicable laws _____

Subtotal _____

## FINANCE PILLAR:

Accurate and timely financial reporting _____

Budgeting _____

Financial controls _____

Collection systems for accounts receivable _____

Effective management and use of financing _____

Cash flow management in general _____

Subtotal _____

## EXECUTIVE LEADERSHIP PILLAR:

Each team member has a clear understanding of the mission, values, and goals of the company, and how her individual role contributes to the bigger picture _____

Current business strategy _____

Review process for company performance, direction, strategy, and development _____

Troubleshooting major challenges when they come up  _____

Leadership training  _____

Company culture and tradition  _____

Subtotal  _____

---

**Complete score for your business (scale of 30–300):**  _____

It isn't important that you score high now because what matters is not where you start but where you finish. To end up where you want to be, it's critical to have a reliable way of evaluating your positions along the way. This abridged Level Three Audit is a simple tool to help you do just that.

If you have an **Early or Middle Stage Level Two** business, chances are your scores are currently quite low in three or more pillars. This is normal. You'll improve these scores rapidly when you follow the Level Three Road Map to progress your business. The two most important pillars at these stages are your Sales/Marketing pillar and your Operations pillar. If either scored below a 20 (out of a possible 60 for each area), then you have concentrated work ahead to improve these two critical pillars. At this time in your business, if you score low in reliably generating leads, closing on sales, fulfilling on your client promises, and collecting on what you are owed, you need to immediately remedy that situation. *These functions are the minimum requirements to have a sustainable business.* Remember, basic survival is the first hurdle to get to Level Three.

If you own an **Advanced Stage Level Two or Level Three** business, chances are your scores in most pillars are high (above 40 for each pillar). Look for any specific pillar in which your score was below 20. This area of your business needs immediate attention.

We encourage you to repeat this Five-Pillar Audit each quarter. Make sure to date and save your scores so you can note your progress over time. This tool is a simple, structured way to know where and how your business is progressing, and determine where it needs more of your attention.

Now it's time to go back to your business—pillar by pillar—and look for ways to refine each core pillar to create and sustain rapid growth.

> **SCALING PRINCIPLE SIX:**
> **REMOVE THE PREDICTABLE OBSTACLES TO GROWTH, PILLAR BY PILLAR.**

# YOUR SALES/MARKETING PILLAR

## BUILD SCALABLE LEAD-GENERATION AND CONVERSION SYSTEMS

Every company has to generate leads; every business must convert leads into sales. The fact is, if you want to sustainably scale your business, you are going to have to evolve from growth based on your personal production to growth based on the stable base of systems, team, and controls we've been emphasizing throughout this book. With respect to your Sales/Marketing pillar, this means building with the end in mind—the day when you personally are not needed to generate leads or close sales. In this chapter, we'll keep linking our suggestions for tactics and strategies to grow sales with systematic ways to implement each.

Take the example of Dominique Molina, owner of Certified TaxCoach.com, a specialized training company that trains CPAs in tax planning. She's grown her $1.2-million-a-year business primarily based on two things: giving public talks to industry groups (lead generation) and selling her training program memberships via live webinars (lead conversion). The downside was that her lead generation was heavily reliant on her getting on a plane to go speak at business conferences and industry meetings. As the mother of a young son, she wanted to scale her company without its being so reliant on her being away from her family.

When we met with Dominique during a coaching session, we learned she had never used any kind of tele-sales team to follow up with all the prospects she had gathered from her public talks who either didn't attend her webinars or didn't buy on them. Our advice to her on her sales challenge was twofold. First, based on our past experiences with her type of business, we recommended that she develop a tele-salesperson (or team) who could follow up with all her leads that weren't buying on the webinars. At conservative estimates, we projected she could double her sales using her existing lead flow. The second prong of advice we had for Dominique was that developing her tele-sales capacity would also allow her to radically enhance her "back end" sales opportunities to add higher-value offerings to her existing clients. After running the numbers, we calculated she could grow her sales by another 50 percent. These two simple "sweet spot" strategies could create 150 percent growth for her from her existing lead pool. Further, both would dramatically reduce her business's reliance on her to personally close business since they would be done by a trained salesperson following a clearly written sales script. This is the power of enhancing and systematizing your sales/marketing pillar.

The first step in removing your sales/marketing pillar's obstacles to scaling is to pinpoint your company's most costly lead-generation weaknesses. Use the ten-point checklist below to evaluate your company's lead-generation challenges. Check the box for any of the challenges that currently hurt your business. If you check more than three boxes, which is very common if you're an owner doing this assessment for the first time, go back to the list and circle the *one* pain point that hurts your business the most. This is where you'll put your initial focus.

## LEAD-GENERATION TROUBLESHOOTING CHECKLIST

❏ **You don't have enough leads to sell to.** Or your lead generation is erratic and you don't have a consistent lead stream you can count on.

❏ **You don't have a system to organize and manage your leads.** As a result you don't consistently follow up with leads in a timely way and many of your sales opportunities slip between the cracks.

❏ **You don't have a structured lead-scoring system.** You waste your sales efforts by squandering your best sales resources on variable leads rather than being able to quickly and easily sort your lead pool to separate your highest-quality leads for follow-up first.

❏ **You don't systematically track your lead-generation efforts.** Without hard data you have no way of determining which of your lead-generation tactics are producing and which aren't. Raw intuition or anecdotal observations are not enough.

❏ **You don't have a *system* to generate leads.** You or a key staff member has all the "know-how" for implementing a marketing tactic in your heads versus a concrete business system. Your company is vulnerable should the key person not be available to do the marketing.

❏ **Your current lead-generation processes aren't scalable.** Either the prospect pool you work with is too small or the system itself is limited, and as such you can't scale the basic lead- generation system(s) that you have.

❏ **Your current cost per lead is too high.** The leads you generate are just too expensive to make sense considering your current conversion rates and average unit of sale. You need less expensive ways to generate leads or better conversion systems to get more from each lead you do generate.

- **Your lead quality is just too poor.** It's like looking for a needle in a haystack of junk leads who either aren't qualified or aren't motivated to buy your product or service.

- **You have a ton of lead-generation ideas but you just don't seem to be able to effectively *implement* them.** You have half done many different marketing ideas, but never seem to finish implementing the majority of them so that they actually produce leads for your business.

- **Your marketing is too reliant on you, and as such you "start/stop" it as other demands in the business pull you away.** As a result, you regularly go through cycles of feast or famine where you alternate between focusing totally on producing your product or service offering with no time to market, and likely no real capacity to take on more work, followed by periods of panic where you see your funnel running low and you scramble to start up your marketing again to quickly bring in more business. Not only does this constant cycling back and forth between the two exhaust you, but you never seem to build enough momentum to break out of this trap.

In our experience working with small and midsize businesses, many mistakenly believe their lead-generation woes are about volume: "If only we had more raw, fresh leads to work with . . ." However, lack of leads is generally a result, not a cause. It's almost always a by-product of one of the other lead-generation pain points. For example, maybe you don't have an organized sales database so the leads you *do* generate get a poorly crafted sales effort and almost no organized sales follow-up. Or perhaps because you don't systematically track your marketing tactics, you can't rationally compare lead-generation tactics so that you end up wasting thousands and thousands of dollars on poorly performing tactics when those same dollars could be reinvested in your best lead-generation producers to scale those winning efforts. Still others may find they regularly go through periods where they have to turn attention away from marketing to other areas of the business, and as a result never seem to build any marketing momentum. To build a Level Three business, you need a lead-generation *system* that you can count on to produce for you regardless of whether or not you personally were there to be the driving and directive force.

Jeff once worked with a company that sold products and services to hotels and hotel chains. They weren't hitting their sales numbers, so they paid to buy more sales leads. The next quarter they still didn't hit their numbers, but by then they had spent so much money on lead generation that their business was in a vulnerable place. Their real problem wasn't that they lacked leads, though; rather, it was that they had no system for scoring or ranking their sales leads. They had no way of knowing which leads should get their best sales efforts and which weren't worth the costly investment of sales energy. Their lead-generation pain point could have been solved with a lead-scoring system that allowed them to filter and rank all incoming sales leads by factors like: Is their budget to buy already approved? Can they afford our product or service? Have they bought this type of product or service before? Can we get to the actual decision maker?

Don't stop at the surface pain point—you've got to go deeper and ask what causes this lead-generation challenge so that your company invests its limited resources in solving the *real* problem.

With this understanding, it is time to look at your core system for generating leads.

• • •

# The Five Steps to Building Your Baseline Lead-Generation System

It's not enough that you learn new tactics to generate leads or close sales. You also need to learn how to build the *systems* that help you generate leads and close sales. That is why we keep emphasizing the importance of systems to help you scale. The problem with informal systems you keep in your head is that they leave your business vulnerable. If you get hurt or busy, no one else knows how to do that key process. Plus, it's hard to refine a system when you can't see it written out. Perhaps most damaging of all, informal systems that are locked in the minds of you and your key employees just aren't scalable.

Here are five steps to building out your baseline lead-generation system. You've likely already created parts of this system but haven't done so formally.

1. **Determine which marketing tactic(s) to focus on first.**

   Pick your single most important lead-generation tactic. This is the one you'll want to systematize first. If you're not sure which of your various lead-generation tactics are most important, ask yourself the following: *If you could only do one thing to generate new leads for your business, what one tactic would you pick?*

2. **Draft the "process layer" of how to implement that marketing tactic.**

   Grab a pad of yellow sticky notes and lay out the steps to implement this marketing tactic. Put one step on each sticky note. The reason this is such an effective way to document your process is that it frees your mind to lay out all the steps, and even edit the steps as you go, into a simple flow of yellow stickies. Don't like the order or missed a step? No problem; just move around the stickies to suit your needs. Once you have the process of executing this marketing strategy or tactic clearly laid out in your yellow sticky notes, write it up into a simple, step-by-step recipe.

3. **Create a rough scorecard to track this marketing tactic.**

    The key here is to make sure you're gathering relevant, objective data that will tell you how well your marketing efforts are going and allow you to compare tactics in order to make smart strategic decisions about where to invest your company's time and money. These numbers will root any forecasts or projections you make in reality versus the "go by the gut" fantasy too many entrepreneurs accept. (We'll have more to say about your sales/marketing metrics in a moment.)

4. **Package your "process" in a way that ensures your team and business consistently follow the steps to get the results you want.**

    As we discussed in chapter 2, every system has two layers to it—the process layer and the format layer. In step two, you wrote out your process layer to this system. Now it's time for you to give some thought to the best way to package each of these steps so that the system is easy to use and works. For example, if the system you're focused on is search engine optimization, tools to package your system could include a one-page "cheat sheet" list of the top keywords; a weekly checklist of the seven most important tasks you want your marketing team to do; an instruction document, including annotated screen shots, that shows exactly how to post text or video blog posts to effectively emphasize keywords; etc. If the system you're focused on is direct mail to targeted lists, tools to package your process could include a tracking spreadsheet to measure the results; your direct mail control letter; a list of your key direct mail vendors with past pricing, terms, and notes; etc.

    The essence of this step is to ask yourself, "What is the best format to package the key steps of this system so that our team can more easily follow it to consistently produce quality leads for our company?"

**5. Implement, track, and refine.**

By paying close attention to the results you're getting from your lead-generation efforts, you'll spot opportunities to improve your system. Whether it's the addition of a new tool like a sales video for your website, or a five-email follow-up sequence that automates part of your process, you and your team will constantly be finding ways to tweak and improve your baseline lead-generation system so that it consistently produces more and better-quality leads. You need to look for ways to improve both the process and format layers. We suggest that each quarter you and your marketing team (if you have one) sit down and conduct a Sweet Spot Analysis to choose the highest-leverage improvements to your lead-generation system(s) to work on that quarter. Then break down and timeline these upgrades over the quarter, staffing out exactly who is responsible for what results and by when. It's this kind of consistent refinement that, over time, will result in a finely tuned lead-generation machine.

# The Four Most Important Marketing Controls

As we previously defined, a control is simply a specialized system that your business uses to make sure that the right steps are being taken, at the right time, to get the right results. Here are the four most important marketing controls to make sure that your marketing system is operating smoothly to consistently produce quality leads for your company.

## Marketing Control One: Marketing Calendar

Lay out your key lead-generation campaigns for the next 90 days on a standard calendar. Then add the deadlines for any key steps required to successfully run those campaigns. For example, one retail service business we coached laid out its quarterly marketing calendar, which included a "front counter upgrade" campaign to enroll clients in its Concierge Level service, and a campaign for add-on service. This latter campaign showed up on the calendar with deadlines for completing the draft marketing flyers, printing the information sheet for its counter team about the special promotion, and posting the new point-of-purchase signage in the store.

Your marketing calendar is a great visual control to make sure you are on track with all the precampaign steps necessary to make your lead-generation efforts successful. It also helps make sure you keep the most important steps front and center to your business so that other urgencies don't pull you away from the consistent marketing necessary to build momentum. Perhaps the most important thing your marketing calendar does is allow you to delegate ownership of many (dare we say all) of the steps to your team, since it gives everyone a powerful way to make sure that all your marketing efforts are on track.

It's often useful to compare your marketing calendar with external calendars as well. David once spent $15,000 promoting a business workshop in San Diego only to learn that he chose a date when the local football team was competing for the division championship. You can likely anticipate the outcome—dramatically lower attendance that he could have avoided if he had only checked the dates against local and national events. Make sure you run your marketing calendar through the filter of outside events and holidays to avoid this same costly mistake.

## Marketing Control Two: Standardized Marketing Collateral

Whether it's a template email sequence you send to everyone who registers on your website, the glossy sales brochure your field sales team uses when prospecting at trade shows, or a white paper prospects can download from your website, standardized marketing collateral is an effective "embedded" control to make sure your prospects get your best sales messaging. Not only will your marketing collateral help your prospects learn about your products or services, but they are also great tools to help train new team members in the company and product knowledge they need to be effective on your team. Further, future vendors will many times use your collateral to help them learn about and produce a better result for your business. For example, a new online marketing company you hire to help you improve lead flow from your website will likely start by looking at your existing marketing collateral to best understand who your target market is, what their most sensitive hot buttons are, and the branding and positioning of your company.

Don't think of this building out of your marketing collateral as an all-or-nothing proposition. Instead, start small and build out your collateral in bite-size bits. What one or two marketing collateral pieces does your business need most? Create your best version of those items first and get your team to consistently use them. Over time you'll flesh out your marketing collateral with better and better brochures, product slicks, web pages, catalogs, direct mail pieces, point-of-purchase signage, and much more. You'll get more talented people involved in helping you create the refined versions of these marketing tools. The key is to start where you are and take the first step to pick the highest-value marketing piece to create first. The rest will come later.

## Marketing Control Three: A Simple Marketing Scoreboard

Building on the theme of simplicity, we want to suggest that you create a simple scoreboard that gives you the high-level results of your marketing efforts. In fact, we'll go one further; we recommend that unless you already have a marketing scoreboard, you start by measuring just three numbers:

**Marketing Metric #1: Your "Cost per Lead."** Measure the total cost of a particular marketing tactic (e.g., pay-per-click advertising, direct mail, trade show booth, etc.) and divide that by the total number of leads that tactic generated in a specific period of time. If you spent $10,000 on your trade show booth, travel, and staff cost and generated 100 new leads, your cost per lead is $100 ($10,000/100 leads). Knowing your cost per lead helps you compare which lead tactics are most cost-efficient, and gives you feedback so you can refine a specific lead-generation tactic to perform better. Plus, any big change in your cost per lead can be a critical leading indicator, good or bad, that you must pay attention to in your business.

**Marketing Metric #2: Your "Cost per Sale."** This measure is simply the total cost of a particular marketing tactic divided by the total number of sales you made from that tactic. Continuing with our trade show example, imagine that of those 100 leads you got from the trade show, you closed 10 sales. That means your cost per sale is $1,000 ($10,000/10 sales). Knowing your cost per sale helps you get a sense of which marketing tactics yield leads that are higher-propensity buyers relative to your cost to acquire these leads.

**Marketing Metric #3: The "Return on Investment (ROI) $1 Spent on Lead Cost."** This final number is a powerful way to equalize various marketing tactics so you can see which one has the greatest return on investment. You calculate it by dividing the total sales you made with this tactic by the total amount you spent on that marketing tactic. Using the trade show example, if your 10 sales each purchased $10,000 from your company, that means that your $10,000 investment in the trade show yielded $100,000 in gross sales (10 sales × $10,000 per sale). In this case, your ROI per $1 spent on lead cost would be $10 ($100,000 in total sales/$10,000 in lead cost for those sales). In essence this means you had a *gross* return of 10x (1,000 percent) on the money you spent on the trade show. Depending on your margins, and how much future business these 10 customers will yield, and a few other factors, you'll know if that return on your marketing dollars for the trade show was worthwhile or not.

**Marketing Control Four: Your Sales Database or "CRM" Solution.** Your CRM (customer relationship management) solution is the system you use to organize your customer and prospect data and manage those relationships over time. Don't let the term intimidate you if you're unfamiliar with it; you've likely been using one for years now even if you didn't realize it. Whether you use Salesforce.com, Infusionsoft, Zoho, Microsoft Dynamics, a custom Oracle database, or another system, your CRM solution is simply the contact management tool that holds your customer and prospect list and also helps you use that information to create and service sales over the long term.

The most rudimentary sales database is a spreadsheet of prospect information that includes a name, address, email, and phone. As your business grows, the spreadsheet solution isn't likely to be your ultimate solution because it is limited. When multiple people use it, the data often become messy and inconsistent as people fill in certain fields in their own styles. Plus, a true CRM solution allows you to automate and systematize much of your sales process, including building in prompts and automated steps or reminders for follow-up, standardized reporting to tell you how your sales efforts are going, and filters that allow you to easily pull marketing lists together and make sure leads are properly assigned to various salespeople.

This isn't a technical book about sales databases. We simply want you to realize that your sales database (spreadsheet or CRM solution) is a form of a marketing control that, when used correctly, helps your business ensure that leads are properly captured and followed up with on a timely and effective basis, and that all the insights gleaned along the way are recorded for future use in a standardized way.

# The Four Fastest and Least-Expensive Marketing Tactics to Generate Additional Sales

With all this talk on lead generation, we want to help you avoid one of the most expensive mistakes that too many business owners make—thinking that their marketing efforts should be focused on finding new, fresh sales prospects.

The "new" and "fresh" labels are seductive. After all, don't you want fresh and new leads versus stale and old? The truth is, though, for most existing businesses, the fastest and least expensive marketing tactics to create rapid growth don't focus on finding new and fresh prospects, but rather on more creatively and systematically getting more from their existing customer base.

When Jeff was building his first company, CTI (which he eventually sold to American Express), it developed and sold desktop travel booking systems to corporations. Every day Jeff's team would search for fresh new leads, hoping to find new corporations to go visit. One day Jeff and one of his salespeople were at a customer site when they heard the customer say, "I wish our expense management vendor was as good as you guys." Jeff and his salesperson both had the same thought. Here they were so busy looking for new customers once they closed a sale that they had never asked their existing customers if there was anything else CTI could do for them. It turned out there was. Adding additional service to their existing contracts was far faster and much cheaper than finding new clients and starting the sales cycle over from the beginning.

Here are four tactics to tap into your *existing* client base to grow your sales. As you read through each tactic, ask yourself how you could profitably apply it to scale your sales.

· · ·

## Tactic One: Formalized Referral Systems

We all know that referred prospects are generally faster and easier to enroll, buy more frequently, and are more loyal. Most business owners we work with tell us that a good portion of their business comes from customer referrals. Yet when we dig a little deeper, we discover that 95 percent of those referrals came to the business by word of mouth. Word of mouth is *passive*. Your business didn't do anything to spark it other than to deliver on your service or product promises (as if that were an easy thing!). A formalized referral system is an *active* referral strategy that you intentionally craft to spark and prompt your existing clients to help you find more prospects.

Bill owns a driver's education company that primarily teaches teens safe driving skills through on-the-road, one-to-one driver's instruction. The primary reason parents sign their teens up for and pay for these lessons is because they want to prevent their kids from getting in an accident. We suggested that Bill tap into this desire to protect their teens from auto accidents by creating a "Safety Circle Program." After the second lesson with a teen, Bill meets with the parents and explains that their son or daughter is more likely to be driven by one of their three or four closest friends than they are to be the one driving. To really protect their teen, it's not enough for their teen to get trained; his or her closest friends need to get the same training so that when their teen is driving with these friends, parents can feel confident that they've done all they can to keep their teen safe.

To this end, Bill goes on to explain, his company created the Safety Circle Program. Bill helps the parents identify the four closest friends of their teen and gives them a special coupon certificate that their friends' parents can use when they bring in *their* teens to get trained. Bill shares the certificate and a simple one-page flyer, then coaches the teen's parents on how to have a direct conversation with the parents of the other teens, suggesting that they work with Bill's company to get their teens trained too. The net result is that Bill turns his customers into allies in generating more business for his driving school.

## Tactic Two: Formal Reactivation System

If you've been in business for more than two years and provided great value to your customers during that time, you should strongly consider adding a formal reactivation system to your marketing mix. A formal reactivation system is a process whereby you systematically go back to those past customers or clients who used to buy from you, but for one reason or another haven't purchased from you in a while, to powerfully invite them to buy again.

At uBid.com, Jeff saw lots of customers register an account, then disappear soon after. When Jeff and his team looked at the data, they saw that there were many customers who could not find the product they wanted at the price they wanted, so they left the site without buying anything. But uBid.com knew what these customers had been looking for, so they created a reactivation campaign that sent follow-up emails to these people, asking them if they would come back if the site offered a slightly different product but in the price range they were seeking. This generated significant incremental sales from a group of customers who otherwise would not have made these additional purchases.

Creating your formal reactivation system is simple. First, gather your pool of past client leads into one list. Whether you compile a spreadsheet of contacts or create a memorized report in your CRM database, pull your list together and document how you gathered this list so that the next time you repeat this process next quarter or next year, your team can follow this process to do it better and faster.

Next, create your outreach strategy. This is going to depend both on the number of past customers you are going to reach out to, and also on the makeup of that list. If the list is small enough, and the dollars make sense, you might arrange to meet with each of them in person to follow up or perhaps divide up the list for your sales team to call through. Maybe you'll send out a series of letters or emails. The key here is to consistently reach out to these former clients and give them a crafted "come back to the fold" offer with a logically compelling reason why you are reaching out to them at this time.

Once you've determined your outreach strategy, the third step is to craft your reactivation message. You need to reconnect first, then make sure to end the conversation with the clear next step you want the customer to take. Do you want them to come back in for an office visit? To have you bid on more work? To place an order right there? Formally script out what you want your team to say when they make this call or visit, or write out the letter or email you'll send.

Once you've gotten your reactivation message ready, it's time to pull the trigger on the campaign. Start making your dials, sending your emails, or arranging your on-site visits. Make sure you track your efforts so that you can measure the impact of the campaign.

The final step is to evaluate the campaign to refine it for the future. If you are smart, you'll not only have your team looking to increase sales, but you'll use your interactions with your former customers to gather valuable insights into the hearts and minds of your market. Is there a consistent trigger for why they stopped buying that you could fix? Were there two features they were dying to have that could be the spark for you to innovate around? This way you will profit not only from the sales you make, but also from the insights you gain in digging into why your customers use your services, and why they might leave.

Let's look at a formal reactivation campaign we helped one of our clients create and implement. Dr. Kim owned two successful dental clinics. Over her 15-year history, the practices had accumulated a large number of patients who kept putting off their regular dental examinations and cleanings. Dr. Kim's office team pulled a list of all their past patients who hadn't been in to see them in more than nine months. Then, in quiet times in the day, her office staff would spend a few hours calling these patients, using a simple script with the express goal of scheduling them to come back into the office for a dental exam and cleaning. Of the people her team reached, 25 percent immediately reactivated and scheduled an appointment on the spot. Another 15 percent of them asked the office to call them in 30 days to schedule an appointment at that time. Not only did this generate thousands of dollars of service volume for Dr. Kim's practice every month, but it also helped her business fulfill its mission of caring for the oral health of its patients. Best of all, this formal reactivation system is now a staple in her office that allows her team to fill in any lulls in treatment hours so that the practice always stays full, utilizing its capacity to best effect.

## Tactic Three: Retention, Retention, Retention!

Over time, every business sees some of its clients leave. This attrition is expensive because in most cases the cost to attract, close, and support a new customer is many times greater than the cost to service and support an existing one. This is the primary reason why a formal retention system can have a great impact on your business. For example, Brad, who owns a commercial insurance business, has to pay five times greater sales commissions during the first year one of his team sells a policy than in year two, when they get the renewal. Patty, who runs a professional service firm, estimates that her support costs in the first 90 days of a new client are 30 percent higher than for her established clients, as she must train her new clients in how to use her services and communicate with her team.

Unless your business is built on a "one sale" model, you'd do well to revisit how your company retains its existing customers and look for ways to systematically enhance how you keep your best customers doing business with you.

First, measure what your baseline retention rate is. You might measure the average number of months a client stays with your service, or the percentage of customers who continue buying your products a second, fifth, or tenth time. The key is to pick one number to measure that gives you an accurate sense of how well your business is doing retaining its customers. Once you have this number, formalize a process to keep it front and center in the minds of your team, ideally on a weekly basis, but at least on a monthly basis.

Next, pull several of your key team members into a conference room and analyze what you think are the two or three biggest "drop points" where you commonly lose customers. What causes them to drop? Why do other clients instead choose to stay? Conduct a Sweet Spot Analysis to pick the best ways to formally plug these drop points so that you retain more of your clients. Could you strategically schedule a visit or phone call on day X? Pre-complete a key step for them so that you help them skip right over a drop point altogether? Add a visual tool that helps them see the progress they've made?

Finally, implement the Sweet Spot enhancements you come up with and track their effectiveness. Then, in several months' time, repeat the process. The end goal is that over time you'll be able to plug the gaps and keep more of your customers buying from you for longer.

Probably one of the most effective examples of a retention system is the airlines' frequent flyer mileage programs. They are so effective that customers will often choose a more expensive fare just to get the miles on the airline where they have already accumulated the most miles. Airlines have continued to enhance these retention programs over time by allowing customers to use their miles to book hotels or spa services, donate them to friends as gifts or to charity, trade them for gift cards, and more. A loyalty program is a powerful retention tool that rewards your best customers for sticking with you, and makes the switching cost of leaving you even higher.

## Tactic Four: Up-sell, Cross-sell, Re-sell!

A company that we worked with in the early days of the Internet specialized in antivirus systems. Their product was one of the best on the market and they sold it well. However, they didn't tell customers that antivirus alone did not provide complete protection for your computer. You also needed a firewall product (which they actually had, but which was sold by a different team), and a malware scanner (which they could have easily offered by partnering with another company). Their customers got annoyed when they discovered that they really needed all three products. As soon as a competitor began bundling and cross-selling these three products, their business quickly died.

Stay vigilant in what you can up-sell, cross-sell, and re-sell to keep your customers committed to the services and products you offer. Strategically map out how you can enhance your customer results by getting customers to buy the optimal selection, choice, and frequency of your product or service.

**Up-sell:** An up-sell is when you offer your customer a richer total package or premium service level or other upgrades that directly relate to what your customer originally purchased from you.

For example, David's business coaching company created a special service level ("Diamond") for companies doing over $20 million a year in revenue, for which his company coaches not only the business owner, but also the entire management team, and facilitates private on-site company strategic retreats. Most clients come to his business because they want help building their company and reducing its reliance on key team members, and for a percentage of these businesses this upgraded service level delivers an exponentially more valuable result.

Generally an up-sell happens right at the point of sale or soon thereafter. In fact, many times your prospect may come to you looking for your base-level product or service, with no knowledge that you even have an upgraded option. As part of the sales discovery process, you'll need to pull out your prospect's needs, desires, and budget, and with that information make the decision of whether that customer would be best served by your upgraded offer or not. Here's the best part: Done right, even if your prospect turns down your up-sell offer, it can often create the contrast you need to make your base-level product or service feel much more affordable and, as such, enhance your sales closing rate.

Think about your own business now. What upgraded product or service offering could you present to your customers, or perhaps just to a subsection of your customers? Keep in mind that packaging your own products together is not the only option. Are there opportunities to bundle in or offer complementary products from other companies?

Here are a few suggestions to spark your thinking:

- What could you bundle together to make an upgraded package to get your client the optimal result?
- What service(s) could you add to this package to get your client an amazing result?
- What product(s) could you add to radically enhance the client experience?
- If you knew that for 5–15 percent of your customers, price was no barrier, and that they just wanted the highest value and level of service and quality consistent with your brand, what could you profitably offer them that would delight and thrill them?

**Cross-sell:** A cross-sell is when you offer your client complementary and related products or services that may or may not be direct enhancements to what your client originally purchased from you. This often happens at the point of sale or soon thereafter, although the timing of a cross-sell can be much later.

Jeff's former company, Priceline.com, was able to significantly accelerate its revenue growth by adding cross-sell products to its original product line. Its initial focus was on selling airline tickets, but many of its customers also needed a hotel room or rental car for their trip. By offering these complementary products, and later bundling them and offering package deals to make the cross-sell even more attractive, Priceline.com rapidly grew sales.

When someone buys from you, what other products or services will they often go on to buy? What other products or services complement or enhance their purchase from you? Could you offer to sell them these items yourself? Or refer out to a third-party company that you have vetted and with which you have arranged a revenue split or referral fee? Or arrange a "lead swap" whereby you reciprocally share leads with one or more of these third-party providers?

**Re-sell:** A re-sell is when you help your customer repurchase (once or many more times) essentially what they purchased from you the first time. This action requires strategically mapping out the optimal repurchase timeline for your customer, and prompting them to follow that timeline.

For example, Kimberly Ackworth, the owner of two successful beauty salons, knows that to keep her clients looking their best, they should come in for treatments every four to six weeks. That's why her salons have a scripted-out process (re-sell system) to schedule the client's next beauty appointment at the conclusion of the current appointment. She starts this right from the first visit with a new client, measuring her system's efficacy by tracking "New Client Retention Score" and "Rebooking Rate." She has between 30 and 50 percent of her clients book their next appointment right there at the time of service. For those clients who don't book their next session as they leave, her business has a powerful direct mail system of postcards and email that it uses to prompt clients to come back in more frequently.

Too many business owners passively wait for their customers to ask to buy again. Not only does this underserve the customer, but it also potentially costs the business many thousands of dollars of easy, high-margin revenue. If your business is one in which your customers buy the same product or service from you multiple times, take two minutes to ask the following three questions:

1. What is the best purchase timeline to help your customers get the optimal result with your product or service?
2. As your business currently does things, what is the average actual repurchase timeline?
3. What simple, leveraged steps could you take that would effectively prompt more of your customers to follow the optimal purchase timeline? (We suggest you use the Sweet Spot Analysis tool we shared in chapter 4 to pick two to three Sweet Spot ideas you could implement this quarter to grow your repeat business.)

## Lead Conversion: Converting Leads into Sales

If the marketing half of your Sales/Marketing pillar is primarily tasked with generating a steady stream of qualified leads to your business, then the sales half is focused on converting those leads into paying customers.

Whether you employ an inside sales team working with customers who come to your location to generate business, an outside sales team that works in the field, a web-based model that sells online, or even a wholesale network whereby other companies generate most of your sales, every business needs a trusted process whereby it effectively converts leads into sales. We call this trusted process your "lead-conversion system." In a moment we'll walk you through exactly how to build your baseline lead-conversion system, but first we want to step back and look at your current system. You already have one; your system may be ad hoc and wholly housed in your head, but you do have a process of some sort, otherwise you wouldn't have been able to generate the business you have.

Before we share with you our process to formally build out your baseline lead-generation process, use the ten-point lead-conversion checklist below to help you diagnose what your most painful and costly lead-conversion challenges currently are. The more clearly and concretely you can pin this down, the better your lead-generation system will be, since you'll better understand the current constraints and needs of that system. Review the list and check the box beside any of these ten challenges your business is currently struggling with.

### LEAD-CONVERSION TROUBLESHOOTING CHECKLIST

❏ **You don't have a focused understanding of your product or service that you can powerfully communicate to your prospective customers.** Or if you do have a clear understanding, your prospects just don't find the way you communicate it to them compelling or enticing.

❏ **You don't have a defined sales process to lead prospects through clear stages to close the sale.** You've never strategically laid out all the steps in your sales process in a visual way so that you could formalize your sales process and work to optimize it.

❏ **You, the owner, are the only salesperson for your business.** All the essential sales know-how is locked in your head (or in the head of a single key employee). If you (or your single key employee) aren't there, no one else would be able to close business.

❏ **You lack the sales capacity to actually process and sell to all the leads you already have.** As a result, many leads spoil for lack of someone to follow up with them.

❏ **You have no reliable control in place to accurately track, measure, and refine your sales system over time.** You don't know what your key conversion rates are at each critical step in your sales process, and as a result you're flying blind, not really knowing if a change you make is working as intended or not.

❑ **Your sales system simply isn't scalable as it exists at present.** It works at your current business volume but it won't scale as you grow.

❑ **You don't have effective standardized sales tools** (e.g., testimonials, sales collateral, scripting, sales contracts, etc.). As a result, you waste valuable time creating improvised sales tools as you go that never seem to turn into the refined sales tools you know you eventually need.

❑ **You lack an organized follow-up system to coherently nurture leads that need more time to close.** You attempt to sell once and if they don't buy, you move on to your next prospect.

❑ **You don't have a back-end offering to up-sell/cross-sell your customers.** Once your customers buy from you, you have no real next-step offering for them to keep buying.

❑ **Your sales scripting is weak and/or your sales team is poorly trained.** You sell based on price with no real scripted process to develop your prospect's need, pain, and aspirations. You don't systematically help your prospect quantify the cost (emotional and financial) of their status quo, and the real value of a solution.

## The Five Steps to Building Your Baseline Sales System

Our guess is that you found the preceding lead-conversion pain-point checklist a bit uncomfortable. It is very common to have checked many of the boxes. Have no fear; this is just your starting point. Now that you are aware of the weaknesses, we can help you deal with them. The place to start is by building out your baseline sales system to convert prospects into customers. Here is a simple five-step process to do just this:

1. **Lay out your current sales process in a flowchart.** Make each step in your sales process a box and link that box to the next box(es). Every time you draw an arrow from one key step in your sales process to another key step, that arrow represents a key conversion point when your prospect can say yes or no. Label that conversion point with a letter; you'll use these in step two when you build your scoreboard. (See Figure 7.1.)

FIGURE 7.1: SAMPLE TWO-STEP SALES PROCESS VISUALLY MAPPED OUT

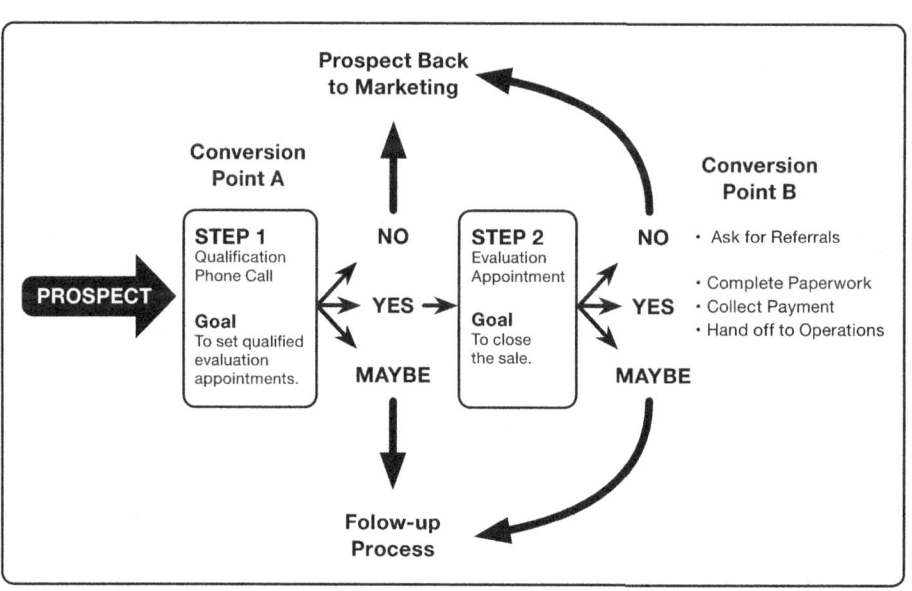

2. **Create a rough scorecard of how you track each key conversion point.** Count how many prospects made it into and out of

each key conversion point and do a simple division of *leads out* divided by *leads in* to calculate the "conversion rate" of that step in your sales process.

3. **Pick *one* conversion point to focus on first and brainstorm leveraged improvements you could make to it over the next 90 days.** For example, if you choose the conversion point B in Figure 7.1 (your closing ratio at your "Evaluation Appointment"), potential improvements could include:

   - Refined sales collateral (e.g., brochure, flyer, sales presentation deck, etc.)
   - Improved sales scripting (including how to preempt, reframe, or overcome common objections)
   - Product samples or photos
   - Recorded sales presentation to help your sales team model your best practices

   The key here is to start small by focusing on one conversion point at a time. Remember, fewer better ideas that you actually implement are better than a whole host of ideas that you do only partially.

4. **Create a mini–action plan to implement the top leveraged improvements you chose in step three.** Clarify who is responsible for doing what, by when, to what standard, and how they are going to be held accountable. Make sure someone in your company is responsible for this area of your business as a whole, and as such, is tasked with following up to ensure that your team effectively executes your mini-plan.

5. **Implement, track, and refine quarterly.** Each quarter, repeat this process. We know it isn't the sexiest thing in the world, but the sales it will help your company consistently generate sure are. Plus, each quarter you'll be taking powerful, leveraged action to consistently reduce your company's reliance on

you or your key salesperson, protecting your business and making it more scalable.

Patricia, a chiropractor building a multi-clinic practice, realized that she was her business's best salesperson. To deal with this bottleneck, she selected two of her doctors to do the initial examination with new patients (where the "sale" occurred for her business) and trained them in how to replicate her sales success. She scripted out the sales process, videoed herself in action in mock exams, role-played with her exam doctors, and designed a simple scorecard that told the doctors how they were doing on their conversion rate at any given moment. Her two exam doctors saw their conversion rates go up by over 40 percent in less than 90 days! Now Patricia has a scalable training program that teaches a new doctor how to sell her way in less than 90 days.

We know you'll use these tools and techniques to help you blow through the obstacles standing in your business's way of scaling its Sales/Marketing pillar. In the next chapter we'll share with you three breakthrough tools to help you scale your Operations pillar without sacrificing your life to do so.

# YOUR OPERATIONS PILLAR

## THREE BREAKTHROUGH IDEAS TO SCALE YOUR CAPACITY

The Operations pillar of your company creates your product or delivers on your service. It is responsible for fulfilling on the promises you made to your customers in the sales process, along with performing the general and administrative back-end functions of your business.

In this chapter, you'll learn three breakthrough concepts to efficiently produce more and better value for your market as your business scales. First, we'll give you a powerful blueprint to build out your most important business systems, which we call your "Expert Systems." Then, we'll give you a framework—we call it your "UBS"—to organize, house, access, and refine your business systems. Finally, we'll share with you one more critical component for sustaining growth over the long term, called "business linkages." This final tool will help you reduce the number of things that fall between the cracks as one pillar of your company hands off to another pillar of your company, and speed up the pace at which your business produces results internally as you script out and reinforce critical business linkages.

The place to start is with building your Expert Systems.

## Expert Systems

Your ability to scale is directly proportional to your company's ability to create cookie-cutter processes for mission-critical areas. Your Expert Systems capture the hard-earned wisdom of *how* to perform your company's core business functions. They replicate that expertise in a formalized process and connected set of tools, training, and controls to make it possible for the *business* to own that expertise versus the know-how being held in the brain of a key employee. Not only does this protect your business from the loss of a key employee, but it also allows you to replicate this formally expert-level-only process in a coherent system. This means you can scale an Expert System because one person is no longer the bottleneck. It also means you can lower your costs as you push down the level of expertise needed to reliably produce the desired result, perhaps even automating a large chunk of it. Because you are freezing the formerly impromptu process into a *formal* process, you can also optimize it, increasing the speed and value of the output. And finally, because you now have a readily reproducible recipe to focus your efforts on, you can control for consistency and quality, even creating simple business controls to ensure the process runs right.

In a perfect world, you'd love to have a business that runs by itself; while you're at the pool, your company takes orders and delivers products. While this fantasy may not be possible, using this filter to look at your business prompts you to constantly find ways to automate, streamline, and improve operations instead of just adding more people when more work comes in.

Here's an example of how Expert Systems work in the real world. In January 1997, David launched his first business-coaching company. In the beginning, he and his business partner did all the coaching, were responsible for most of the sales, and oversaw all the other core functions of the business. In essence they were the typical start-up entrepreneurs, working long hours and wearing all of the hats. As the business started to grow they faced a major hurdle—finding a way to deliver a world-class business-coaching service that didn't rely too heavily on them to personally do the coaching.

David eventually sold this company in 2005, but not before he scaled the coaching division to work with more than 1,500 clients a year. As you can imagine, he and his business partner maxed out individually coaching at the 50-client mark. To go beyond this number, they had to create a formal process where they froze their method for working with a coaching client to deliver great results in a collection of tools. These tools included the process to find, hire, and train new coaches; the diagnostic tools to work with a new client; the accountability tools to keep clients on track; the ongoing training process to continually grow their coaches over time; and the technology to automate many of these processes. Collectively, all these tools and processes evolved into David's Expert System for producing coaching services. The most amazing part was that once they had built this Expert System that essentially replicated and replaced David and his partner in direct client coaching, by every measure of success (e. g., growth in client sales, growth in client profits, client satisfaction ratings, client referral rate, etc.) the Expert System produced a *better* result!

Expert Systems don't have to be just about production; they can be critical components of *other* parts of your business. Take the example of L. H. Thomson Inc., a contract manufacturing company in Macon, Georgia, that makes components for airplanes. One of their Expert Systems is their system for filtering, pricing, and responding to bidding opportunities for new manufacturing contracts. Since most of their aerospace manufacturing contracts run for five years and are for half a million dollars or more a year, choosing which contracts to bid on and at what price is a critical part of their business success. Once upon a time, all this know-how was locked in the heads of their CFO and CEO. Today, they have formal, written criteria for which contracts they will and won't go after, a clear methodology on how to accurately price the bid that ensures the job will be profitable, strong boilerplate contract language that protects them from fluctuations on raw materials, a software tool that speeds up the number crunching and allows them to respond quickly and accurately, and a training process that captures their best practices and brings team members up to speed on effectively using this system. Collectively these tools are their Expert System for bidding on new work.

Your company may have an Expert System for producing its core product or service offering, or for effectively converting leads into sales, or managing your collections process. In fact, most businesses will ultimately want to build three to five Expert Systems that help them clearly lay out how to handle the critical parts of their business in a stable, scalable way.

Here is a six-step formula for building your core Expert Systems.

## Step One: Define All Deliverables

A deliverable is any result your Expert System needs to produce to meet the expected or promised outputs of your system. This is just a fancy way of saying that you need to clarify what exactly your system is supposed to produce for its customer. This may include getting a certain number of physical products to your customer by a certain date, making a report or recommendation on a course of action to your client on how to best handle a specific challenge, or some other output your Expert System has promised to fulfill.

There are four types of deliverables you need to concretely define: external deliverables, internal deliverables, phantom deliverables, and reverse phantom deliverables. **External deliverables** are what most of us think about when we think of a deliverable—products or services we've promised to our customer, like fulfilling a hundred-widget order by Friday or completing a full-day training program. **Internal deliverables** are those things that you have to produce, create, or deliver behind the scenes in order to meet your external deliverables for your client. They may include collecting certain customer information and entering that into your system, holding an internal project meeting, handing a project step from person A to person B, or even subcontracting certain portions of the finished "product" and managing your subcontractors to deliver their pieces on time and up to standards.

**Phantom deliverables** are those deliverables that you haven't actually promised your customer but they *think* you have. This could include their belief that your product will come ready to use out of the box, or that you'll provide follow-up support after the contract formally ends. You need to clarify all your phantom deliverables so that you can either clarify that they aren't included, or make sure that they are delivered, because if your customer thinks you've promised them something and you don't clarify or deliver that deliverable, then they will leave feeling dissatisfied. While this may not be fair, it is accurate. Finally, there are **reverse phantom deliverables**—those things you *think* you promised your customers that not only you didn't, but that your customer simply doesn't care about. Maybe you deliver weekly reports that your customer just deletes, or product features that your customer never uses. Take the time to reassess all your current deliverables to make sure they are still relevant to your business and add value to your customers. We have seen companies build Expert Systems that incorporate all of their current deliverables, when in fact some of those deliverables were old legacy requirements that nobody had questioned in years.

As you can imagine, the more complicated the Expert System you are working on, the more deliverables you'll capture on your list. While this may seem overwhelming at first, this should actually comfort you. You've already been producing all of these deliverables, but you were doing so in an informal way that one or two key people in your company just "did." By concretely defining your deliverables, you're taking that key first step in building out a system that will effectively produce them. After all, how can you produce what you haven't consciously identified you've promised to create? And without documenting all these deliverables, how can you get customer sign-off that you are actually doing your job well and delivering on your promises?

## Step Two: Lay Out the Process

Now the fun begins. Grab a pad of yellow sticky notes and your list of deliverables. Placing one "step" on each sticky note, lay out the process your company will use to create and deliver on all those deliverables. Using sticky notes keeps you fluid and loose as you design and document your process, allowing you to move them around, add steps, combine steps, or delete steps.

Once you've got a rough layout of your steps, it's time to ask yourself a series of questions to refine your draft process:

- Which deliverables *really* matter? Which deliverables are nice but not essential? Which deliverables do your employees *think* your customers want or asked for but didn't? How can you eliminate these deliverables that actually just get in the way and are not wanted?
- How can you reduce the steps and still generate the desired results? And generate an *improved* result?
- How could you decrease the resources needed and still generate the desired results? And generate an *improved* result?
- How can you speed up this process?
- How can you automate or template this process (or part of this process)?
- How can you lower the costs of doing this process without impacting the value of the output?
- What simple changes or improvements can you make to increase the value of the output? How could you marginally increase your cost to produce but in a way that so enhances the value of the output that you can get a price increase for the value you're offering now?

- Who else in the world has a related process or tool you can learn from to help you better design this process?
- Could you outsource any parts of this system? Does it really make sense long-term to do this?
- How could you make the system more robust? More stable? Less prone to error?

Once you've thought about and answered these questions, return to your sticky notes. Based on your answers, move, add, delete, and play with the steps of your system until you lay out a process that promises to be faster, cheaper, of better quality, of greater impact, and more scalable.

When you've drafted these improvements into your sticky notes, you'll type out the finished process into a complete and neat recipe to produce the desired outputs. This recipe will be a simple longhand list of each step in the process (e.g., Step One . . . Step Two . . . Step Three . . . etc.).

Once you have this clear process laid out it is time to move on to step three.

## Step Three: Determine the Optimal Level of Expertise for Each Step

When Jeff consulted to the Cleveland Clinic, one of the world's top-rated medical institutions, their goal was to get every doctor to practice "at the top of their degree." To do so, they had to review everything a doctor in their institution did to identify those nonspecialized things that should have been done by support staff. The closer they got to this goal, the more efficiently their institution ran.

As a business, you want to find ways to relieve your most expensive and experienced employees from doing lower-value work. The hospital example is very clear. A surgeon is most useful to the hospital, and generates the most value and revenue, when she is performing surgery. The same thing applies to your business, even if your "experts" aren't surgeons, but rather just your most experienced and expensive team members. To sustainably scale your business, you must commit to push as much of the work of each Expert System down the value chain so that your experts do less of your Expert System. Not only does this immediately increase your capacity because your expert can now be spread over a larger volume of total work, it also drives down your costs as the work performed at a lower level is much less expensive.

There is a hierarchy of expertise for each step in your Expert System. At the bottom, you have those steps that can be automated, semiautomated, or made into a template. Next, you have those steps that require a person to complete them, but not necessarily a skilled person (e.g., clerical, administrative, unskilled laborer, etc.). The next level up is for those steps that need a semiskilled team member to perform them (e.g., paralegal, nurse, journeyman, etc.). Above this is the level of skilled, which requires a basic expert to produce these steps. Finally, the top level of the pyramid is for those steps that require a top expert to produce for the business, which in most small businesses is the owner or one or two key employees.

Let's look at an example of how this hierarchy of expertise plays out in a law firm to make these levels clear. Automated, semiautomated, or templated refer to things like the standardized engagement letter that gets sent to any new client or the library of boilerplate contract templates on the company's server. Nonskilled tasks include those tasks that a clerical worker without legal training could handle, such as scheduling meetings, collecting client data, and gathering historical documents to give to the attorney. Semiskilled tasks in this context would likely refer to those items that a paralegal could produce as opposed to an actual attorney. Basic expert tasks are those that only a licensed attorney could do, although they could be done by a less expensive, less experienced associate attorney. Top expert tasks are processes and functions that require the best legal talent at that firm in that area—things that likely need years of experience to understand and do properly.

The goal of your Expert System is to identify the best level of expertise to match up with each step of your Expert System. What you'll likely find is that there is a vast gap between what you intellectually know to be the optimal level of expertise for a particular step and the actual level at which you currently perform that step.

For most existing businesses, the biggest immediate reward of drafting their Expert System in a given area is how this exercise reveals where they need to push steps down from the top two levels (Basic Expert and Top Expert) to lower levels. In many cases, a business can quickly increase its capacity by 30 to 50 percent or more simply by staffing down many of the steps in its Expert System to a lower level in the pyramid.

In the example of our hypothetical law firm, this would include things like getting clerical staff involved in scheduling meetings and reminding clients of information they need to get to the firm prior to that meeting, using better software that automates or semiautomates the invoicing of clients for work performed, or standardizing the core legal services to allow a less experienced attorney to do tasks previously performed by the senior partners of the firm (but that don't require the latter's deep expertise).

From all our years coaching business owners, we consistently see that most businesses have their best, most expensive "experts" doing too many of the steps of their informal Expert System. As a result they struggle with capacity issues and poor margins, and are vulnerable to that "expert" getting hurt or otherwise leaving the business, taking with her all the know-how and institutional knowledge she gained from years of being the wizard inside the black box producing in this area of the business. If you want to scale your business exponentially, then you must reduce your company's reliance on any one expert with formalized Expert Systems upon which you have trained and cross-trained your team.

• • •

## Step Four: Control for Consistency

Now that you've got your written process, and have identified which level of expertise optimally goes best with each step, it's time to refine your process to control for consistency. This is just another way of saying that you now need to look for ways to improve quality and reduce variability. Here are several key thoughts to help you do just this:

- **The more you can automate, semiautomate, and template, the easier it is for you to control for consistency.** All it then takes is a sharp review of your template or automated steps to make sure they are accurate. These processes become great "embedded controls" to protect your business.
- **Streamline the process.** The fewer the steps in any complete process, performed by fewer people, the fewer the potential problems.
- **Pay particular attention to the critical linkages.** Script out the critical linkages between tasks and reinforce them. (More on this at the end of this chapter.)
- **Standardize wherever you can.** This will help you accelerate the process, increase efficiencies, lower costs, increase impact, and improve quality.
- **Create your three "master" documents:** your master timeline, your master checklist, and your master budget.
- **Capture institutional knowledge in a structured, searchable place.** This includes detailed client notes not in the heads of your staff, but in searchable text in your CRM. It can also include an organized file of the associated documents for a specific project or client. If you don't take steps now to capture this essential past history, there will come a day when a key team member leaves your company and you'll have to scramble to re-create the institutional knowledge they took with them. Not only will this

be financially expensive, but it will also be incredibly stressful and emotionally painful.
- **Train and cross-train your team.** Make sure that every key role in your Expert System has at least one fully trained understudy. Redundancies aren't glamorous, but they give you incredible peace of mind and business depth.

## Step Five: Map Out the Key Components of Your Expert System to Refine First

Likely you don't have any formal Expert Systems established right now, but you do have an informal collection of best practices that are in the heads of your key team members. Now that you've followed steps one through four to formally lay out your Expert System, it's time to flesh out the system with the tools, training, and controls you need to enhance your Expert System.

Don't worry—we won't ask you to do this all at once, as likely your Expert System is a complicated thing, and the tools you want will best be created and phased in over time. For example, when Pete Fowler, owner of a construction-defect litigation company, first applied the Expert System concept to his business, he started by looking at the inspection process his highly trained team used to review a building. He took his top three team members off-site for two days to create both a detailed inspection template and a workflow map of all the steps in this portion of their client engagements. Then, over the next two quarters, they built out the other tools they needed to complete their Inspection Service Expert System.

Pick the piece of your Expert System—the "block"—that you think either would be easiest to refine, or would have the biggest impact for your business. Picking a block that you know you can successfully model in an Expert System gives your staff a visible example of the value and operation of Expert Systems, and increases their confidence in attacking the next, more complex block. Give this block a name (e.g., The "New Client Launch," the "Quality Review Process," the "Bid Selection Step," etc.) to make it easier for you and your team to talk about.

Now we'll approach this block from four specific directions:

**Critical Knowledge to Institutionalize:** What is the critical know-how about this block of your Expert System that is locked in the heads of one or more key team members? Identify this institutional knowledge and brainstorm the best way to capture, store, and share it. Perhaps you could have a checklist of items to note in the client record each week during a longer project. Or you could make sure that you have well-thought-through custom fields in your CRM to input key parameters for a project. Or maybe you build a searchable company wiki or discussion forum to take essential conversations out of email and capture them in a more permanent and accessible way. The idea here is to ask yourself what information or knowledge would be the most costly and painful to replicate if you lost your key expert, and to look for ways to reduce that expert reliance.

**Tools to Enhance and Leverage:** What tools, templates, and automation would make this block of your Expert System faster, cheaper, better? Would an automated sequence of welcome emails help bring on a new customer more smoothly? Would an online web survey allow you to gather key client information? How about a CRM solution that lets you record all client or project email, and select from a library of email templates, to reduce the time and expertise needed for specific steps?

**Training to Design and Implement:** What training and cross-training will team members need in order to be successful in using this Expert System (or at least this block of your Expert System)? How could you formalize or "freeze" that training in easily accessible, updatable, and scalable systems? Could you create a series of short video training modules, a process document with annotated screen-shot images, or maybe a formal mentoring system inside your company? Remember, you are not just looking to one-off train one team member to be able to back up one "expert." This may help reduce your reliance a bit, but it doesn't go far enough. You are looking for longer-term ways of building your training system so that you can train the next, and the next, and the next team member you need to perform in this area of your business. A good test of your eventual training tools is asking a member of your team who hasn't been involved in this area of the business to review your Expert System. If he or she is able to follow the documentation, training, and tools to perform useful work quickly, then you're on the right track.

**Controls to Monitor and Ensure Quality:** Consider what internal controls (visual, procedural, or embedded) would best help your business ensure that this block of your Expert System consistently works exceptionally well. Do you need a master timeline to lay out all the key steps and milestones in a time-coded sequence? Automate key steps into your software so that they happen regardless of which team member is handling that stage of the project? Implement a simple metric to let you see that things are running smoothly at that step? Considering how mission critical your three to five Expert Systems will be to your company's success, you'll need to incrementally develop, test, and refine the business controls you implement for each of them.

## Step Six: Each Quarter Reevaluate Your Expert System to Prioritize the Next Block to Enhance and Refine

Each quarter, revisit your Expert System and pick the next "block" to focus on and refine. It's normal to take three to four quarters to really nail down a complete Expert System for your company. Because these are the processes that produce the most value in your business, you'll find your company greatly benefits from the time and attention you invest on each block as you and your team iterate and refine over the long term.

Now that you have a clear process to build out your Expert Systems, it's time to focus on the bigger picture of how you store, organize, and access *all* your systems.

## Building Your Master System— Your "UBS"

One of the most powerful operational secrets we've discovered after decades of building successful companies is a concept called your "UBS." UBS stands for your "Ultimate Business System," and it is the master system for how you structure, organize, store, access, refine, and, if need be, delete, your company's systems.

Most owners will hear this and say, "Oh, you mean our policies and procedures manual?" We most definitely do *not*. After surveying thousands of businesspeople about the usefulness of a policies and procedures manual, we've come to one firm and irrefutable conclusion—no one *uses* or refers to a policies and procedures manual, especially after the first 30 days on the job.

We want you to think of your UBS as an organized collection of tools that captures the actual, everyday know-how of your business in a searchable, accessible, and editable way. Generally this means a collection of cloud-based file folders into which you organize and put your checklists, your worksheets, your templates, and your archived files. As technology progresses, more small and midsize businesses are able to put part of their business processes into enterprise software that runs their companies. As this trend accelerates, expect that your UBS will increasingly live inside the enterprise software you develop for your company. Even still, there will likely always be a place for the other systems that aren't easily captured in your software: systems for how you hire, how you generate leads, how you process sales, and how you pay your vendors. The UBS concept is timeless.

The goal is to make your UBS a living, breathing way of doing business in your company—an ongoing practice. You'll know you've won when you regularly hear your team say things like, "Did you add that to the UBS?" and "Great solution to that problem, can you UBS it?" This is not something that you sit down and "do" in one sitting. Your UBS is a discipline that your team will cultivate and refine over the long term.

Here is our four-step process for building your UBS.

## Step One: Create Your UBS's File Folder Organizational Hierarchy

If you had to cluster all the functions of your business into five to nine main headings, what would those headings be? Further, how would you break each of these folders into five to nine subheadings? This is the first step in creating your company's UBS.

In Figure 8.1, we show you what this might look like. In the example, we've used the five functional pillars of every business. This is a great default place to start from. Too many file folders creates too much complexity, and your team won't know where to put things, where to find things, and soon your UBS will devolve into a mess that people ignore. Instead, limit your UBS to between five and nine headings each, with only five to nine subheadings, so that your team becomes intuitively able to know which main folder or subfolder to use to access and store your systems.

In the sample UBS below, notice how we used the numeric system to label each main folder and subfolder with a number—a useful shortcut to organize your UBS. You may be tempted to extend this numbering system beyond two levels. DON'T! We can tell you from direct experience that if you push the numbering system too far (e.g., "2.3.2.9"), you'll end up with a mess of a UBS. With the ability to search folders easily, and with the way our brains have been trained to think about keyword search, you're better off with a simpler folder hierarchy that allows you to find the tool you want, when you want it. As you name the files and tools in your UBS, standardize the keywords you use in your naming so that people save things in a way that lets other people know how to search for them. The UBS hierarchy should be intuitive. We suggest that you also use complete names that spell out exactly what a document or tool is so that when searching for it brings up a few possibilities, the correct document is obvious. For example, when you need to pull up the lead-conversion scorecard to enter your daily numbers, you'll pull up the spreadsheet named "1.5 Daily Sales Team Tracking Spreadsheet March 20XX," enter your numbers, save the document, and then close it. Now anyone else in your company who wants to review the numbers can pull up the spreadsheet and see where things stand. (We'll get into the software choices to house your UBS in a moment.)

What matters most is that you strictly map out the architecture of how your UBS will be organized. Try to develop a structure that looks more like your actual business than a computer database. Only your IT team thinks in database terms; everyone else just understands the business by category, assignment, or workflow. If you design the UBS with this in mind, no matter which software or hardware you use to store it, you'll have a good start on an organized, useful way to create, store, access, and refine all your business systems.

**FIGURE 8.1:** A SAMPLE OUTLINE FOR A COMPANY UBS

**1.0 SALES/MARKETING**

1.1 Lead Generation

1.2 Lead Conversion

1.3 Sales Team Tools

1.4 Sales Planning and Strategy

1.5 Sales Metrics and Reporting

2.0 OPERATIONS

2.1 Production

2.2 Fulfillment

2.3 Purchasing

2.4 Facilities/Infrastructure

2.5 General Administration

3.0 FINANCE

3.1 Accounting/Financial Reporting

3.2 Collections

3.3 Accounts Payable

3.4 Budgeting

3.5 Financial Controls

3.6 Cash Flow Management

4.0 TEAM

4.1 Hiring and Orientation

4.2 Training, Review, and Retention

4.3 Benefits Administration

4.4 Labor Compliance

4.5 Exit Processes

5.0 LEADERSHIP

5.1 Strategic Planning

5.2 Leadership Development/ Succession Planning

5.3 Company Culture and Traditions

5.4 Communications Company-wide

## Step Two: Rename and Store Your Existing Systems and Tools

If you've been in business for a while, you likely have a hodgepodge collection of systems and tools in place already. You might have a scheduling spreadsheet you use to organize which staff are on which shifts month by month, a nine-step checklist to open up your store for the day, and even a database of potential suppliers to get bids from on new product orders.

Step two in the UBS process is to go through your computer and files to gather your existing systems and tools and put them into your new UBS. This is a perfect time to identify which tools are outdated or inadequate, which work well, and which tools your system desperately needs. Only save to your UBS those documents and tools that you want your business actually using going forward. (You can always store anything no longer current in an "archive" folder in each section of your UBS on the off chance you need to access it later.) Rename files and tools in the hierarchy and naming pattern you determined previously, so that finding them is easy and fast. Append the word "temp" to the name of each document or tool that you know you need to upgrade to cue your team to refine or replace that system at some point in the future.

## Step Three: Create a Prioritized List of the Three Systems You'll Build This Quarter (and get to work building them)

Brainstorm which systems your company desperately needs. Then from that list pick three (yes—just three) to build this quarter. We recommend choosing only three because we've both seen far too many business owners get excited by this concept of building systems and launch 22 different business improvement projects all at the same time, only to never finish any of them. Building systems sucks up resources, so make sure not only that the systems you build are worthwhile, but that you actually finish them and get them to a place where they produce results for your business.

Here is a short list of questions to ask to help you pick which three systems to begin building first:

- Which system would yield the biggest return?
- Which system would best help us push back our current number-one biggest Limiting Factor?
- Which system costs us the most for not having in place?

You've got the rest of the quarter to create your first (or next) version of these three systems.

## Step Four: Repeat Step Three Every Quarter

Each quarter, you'll go back to step three and pick the next three systems to build. As you grow your team, you will have help in building out your systems and will likely be able to build many more systems each quarter than just three. Still, we recommend that each quarter you clearly identify the top three systems that your company is committed to building. If the systems are too big to complete in one quarter, which might be true if you're building out one of your core Expert Systems, then frame out which *part* of the system you'll have done by the end of the quarter. Over time, this process is magic, and you'll find that you consistently make your business more and more scalable and less and less reliant on a few key staff members (including you).

## Picking Your Storage Technology to House Your UBS

Every company needs to come up with its own way of storing its systems for its team to use. The problem is that technology changes so fast that the solutions we recommend today will quite likely be out of date in a very short time. That said, here are the four most critical attributes that any technology solution to house your UBS must meet:

1. *Accessible:* Your UBS needs to be quickly accessible. Usually, this means it's accessible online, but it could be a paper-based system too. In the case of your team's doing work remotely while traveling, ideally your choice would still be accessible when a team member is off-line (with the system automatically syncing up when they go back online). Clearly in today's world, having systems and data accessible even on handheld and mobile devices is a big productivity enhancer.

2. *Searchable:* People have to be able to quickly find what they want in the UBS; otherwise they'll start to keep their own "cheat sheet" systems at their desks or on their computers. This would eventually mean your UBS won't house the best practices but merely return to being a procedural manual that no one uses. Remember, people are used to keyword search as a tool to find answers on demand. Your UBS tool needs a robust search function.

3. *Version Control:* Your UBS needs to be collaborative, which means all users need to be able to edit and improve the data. This requires having version control and also constantly pruning your UBS's outdated information and systems. Systems will change and grow, and if you leave the old one to live with the new, it will cloud the waters and make it harder for people to know quickly which systems to use and when. In many ways, the eraser is mightier than the pen for your UBS.

4. *Security:* Your UBS needs to have security features that allow you to protect your intellectual property both from outside parties and from internal misuse. Your UBS is one of your business's most valuable assets. Ideally, you'd have simple, granular control over who has access to what parts of your UBS. Also, this is a good place to suggest that all your employees and contractors who have access to part or all of your UBS sign strong confidentiality agreements that make clear that this system is proprietary to your company and as such protected under that agreement.

Systems and controls cannot be a fad, but must be an ingrained way of doing things inside your business. If you start the process and don't see it through, your efforts will wither and you'll lose credibility with your team. Your team must see why systems and controls matter to the business, to you, and to them.

And they must see you staying the course by making them a fundamental part of your business.

Here are four more quick suggestions to make systems a part of your company culture:

1. **Train your team.** Don't just expect that your team will know how to build systems, or even use them. You need to make training on how to create the UBS, and how to access and use it, a core part of your business. Explain to them why the UBS is so important, and how critical it is to your company's ability to grow.

2. **Involve your team.** You don't have to do all the work of creating the UBS alone. In fact, if your business already has a much better "process thinker" than you are, get this person to lead the project of creating your UBS. As for building your systems, the best leverage point is to enroll your team to build your systems with you. Your most important job is to cultivate the *discipline* of systems throughout your organization.

3. **Systems must make your team's lives better.** Be on the lookout for silly systems or steps that just add red tape or offer no compelling benefit to the company. A system must make the company and/or your team's lives better.

4. **Start right from the point of hire.** Emphasize your culture of creating and using systems. Make editing and using the UBS part of any new hire's job. Train them on it from day one. Your team will never be as open to doing things the "company" way as they will be at the point of hire.

The bottom line is that you want your team to internalize the discipline and understanding of the value of creating, using, and refining your systems and controls over time.

## Reinforcing Critical Linkages

The final predictable obstacle you'll need to blow through as you scale your Operations pillar is a direct outgrowth of your increased size—making sure details don't slip through the cracks as more of what your company does crosses functional areas (i.e., pillars) of the business. That's why we want to share with you one more tool to help you successfully scale—"linkages."

Linkages are the connections between two or more pillars of your company. Whenever a process crosses over from one pillar to another, there's heightened potential for something to slip between the cracks. The best companies script out and reinforce their critical linkages so that they preempt things from falling between the cracks.

Think of it like a relay race. You have one sprinter racing to hand the baton to the next racer, then the next. The goal is to beat their competition to the finish line. While it seems so simple—just run as fast as you can and pass the baton—it is far from easy. In fact, if you were to spend time watching Olympic-level relay teams train, you'd notice they spend a disproportionate amount of their training time practicing the handoff, because they know that it's the biggest point of failure for a relay team. It is the one place in the race where everything they have worked for can be lost in a single fumble.

In your business, critical linkages include the handoff between marketing and sales when you generate a new lead and ask your sales team to follow up on that lead, the handoff between your operations team and finance when it's time to make sure regular client billing is completed in a timely and accurate way, and the handoff of a new customer order from sales to operations. At these points, it's key to have a foolproof system to make sure the transition is smooth and effective as work flows between pillars in your company.

The keys to a strong linkage include:

- **Get a moving start.** The pillar who is handing off the process to the next recipient pillar of the business has to make sure that certain information is clearly captured and passed along in a structured way. This could mean that your salesperson formally introduces your operations team to the client, or that your account rep sets manageable and realistic expectations with your customer when they turn over the client to your production team.

- **Make the handoff explicit.** In racing, you'll hear sprinters shouting "Baton!" or see them slap the baton into the hand of the recipient so they know the transition has happened. In business, it is just as essential to make sure your team always knows who owns which stages in the process and, most important, which stage the process is currently at. Define each stage and make it part of your process to formally declare which stage the process is at and get both halves of the linkage to acknowledge this.

- **Define the handoff boundaries.** In racing, there is a specific section of the track in which the handoff must occur or the team will be disqualified. In business, you also need to have a clear, formal process that lays out the parameters for the handoff and ensures that all parties have signed off on these rules.

- **Explicitly ask both halves of the handoff what their needs are (and why).** What does the person who is receiving the handoff need to help them succeed? What information, materials, introductions, setup, or support? Why do these items matter to them? What happens if they don't get it? And what about the party doing the handoff—what do they need to succeed? What response, feedback, timeliness, or assurances? And what is the impact if they don't get these items? It may seem obvious that this conversation needs to take place, but in our experience it rarely does. When your team understands the other side of the handoff's needs and the "why" behind those needs, you'll notice your team going above and beyond to be better team members and meet those needs. This in turn will lead to fewer fires and better teamwork.

- **Formally process out the handoff.** Pull out your sticky notes and process out the exact steps in the ideal handoff. Try out this draft process and observe where the wasteful steps and rough edges are. Then, in version two, simplify the process and sand down the rough edges. Consider adding a simple control (e.g., checklist, visual timeline with marker of where you stand in the process, etc.) to make sure the process is operating smoothly.

So there you have three powerful operational tools to help you scale your operations pillar: Expert Systems, your UBS, and critical linkages. In the next chapter we'll look closely at the obstacles to scaling in your Financial pillar.

# YOUR FINANCE PILLAR

## CFO SECRETS TO MANAGE CASH FLOW, IMPROVE MARGINS, AND FUND GROWTH

The Finance pillar of your business encompasses all the essential functions of collecting, tracking, distributing, and reporting the flow of money in and out of your business. It includes your billing procedures, collection practices, accounts payable processes, all financial reporting from balance sheets to profit and loss statements, and your management of cash flow. As your business matures, this pillar will also include the sourcing of capital, management of risk, and the forecasting necessary to help your management team make better business decisions.

At Level One and Early Stage Level Two, chances are you have few financial systems in place. This is normal for a small business scrambling to survive. At the very least, we suggest that you outsource your bookkeeping to a part-time service so your financial transactions are accurately entered into an accounting software program.

Once your business enters Middle Stage Level Two, you need to put your financial house in order. Whether you outsource your accounting to a part-time controller or employ someone on staff full-time, it's essential that you enlist help to organize your

Finance pillar and begin establishing the intelligent financial controls that your business will need as it grows.

At Advanced Stage Level Two, you'll most likely have a full-time controller overseeing the finance part of your business; as you enter Level Three, you'll probably transition to a full-blown CFO (Chief Financial Officer), not just a controller. What's the difference? A controller is expert in following the financial systems you have in place; a CFO is expert in helping you build them. A controller can help you make sure you have accurate reporting and can maintain your existing financial infrastructure; a CFO can help you with higher-order financial thinking, such as running pro forma analyses and managing your capital sources. A controller can help you execute existing plans in the here and now; a CFO will help you plan for the future.

Regardless of which stage your business is at or whom you have helping the financial area of your company, as the business owner you still must understand how to manage cash flow, how to fund growth, and the basics of financial controls. While you can leverage your financial team, you cannot abdicate responsibility. In this chapter we'll give you the essential finance short course you need to safely and intelligently scale your business. Let's begin with cash flow.

## Managing Cash Flow: The Seven Cash Flow Commandments

One of the biggest obstacles to scaling your business is poor management of cash flow. That makes sense when you consider how a typical product-based business works. The business pays to manufacture or purchase its products and then inventories the products until customers purchase them. Buying or producing that inventory ties up the business's cash and increases its risk (e.g., damage to inventory, obsolescence when upgraded, etc.). And when they *do* ask for payment, most business owners never create a clear, measurable collections system that sends invoices in a timely manner and relies on a formalized follow-up system to make sure they are paid.

Here are seven Cash Flow Commandments, along with our suggestions to effectively apply them, to give you a rock-solid financial base upon which to scale your company.

## Cash Flow Commandment #1: Thou shalt collect more of what you're owed.

It's our observation that most business owners are simply uncomfortable or even afraid to look clearly at their collection practices. They bury their heads in the sand and passively wait to get paid. Many are even afraid of upsetting clients by asking for payment and push it off onto their bookkeeper or another poorly equipped member of their team.

When you are delivering value to your customers you should never be afraid or apologetic about asking to get paid. Your customers wouldn't pull up to the gas station and expect to get their tank filled for free. Likewise, they knew they would be paying for your product or service when they ordered it.

The costs to most small businesses of not collecting money due to them are huge, and only compound as the business grows. If a business is struggling with cash flow, one of the most common causes isn't lack of sales, it's poor collections. Generally, by focusing on this area of a business, an owner can get a 5 to 15 percent boost in his *collected* gross income within 90 days.

Think about this for a moment. If your business operates at a 33 percent profit margin, then that 5 to 15 percent increase in gross income actually translates into a 15 to 45 percent increase in operating profit. That's the power of Cash Flow Commandment #1, and why you *must* pay attention to it.

Take the example of Brett, who owns an IT services company in Colorado. He came up to us at a break during a workshop we were hosting and asked our advice on a collections issue he was facing. He was embarrassed to admit that he was guilty of ignoring this part of his business. It turned out that Brett had become so busy in the day-to-day of his business that he hadn't billed several large clients for more than six months! He went on to say that he didn't want to upset them with a large, late bill so he was planning on writing off the past-due invoices. We strongly pushed him to send the past-due invoices right away, along with a letter and phone call to explain the situation and ask for full payment. He collected more than $30,000 in immediate revenue by doing so.

Despite what you might think, most people just want to do the right thing. Your customers are not trying to avoid paying you—you just didn't bill them. Nor are they trying to cheat you by not paying. So while a late invoice and an apology might be a little annoying, they're more likely to get you paid than you might think. After all, it's money that they truly owe you.

The first foundation of your collections process is to collect all that you are owed. The only thing worse than not making the sale is making the sale, but not getting paid. After all, the moment you make the sale you now have your cost of goods sold, any sales commissions you're paying, and other expenses. If you don't collect on what you're owed, the sale is a negative drain on your company's cash flow. Here are some specific suggestions to help you collect more of what you are owed:

- **Accurately track who owes what.** Many collections issues aren't about poor practices in asking for the money, they are about poor operational systems to track what money is actually owed, and where you stand in collecting that money. If this is true of your business, make sure that your collections Expert System is something you focus on building.

- **Invoice more frequently.** Asking for more frequent payments means that the amount of payment is smaller and therefore easier for your customer to pay. It establishes a professional pattern of asking for and getting the money you're owed. Furthermore, by invoicing more frequently you get the added benefit of a steady stream of income for your own cash management, instead of struggling along between each large payment over time.

- **If you have to escalate your collections efforts, compress the timeline.** Don't let slow-paying customers stretch out payment for another 60 to 90 days. Front-load your collections efforts.

- **Be smart about the people you task with asking for payment.** By default, most companies assign their bookkeepers or controllers to ask for payment. But these people tend to have weak interpersonal skills. Instead, consider involving a mix of people in your business to collect what's owed. For example, when the receivable is fresh, ask your sales team to make collection calls. Because many of them are compensated on a commission basis, they have a strong financial incentive to help you collect on the sales they make. Also, paying salespeople when money is actually collected, as opposed to paying them the day a customer just says yes, is a smart way to keep salespeople vested in the collections process.

- **Pay attention!** As simple as it seems, just paying close attention to your A/R reporting on a weekly basis helps your business collect thousands of dollars more of the money it's owed. The result? Increases to your cash flow and better effective operating margins for your business.

## Cash Flow Commandment #2: Thou shalt collect faster.

One of the most important lessons with respect to managing cash flow is this: **The faster you collect from your customers,**

**the easier it will be to manage your cash flow.** Most businesses carelessly fall into cash crunches because they let their receivables slip longer and longer before being paid. Not only does this put the revenue in jeopardy because the longer it takes you to collect, the lower your odds of getting paid, but also because your collections costs rise, cutting into your margins. That is why you need to do all you can to accelerate the pace of your "collections cycle," the average time from the moment you have cash going out the door for "cost of goods sold" to the time you collect on the sale of that product or service.

Consider a manufacturer like Brian Thomson. His company designs and manufactures a high-end line of bicycle parts. Their collections cycle starts when they buy raw materials to produce their parts and continues until three to four months later, when they collect from their distributors and other wholesale customers. As you can imagine, Thomson and his team do everything they can to reduce the collections cycle to free up a tremendous amount of cash with which to operate and grow the business.

The same concept of a collections cycle applies to service businesses too. Far too many service providers make a sale, perform the work, and only then invoice for payment, often waiting 30 to 90 days to be paid after the work has been completed. In many cases, this means that the service business has had the cost of goods sold from labor, materials, and other out-of-pocket expenses to fulfill on its service offering for 60 to 90 days or longer. Remember, the longer your collections cycle, the more operating capital you need to run your business. Our goal with Cash Flow Commandment #2 is to shorten the collections cycle and free up operating capital to grow your business. Here are some concrete suggestions to do just that:

- **Get paid in advance!** The best way to reduce your collections cycle is to get paid up front. If you can't collect in full, can you at least collect a deposit, retainer, or up-front fee? Getting paid before you fulfill your product or service helps you eliminate the hassle and additional cost of chasing down payment later.

- **Consider incentivizing customers to pay in advance if you struggle to collect in advance otherwise.** You could offer a discount on advance payment, moving the customer to the front of the delivery line, or adding a bonus to their purchase they wouldn't otherwise get. More customers are willing to pay in advance than you might think if you offer them an appealing incentive. Many business owners just assume customers will say no, so they don't even ask. Don't answer for your customers—give it a shot and see what happens.

- **Don't wait to bill; collect right at time of service or delivery.** If you can't bill before you fulfill, why not ask for payment upon completion of the work or at the time you deliver the product to your customer? Smile and say you'll wait while they grab their checkbook or credit card. At the very least, give your customers a bill at the time the services are rendered as opposed to waiting several weeks.

- **Build a "cost" for your clients into your standard contracts.** If you are financing your client's purchases, then you should get paid for your trouble. Make sure your contract includes a monthly financing charge for all accruing bills. This clause should also state that the client is responsible for all reasonable costs of collection. Finally, where possible, get the business owner to sign individually and not just in the name of the business.

- **Accelerate your production and delivery cycle.** Assuming your business gets paid in part or entirely after you have produced and delivered your product or service, then the faster you finish that production and delivery cycle, the sooner you'll get paid.

- **Make it easy for your clients to pay.** Accept credit cards, PayPal, and other online payment options. Set clients up on auto-pay through an ACH bank draft or credit card. Take payments by phone or through your website. Make sure your invoice clearly says to whom they should make the check out and for how much. Include a self-addressed envelope with your invoice. The easier and more convenient you make it to pay you, the faster you'll get your money.

## Cash Flow Commandment #3: Thou shalt maintain timely and accurate financials.

Your cash flow is like blood circulating through your body—it is the very essence of life flowing through your business. Yet too many businesses have poor bookkeeping practices that either distort their real financial picture or, worse, keep them operating totally in the dark.

We spoke with the owner of an $11-million-a-year promotions company who shared with us how she discovered that her financial bookkeeping was off by more than $3 million because her controller had mis-entered critical information into their accounting software! Another business owner with a $5-million-a-year convenience store business found out, after he fired his bookkeeper, that she hadn't reconciled the company bank statements for over a full year. Sadly, these examples are all too common.

Successfully scaling your company requires that you have good information with which to make smart decisions. Your financial information is one very important view of your business. So let us ask you a blunt question: Is your financial record keeping up-to-date and accurate? Is it timely? In other words, can you look up your profit and loss statement from last month and know that it accurately reflects your income and expenses for that period? What about your balance sheet and statement of cash flow?

If you don't have accurate and timely financials, managing cash flow is almost impossible. You need this information to base your decisions on and to guide the moves you and your team make.

## Cash Flow Commandment #4: Thou shalt work to stabilize income and expenses so that they are more predictable and consistent.

The more accurately you can predict your income and expenses, the easier it is to effectively manage your cash flow. As you make financial projections of income and expenses, work hard to learn from each round of predictions so that with time you become more and more accurate. Think of your financial projections like your weather forecast. Back in the 1970s, weather forecasts were notorious for being more like fiction than fact. But with the advent of satellite weather data and more powerful computers with which to model the weather, today the forecast is incredibly accurate—in the short term. With some effort, your business cash flow forecasts can become very accurate in the short term (over 90 to 120 days), but the farther out you go, the more that can go wrong with them. This is why you must update your projections regularly—monthly in normal times; weekly in crunch times.

Once you have an accurate picture of your cash flow—past and projected—you can begin to clearly identify and deal with patterns you see. For example, do you have seasonality issues that cause your business to slow down in certain seasons? If so, you can make sure you don't build up assets, inventory, or staffing at a time when your business is about to slow down. Also, when you know about a downtime, you can proactively come up with ideas to stabilize your income.

Klayton Tapley, who owns The Fireplace Place, an indoor/outdoor fireplace and patio grill company, did just that. His company's busy season starts in spring and runs through fall, which is tough on his business as he has a full-time sales and technical staff with all the overhead that entails. This past year, Tapley implemented a new strategy to go after the multifamily building market, which included both service and repair work as well as major capital improvements for these buildings. In his first four months of implementing his seasonal strategy, his dedicated multiunit salesperson had signed up more than $250,000 of business, much of it during his historically slow season.

Another important exercise to stabilize income and expenses is to make a list of external factors outside of your control that could affect your cash flow and your forecast. We worked with a company that sold tires for cars, and it had developed a solid sales and cash flow forecast. But then something unexpected happened—there was a huge rubber shortage in the primary countries that produced rubber. As a result, prices for raw materials were projected to dramatically increase in the next quarter. Not only did this create a problem for the company's projected margins for the next quarter, it also created an important strategic opportunity. Should they use some of their cash reserves to purchase a larger stock of inventory before the prices changed? While this would impact short-term cash flow, it would also possibly give them an edge over their competitors in the next quarter when everyone else was buying tires at higher prices. Looking at external events and their potential impact is an important step in forecasting cash flow.

Here are some tips on stabilizing your income and expenses:

- **Work to get longer-term contracts in place with your customers.** Can you go from month-to-month or order-by-order arrangements to annual contracts? How about multiyear contracts? If you must have a cancellation clause to let your customer cancel, see if you can include a provision that requires 60- to 90-day (or longer) notice.

- **The longer your sales cycle or production cycle, the more important it is for you to have "clues" that tell you where you** stand on closing the business or producing your product or service. We call these critical clues "leading indicators." For example, one of our clients does a monthly calculation of the potential sales in his prospect pipeline to give him his expected sales volume over the next 180 days. The idea is that if you can spot a problem early enough, you can do something about it. It's those "surprises" that can derail your business.

- **Look for products or services you could cross-sell or up-sell.** If you sell a product or service that is a "onetime" purchase, what can you do to expand on this sales opportunity? For example, is there any service plan that would enhance customers' ownership of your product? Could you create and offer a next-phase service to follow your product offering?

## Cash Flow Commandment #5: Thou shalt sharply manage your expenses.

Costs matter. Early on, business owners know this and agonize over every penny spent. But as the business grows, you will no longer be able to be the hawk watching closely over every dollar spent. Here are several suggestions to help your company control costs as you scale:

- **Consolidate your purchases and negotiate better pricing.** This is especially important for companies that have gone through a recent burst of growth. Too often we see companies paying prices based on purchase volumes that they far exceed. Renegotiate frequently. Also, check around your community for local buying organizations that gather all the local businesses in the area and use their collective buying power on behalf of all the members.

- **Get vendors to compete for your business.** Make sure they know about each other, without rubbing their faces in it. It's amazing how much better your pricing can be when your vendors feel the hot breath of their competition on their necks. Even if you plan on staying with your current vendor, the very fact that you know and they know that you're getting outside bids will keep their pencils sharp and help ensure you get better pricing.

- **Review your vendors regularly.** Make this a standard practice in your company. Also make sure you flag all automatically renewing contracts to pop up for review and rebidding 60 to 90 days before their renewal. Better yet, cross out the boilerplate language from your vendor's contract that calls for an automatic renewal and instead write in that you have the option to renew, but not the obligation.

- **Train your staff to ask for and get discounts.** A short negotiation course on how your team can get discounts from your vendors, plus consistent recognition for team members who do this, pays off handsomely in increased cash flow. This practice alone could reduce your variable expenses by 5 to 10 percent.

- **Wherever possible, make expenses variable versus fixed.** You can change variable expenses when you need to, dialing them up or down to suit your cash flow situation and business needs. This flexibility is highly valuable. For example, could you use performance-based compensation versus guaranteed payments? Can you rent, not purchase? Can you lock in an option to renew, instead of a contractual obligation?

- **Cultivate fiscal discipline as a core company value.** Symbolic choices you make or allow as the business owner will find their way into the culture of your company. Sure, you can buy that fancy car or travel first-class on your company's dime, but just know that your team is *always* watching your example.

## Cash Flow Commandment #6: Thou shalt relentlessly manage and improve your margins.

The purpose of your business is to profitably create value for the market in a scalable way. In order for you to serve your customers, pay your employees, and reward your investors (yourself or outside investors), your business must be profitable.

Your margins are a measurement of your profitability. There are two "margins" that you the owner must focus on. The first and most easily understood is your **operating profit margin**. This number is simply a calculation of how much of every dollar in sales ends up as operating profit (pretax) for your business. For example, if you had $1 million in sales and ended up with a pretax profit of $250,000, your operating profit margin would be 25 percent. Your operating profit margin is a great measure of how profitable your business is overall. Building on our fictitious $1-million-per-year company, if you were able to go from a 25 percent to a 30 percent operating margin by better managing your expenses, you'd earn $50,000 more profit from that same $1 million of gross revenue. That 5 percent increase in operating profit margin equals a 20 percent increase in profit. Don't worry about the math too closely; what matters is to get a *feel* for the concept of your operating profit margin and why it matters to your business.

The second margin you must understand is your **gross profit margin**. This is perhaps the most misunderstood and least leveraged number in your business. Your gross profit margin is a measure of how much money you have left over from every sale after you take out what it cost you to produce or acquire the product or service you just sold. It's calculated as follows:

Gross Sales (i.e., total sales before any expenses)
– COGS (the "cost of goods sold" for the sales you made)
---
= Your Gross Profit

Continuing with our imaginary $1-million-a-year in sales company, if you had a COGS of $250,000, that would mean that your gross profit was $750,000. When you express that gross profit as a percentage, you get your gross profit margin of 75 percent.

Your gross profit margin tells you exactly how much money you have left after you pay the cost to produce and fulfill on a sale. This lets you know how much you can spend on marketing, sales, fixed overhead, and so on—and still have enough left to make a reasonable profit for your time, effort, and risk. This number is also a good indicator of the overall efficiency of your business. Knowing this number helps you look strategically at your pricing. It lets you know which customers, products, or projects are the best margin business to go after, and which you should consider phasing out (or even immediately cutting).

Here are some tips to improve your margins over the long term:

- **Velocity matters.** The faster your turnaround time (from order to delivery), the lower your overhead cost per unit produced. This in turn means improved profit margins.

- **Up-sell and cross-sell to increase your average unit of sale.** In general, when you increase the amount you sell to your customer at one time, you'll improve your margins because you'll be increasing the purchase velocity and therefore lowering your cost per sale in terms of overhead burden. Plus you're amortizing your marketing cost over a larger unit of sale, which dilutes your marketing cost for each sale.

- **Encourage your customers to upgrade to higher-value products or services.** Explore whether you can get your customer to upgrade to higher-value offerings that serve them better and that generally have a better margin for your business.

- **Cut low-margin clients, products, or services, and invest the saved time and money in higher-producing parts of your business.** This presupposes that you have accurate and timely reporting that shows you which clients, products, or services produce what margins.

- **Retention, retention, retention.** Attrition costs. Do all you can to keep your clients actively purchasing from you. Study the most common "drop points" in your client's purchase history. Can you strategically reinforce your business system to reduce that attrition? Perhaps you need to better communicate with them how to use your product or service? Or give them a well-timed "gift" or make a well-timed visit or phone call? Courting your current customers eliminates or greatly reduces the acquisition or marketing cost on that second and all later transactions.

- **Watch out for scrap, spoilage, and wastage.** Is it a quality issue on production? Are you poor at forecasting, and keep too much supply on hand for an order? Does it take you too long to sell your inventory and you lose part of it to obsolescence? This can also be an issue in areas of your business outside of operations. David once owned a real estate training company that purchased a thousand leads a month from Foreclosures.com at $5 per lead. He thought his sales team was following up on each of these leads with an outbound phone call, but later learned that 90 percent of these leads just weren't followed up on. His sales team had *said* they were calling them, but the reality was that they were earning so much money off the easy inbound leads that they ignored the harder-to-follow-up-with outbound leads. The lack of sound sales controls meant his company wasted $5,000 per month to buy leads that spoiled because they were not effectively followed up on.

## Cash Flow Commandment #7: Thou shalt make smart strategic decisions on purchasing and pricing.

The final part of managing your cash flow is making smart big-picture financial decisions. This includes things like your pricing model, capital investments, staffing, and other strategic investment decisions. Now that you have good financials, tight controls on spending, and a solid understanding of how to manage your margins, you're ready to make the big financial decisions that so heavily impact both cash flow and the long-term success of your company. This is often where the skills and experience of a CFO prove so valuable.

Here are several concrete suggestions to make better strategic financial decisions:

- **Get accurate and timely financial data *before* making long-term financial decisions.** Smart business owners let accurate data inform their mission-critical moves.

- **Review your strategic pricing decisions.** Most businesses set their prices when the business was new and desperately needed business and, as a result, set pricing levels low. Over time, the business may have made nominal increases to pricing every few years, but rarely did the owner ever sit down and fundamentally rethink his pricing model. Do you price in relationship to your costs and your competitors? The most successful companies take both of these factors into consideration, but they also price in relationship to the cost of the status quo for their customers. How much is the problem that your product or service solves already costing them? What is the real value of your product or service? What is the "frame of reference" you could give your customers that would help them immediately see your product or service as both the logically sound and emotionally satisfying solution? The more you are able to provide your market with solutions that other companies can't, the greater your ability to price in relationship to the true value of your solution instead of the race-to-the-bottom commoditization that so many businesses suffer from. While some business owners fear increasing prices for loyal long-term customers, the truth is that customers fear "switching costs"—the cost to leave you, train a new vendor, and go through the whole learning curve all over again with someone new. Often the switching cost is higher than your increase in prices, so they won't leave you just for making changes.

- **Look for the three clues that your pricing may be too low.** (1) You have limited production capacity and a large and hungry demand that exceeds your capacity to produce. (2) Your price is well below market without a compelling reason for it to be so low. (3) You have never *systematically* looked at your competitor's value proposition or your customer's true costs for the problem you solve.

- **Consider changing how you charge.** Is there a way you can move from a one-time charge to an ongoing revenue stream? Perhaps you do have a onetime charge for the initial purchase, but is there a way you can provide ongoing value to service your client on an ongoing basis? The smartest business models allow companies to annuitize their business relationships.

- **Find the optimal staffing level and manage your hiring intelligently.** Look for a simple heuristic that helps you know when you need to hire more production and operational staff (e.g., sales per employee, projects per operations staff, etc.) and when you are too heavy. What are the indicators that alert you to the need to staff up or staff down? What investments could you make in technology, systems, and training that would allow you to produce more with fewer people? Note that generally A players produce *multiples* more value than B or C players, yet cost only a percentage more. Look for ways you can upgrade your team over time so that you can produce more with less.

- **Get perspective before you make a major capital investment.** All too often, business owners find that a succession of small commitment steps lead them over the edge of the cliff when making the big infrastructure and capital decisions. They let sunk costs and vested interests that they are afraid of losing push them to chase bad money with good. After you have gathered all the relevant facts, step back with your leadership team and ask the question fresh: "Knowing all we know today and imagining that we had no sunk costs at this point at all, what is the best decision for the business over the short, medium, and long term?"

- **Know the difference between strategic expenses and nonstrategic expenses.** Strategic expenses are those things that directly help you sell more or produce better. They include marketing campaigns that work, salespeople who sell, technology upgrades that reap real returns and ongoing advantages of significant value, and intellectual property barriers that give you a sustainable advantage for which the market will pay. Nonstrategic expenses essentially include everything else. Outspend your competition for strategic expenses—in good times and bad. Relentlessly cut nonstrategic expenses. And repeat this over and over!

## Funding Rapid Growth

Growth almost always sucks up cash. The faster your growth, the greater your need for sources of capital to fund that growth. Plan in advance of that growth to secure the capital reserves or funding sources to afford that growth.

Here are five sources of capital to fund your growth with important lessons for using each that we paid dearly to learn over the past 20 years.

## Sources to Fund Your Growth

*Customers (the people who buy your products or services):*
- Redesign your collections system so you get paid up front, or at least partially paid up front with progress payments paid along the way instead of at the end.
- Let your customers pay you to be first in line for new features or services that they dearly want.
- Offer a premium deal for cash up front (with a clear reason why you want it). This could include an upgraded value offering or a discounted price for prepayment.
- Revisit your pricing. How could you increase your value and hence increase your pricing?

*Vendors (includes equipment leasing or purchases, supplier terms, etc.):*

- Build your relationship, strategically share information, and ask for input and help from your vendors. They are partners in your growth.
- Get your vendors to increase your available credit and lengthen the period before you must pay them.
- Barter. Find ways to trade products or services to conserve cash for growth.
- Consider engaging your vendor as a strategic partner when you have a big opportunity. After all, your growth will benefit them too.
- Build healthy relationships with your vendors and, if needed, work out win-win ways they can help you get through a cash flow crunch. They can be excellent champions to have on your side.

***Lenders (the traditional institutions from which to borrow money):***

- Make your business bankable before you need the money. Normalize expenses, improve your margins, lock in better customer contracts—then go to your bank for more money.
- Learn how to package your application so banks are competing to lend you money. Smart businesses flip the process on its head by creating competition and soliciting loan proposals from multiple lenders. The better you make your loan package, the easier it is to create a feeding frenzy.
- Understand how a banker looks at your business. (For more on this, see the free training video titled *Business by the Numbers: Margins, Ratios, Key Indicators, and Cost of Goods Sold*. You can access this and two dozen other training videos at **www.ScaleYourBusinessToolKit.com**.)
- Look for ways to enhance your personal credit and financial statement to grow your other bank sources of funding (including credit cards, signature loans, home equity lines of credit, and so on).
- Lines of credit are great sources of liquidity to finance operations, but they can be fickle. If your business relies heavily on short-term credit to finance operations, deepen your banking relationships by consistently and accurately communicating with your bankers. Bankers hate surprises more than anything. Also, plan your contingencies in case your credit line gets reduced or, worse, closed.

***Internal (reinvesting the profits and cash flow of your business back into the business to fund future growth):***

- Build up a capital reserve to help you seize opportunities to grow. Liquid capital at the right time is worth its weight in gold.

- The faster you can accelerate your production and collections cycles the less working capital you need, and the faster your business can grow without external sources of funding. So do all you can to speed up production and reduce your collections cycle.
- Reduce your sales cycle. This will help you generate a faster return from your marketing dollars and hence also lower your working capital requirements.

***Investors (venture capital, private equity, crowdfunding, etc.):***

- Make sure that the extra capital and the growth it can potentially enable you to gain is worth sharing ownership. Does investment capital from venture capital or private equity really serve the long-term goals for your company?
- Money follows people first, and the ideas second. If you are going after investor capital, understand that they will be placing their bet on your team, not just on your business ideas.
- Every capital infusion requires that you set a value for your company. Learn how your business (in your industry and with your model) is valued and take steps early to enhance its value so that when you go for outside capital you get more money while giving up less ownership.
- Do your homework. Research your potential investors. Make sure you are approaching people who have invested in businesses in your industry. Don't try to raise capital to expand your financial-services business from an investor who focuses on retailing.
- Learn to tell a compelling story. Raising capital is a sales process, and you need to capture investors' attention with a story that they understand and covet. Speak from the perspective of your prospective investor's needs, wants, and desires, not your own. Also, if raising money is partially about telling a compelling story, remember the best characters have flaws. Don't hide your business's warts; expose

them to your potential investors along with your concrete plans to fix them. This will build your credibility (they'll likely find them anyway before they stroke that check).
- Because you're looking for money to fund growth of your existing business, make sure you use your existing track record as the springboard to investors' return. Show them how their capital will increase sales and pay them a healthy return.

## Safeguard Your Company from Fraud and Theft

In this final section on removing obstacles to scaling your Financial pillar, we want to look at proven ways to systematically protect your company from fraud and theft. Private companies are prime targets for fraud. According to the Association of Fraud Examiners, in 2010, 42 percent of fraud cases happened in privately held companies. The majority of these cases occurred in companies with fewer than a hundred employees, with the average fraud continuing for 18 months before it was even detected! The median loss in all these fraud cases was devastating: a whopping $231,000 per case. Since your company may be vulnerable to fraud and theft, let's dive in and look at how you can *systematically* protect yourself and your company from being blindsided.

### The "Big Three" Financial Control Concepts

*Financial Control Concept #1: Always have two unrelated parties involved in any money flow in or out of your business.*

This could include one person who opens the mail, lists all checks received on a spreadsheet, and preps these checks for depositing, and a second, unrelated person who double-checks the math and reviews the deposit amounts before it goes to the bank. One person who sets up the ACH payments for the payables period, and another who goes in and approves the payments to go out.

The idea behind this financial control concept is pairing two unrelated team members on a given financial job so they can be a check and balance for each other. This does two things. First, it reduces temptation for fraud as both parties know that the other will likely quickly see any bad behavior and report it immediately. Second, it makes it so two people would both have to collude *and keep the secret* before any serious theft could happen in those areas.

**Financial Control Concept #2: Create permanent footprints in your financial system that cannot be erased so that you always have a clear audit trail.**

This includes numbering your invoices and keeping a separate invoice log of who has which invoice number series. Footprints can also mean keeping checks under lock and key, with a check log clearly showing who is in control of and responsible for which check series, or making sure that your financial software is set up with individual log-ins for any team member who needs to access that information, and that the software permanently tracks any changes to the accounting and who made those changes. (This is an option you can turn on in QuickBooks, one of the most popular small business accounting programs. Other accounting software programs like Peachtree have similar functionality.) We also suggest that you require your financial staff to have private, robust passwords that they change at least twice a year.

What this financial control concept does is make it much more difficult for a person to cover up theft, whether by making it clear who had which checks or invoices, or by keeping a permanent record of who altered what accounting records. By making these things obvious and traceable back to the offending party, you lower the temptation of bad behavior and increase the odds of its being spotted faster.

*Financial Control Concept #3: Show vigilance and actively question things that strike you as strange or out of the ordinary.*

As the business owner, it is your responsibility to actively and regularly review the financial records of your business. Sure, you will have financial staff who do the heavy lifting, but you still need to pay close attention too. Spot-check reports and highlight any line item or general question you might have. Follow up with your staff to get answers. If the answers don't satisfy you, *dig.* Listen to that still, small voice inside that sounds the alarm. At the very least you'll keep your financial team on its toes and at least *thinking* that you are watching closely. Most business owners know roughly what the numbers should look like, and what expenses and sales figures make sense. If you see something that is out of the ordinary, question it.

Here are several more powerful financial controls under four categories for you to consider to make your Financial pillar stronger and more resistant to fraud or theft.

**CASH CONTROLS:**

- Bank statements should be mailed to the business owner's house. The business owner should open and review the bank statement. (And she should mark up the statement so that her controller or bookkeeper sees that she's looked closely at the statement!)
- Perform monthly bank reconciliations, preferably with someone other than the person doing the deposits.
- Use a lockbox or separate post-office box for accounts receivable payments instead of having them sent to a general company address that many more people have access to.
- Consider using a sweep account to take money over a certain amount out of your business's main operating business account. This second sweep account should have

much tighter financial controls around who can access it (usually with the owner being the only person authorized to move money out of that account).
- Do not keep signed blank checks for future use. This practice leaves you vulnerable to misuse.

### COLLECTIONS CONTROLS:

- Any collections write-offs should be approved in writing by the owner or senior-level manager.
- When possible, use prenumbered invoices and maintain an invoice log.
- Collections A/R reports should be reviewed *weekly* by management.
- The owner and senior management should periodically review the master client list for potential fake customers.
- Look for outside ways to verify your sales receipts. For example, compare the attendance numbers at a workshop against the gross income for that event, or the sales for the week against the traffic flow in your store. If something is out of line, investigate.

### ACCOUNTS PAYABLE CONTROLS:

- All vendor invoices over a certain amount should be reviewed by the owner or senior manager.
- Restrict access to corporate credit cards and require receipts and detailed invoices for all credit card charges. Have a formal expensing system that includes a clear, written policy of what expenses are and are not reimbursable, and who needs to sign off on what types of expenses. Also, require that all expenses submitted include a copy of the original receipt. Require your employees to sign their expense reports warranting that they are true and accurate.
- The owner should periodically review the master vendor list for fake vendors (a common way employees steal from

a business). This is a simple report you can pull from your accounting software.
- Hand out paychecks at a job site to see if you have any fictitious employees (especially for businesses with large off-site projects that have employees or contractors there whom they are paying).
- All overtime should be approved by management prior to its being worked.

**OTHER FINANCIAL CONTROLS:**

- Make sure that any software or other purchase that the company pays for be owned and titled in the company name. This includes checking that the company is the one named with the software vendor or other supplier.
- Keep a close eye on your margins and key numbers. For example, if your cost of goods sold or gross margin is off, find out why.
- Thoroughly check employees and independent contractors before you hire them. Consider criminal background checks, drug testing, and credit checks.
- Consider bonding financial team members or getting appropriate insurance coverages.

The reason we laid out this final section of this chapter is not to turn you into a paranoid business owner who is suspicious of all your employees. Rather, the reason is to empower you to be a *responsible* business owner who radically reduces the temptation of some team members' doing something inappropriate because they know that they will be caught. This gives you peace of mind knowing that one bad apple isn't hurting things for your business as a whole.

Now that you have a solid understanding of how to improve your Finance pillar, it's time to turn our attention to removing the obstacles to scaling from your Team pillar.

# YOUR TEAM PILLAR

## ATTRACTING, RETAINING, AND UNLEASHING TALENT

Tim was a good salesperson. He understood the retail flooring industry and could help a homeowner find and purchase the perfect flooring solution for his or her home. But as he grew his flooring company past the $1 million mark, he increasingly found himself behind the scenes in his store, hiring and managing his staff. He had no training or experience to draw on to help him design compensation plans and get his team to buy into the company vision and values, and he certainly suffered his share of expensive staff turnover issues. He was a strong technician who now found that his business needed him to learn and master a completely new skill set.

The Team pillar of your company handles the hiring, orienting, training, assessment, compensation, development, and, if necessary, the exiting of your team. It is also responsible for keeping your company in compliance with all the legal requirements of working with employees.

Most small and midsize companies' Team pillars are fundamentally weak. The causes for this vary from the founder's fear of hiring better, smarter people than himself, to a faulty belief that employees are just a hassle and expense, to a lack of training and experience with hiring and managing employees. As a consequence, most business owners spend too little time strategically deciding whom they need to hire and when, and how to best retain and tap into these talented team members to accomplish the goals and objectives of the company. Yet when this is done well, your team is the ultimate source of leverage for you to create and sustain rapid growth. Their passion, skills, and experiences are often the missing link between your scaling successfully and reaching Level Three, or getting mired in the Self-Employment Trap. Remember the three-legged stool we shared with you in chapter 2? Your team is one of the three essential components of creating a stable base upon which to scale (the other two being systems and controls). In this chapter, we'll share with you our best lessons on recruiting, retaining, and unleashing great talent.

## Common Sense—Where Have You Gone?

When Jeff was in his twenties and the CEO of his first company, he hadn't had much experience managing people. Here he was, this newbie, when one of his older, more seasoned team members asked him about the company's employee manual. Jeff's company didn't have one, so he called everyone from the small company together into a conference room. He asked them all to take out a blank sheet of paper and draw a vertical line down the middle of the page. He asked them to list everything they disliked at other jobs on the left side of the page, from the way people treated them, to the way the company expected them to behave, to all the things that made them want to leave the company. Then, on the right- hand side of the page, he asked them to list the exact opposite: the things they had loved about the companies they had worked for, the policies they wished the companies had had, and the way they wanted to be treated by management and their peers.

Everyone in the room now had a single sheet of paper with two detailed columns, one a list of what they hated about past employers and the other listing how they wanted to be treated. Jeff then instructed the team to all tack their lists outside of their office or cubicle. They had just outlined the company's employee manual. "If I catch anyone doing anything on the left side of the page, including me, you're in trouble," he said, smiling. "And we'll all work hard to do the things on the right side of the page. In fact, I'll make it a point to have myself and any future managers read through the right side of the page every Monday morning as a refresher of how you want to be treated."

While not formally an "employee manual," the two lists gave Jeff a clear outline as to what specifically his team loved and hated. They gave him the simple outline of how he could empower, encourage, and embrace them over the long term.

Here is one of the most interesting parts: Most of what his team had listed on the right-hand side of the page had nothing to do with financial compensation. They wanted recognition, both as valuable people and as contributors to the team. They wanted simple freedoms that kept bureaucratic red tape from wasting their time and hobbling their choices when those choices only helped (or at the very least, in no way hurt) the company reach its goals. They wanted the company to trust their judgment and to actually allow them to make decisions that mattered. And they wanted to grow professionally.

This story illustrates how uncommon common sense has become. When was the last time you asked each of your team members to think about what they wanted from their job? Or the last time you looked at your company's internal systems and controls to see if they helped your employees do their best work? Asking employees what things management can do to motivate them and make them feel valued, and then comparing that list with what your company actually does day to day, is often a shocking wake-up call to leaders.

## Making Your Company a Place Where Great Talent Wants to Work

Companies compete for top talent. One of the most important insights we can give you to help your company create and sustain rapid growth is for you to systematically make your business a place where great talent wants to work. Here are some simple suggestions you can apply today to do just this.

- **Deliberately define and profile your ideal team member.** Establish a profile of your business's perfect team member. Obviously the specific qualifications will vary from position to position, but think about the common traits, beliefs, and drives of your ideal team member. Who would they need to be to fit well into your company culture? How could you build simple filters into your hiring process to weed out any candidates who clearly are not a strong cultural fit for your business?

- **Be selective about whom you invite on your team.** Great talent thrives when working with other talented team members. Keep your standards high as you hire and consider upgrading weak team members as you have the cash flow and opportunity to do so. A great side benefit of this is that birds of a feather flock together. In many of our companies, our best new employees were often friends and referrals of our existing talented employees.

- **See the whole person and manage individually.** Sure, your company needs to have standard HR policies, but use common sense and humanity in applying those standards. Clarify what matters most to each individual team member and manage them in light of their preferences. The goal isn't to treat all team members the same—the goal is to produce amazing results by getting your team to perform at its best.

There is a reason why NBA super coach Phil Jackson coached Michael Jordan differently from Scottie Pippen and Steve Kerr—they all responded best to different coaching and different motivations. And while we're at it, why not have a one-page "cheat sheet" that defines how to coach each individual player on your team? All it takes is a willingness to ask your team what works best for them, what they like least, and to observe them over time.

- **Affirm your team by sharing information, holding high standards, and believing in their ability to deliver results.** Top talent wants to be respected and challenged. Sharing information sends the message you trust them to be competent and integral enough to understand and use the information. Holding high standards and believing in your team's ability to perform is contagious, and helps you create a results-oriented culture inside your business.

- **Remove poor performers quickly.** Give a poorly performing employee proper guidance, coaching, and training, but if after a time it becomes clear that they just can't perform at the level of those around them, remove them swiftly and decisively. It is very demotivating to high performers when they see complacent, low-performing coworkers get a free pass from management.

- **Reward achievements when they happen—immediacy, enthusiasm, and authenticity matter.** The old-school model of evaluating and recognizing performance at annual review time is outdated. When a team member does something exceptional, find a way to applaud that performance right away. It doesn't have to be a raise or promotion, or even cash. Instead, stop everyone in the halls and have them give a team member a standing ovation for work well done, announce the exceptional work in a quick company-wide email, or walk over to a team member's office and tell him or her in person how impressed you are. The key is to show how much you appreciate what the team member did *right now*, when it just happened.

## The Inverted Pyramid of Leadership

Once you've hired great talent, your job as a leader in your business is to serve your talent so that they get great results for your business. Sometimes this means connecting resources; at other times this means removing obstacles. There are times when it will even mean taking on mundane details that support your team in accomplishing its big goals.

Early in the life of his first company, CTI, a travel software business, Jeff was checking in with a development team who had moved into a conference room to finish the final sprint to complete a new product release on time. They were working diligently and Jeff, as CEO, popped in the room and asked, "Is there anything I can do for you to help you meet the deadline?" At this point CTI was a successful business doing $5.8 million per year in sales and had just been named to the *Inc.* magazine list of the 500 fastest-growing small businesses; Jeff was the CEO and owner of the business. One of the junior team members said, "Yeah, Jeff, can you pick up my dry cleaning for me?" There was a palpable pause in the room as the team watched how Jeff would react. Jeff didn't miss a beat. He simply asked for the dry-cleaning ticket and went and got the clothing from the cleaners.

Here's the point: The best thing Jeff could do for his business at that moment was to keep his talent in that room, working on the product, so that they could meet their looming deadline and wow their waiting customers. If you have to go run a few errands so your company wins, then that's what you need to do—ego and personal glory be damned! CTI tripled sales to over $16 million the very next year, and Jeff later sold the company to American Express for an eight-figure payday. That's why one of the most important lessons Jeff shares at large CEO conferences is: "Build a culture and environment where really talented people want to work, and then go get their dry cleaning!"

## Compensation—A Game You Can Only Tie or Lose (Rarely Win)

One of the most stressful areas for most business owners in the Team pillar of their company has to do with compensation: how much they will pay their team. The two prevailing beliefs on compensation are either pay as little as you can to secure the talent that you want or pay handsomely for the best, never letting money stop you from bringing the most talented team on board. We think both approaches are flawed.

First, as to the belief that you should pay the least you can while still being able to sign on the team members you want—we feel that this view doesn't get the way people really work. Over time, people will become resentful if they don't feel like they are being compensated fairly. This may mean they'll leave when a suitor company woos them or that they'll do their work begrudgingly day to day if they stay. Your team is not an expense; they are one of the most essential strategic investments your business will ever make, so use compensation to establish the right relationship with them from the start.

Years ago, Jeff wanted to hire a new programmer for one of his companies. He brought the man into his office. On his desk was a blank sheet of paper. Jeff said, "I understand that you're making $70,000 a year where you're working now and we would like to give you a reasonable increase to take this job and switch companies. There's a sheet of paper on the corner of my desk. I want you to take that paper and write down the salary you would like to join our team." The programmer wrote down $80,000. Jeff then asked him to flip the paper over and read aloud what was written on the other side—$85,000. Jeff explained that prior to the meeting, he had written down what he thought this programmer was really worth to the company. At first, the programmer didn't understand. He said, "But I only asked for eighty thousand." Once Jeff asked him if he really wanted to continue that conversation, the programmer smiled and said no, he didn't.

Business owners who view employees as expenses will say that Jeff wasted $5,000. After all, the programmer would have been happy to take $80,000. But we look at employees as strategic expenses, which made that $5,000 an investment that paid off handsomely. That programmer helped Jeff recruit four of his programmer buddies at zero cost to the company. He also often stayed late to do great work and prove that Jeff was right to pay him the extra $5,000. All things considered, Jeff's company got a huge return on this $5,000 investment.

The point is not that you should pay your team extra, but that you should do your best to nail down the rough range of what each team member is *really* worth to your company and, over time, make sure that you are paying them roughly that amount. By fighting over the last dollar, sometimes you win the battle but lose the war.

Now let's turn our attention to the second most prevailing (and in our opinion, flawed) business owner belief on compensation: that you need to overpay to get a team of stars. To the person who follows this line of reasoning, we would just say that if you overpay, you can often turn a great talent into an entitled, spoiled prima donna who doesn't live up to his or her own hype. Since many small businesses need to be smart with their capital and stretch their dollars, they really shouldn't let money be the leading lure to work for their company. Employees motivated more by money than any other factor are typically not the best employees to have when your company experiences the common ups and downs that all growing businesses go through.

You rarely win with money. The best you can hope for is not to blow it completely. You've got to be in the fair neighborhood. If you come in much too low or too high you'll lose (or pollute) that player. So be fair, and with top talent be generous, but also be strategic. Money is just one of a string of rewards you can "pay" your people with; in many cases it is midway down their list of wants or lower. As a smaller player in the market you can run circles around your competition with the nonfinancial rewards. These include things like:

- Giving your team cool projects and interesting work.
- Letting them *earn* autonomy and real control of many of the details of their work and environment. (Does it really matter how they dress? Can they bring their dog into work with them? Can they work from home several days a week? Can they adjust their hours to make their daughter's soccer game next Tuesday?)
- Sharing information and respecting their insights.
- Helping them find meaning in the work they do.
- Treating them fairly and letting them see you treat others fairly (positively and negatively).

## A Simple Technique to Help Your Team Make the Connection

People thrive on meaning. Companies thrive by creating value. Linking how each team member's role adds value to the company and serves the customer helps your team focus on the right things even when no one is around to "manage" them.

We want to share with you a little-known technique to help team members self-manage and eradicate wasted efforts. We call this technique "making the connection."

Several years ago, Jeff was being shown around the headquarters of 1-800-Flowers by its CEO and founder, Jim McCann. Jim opened up his first flower shop in 1976, and had grown it into one of the world's largest flower and gift companies with annual sales of $700 million. As they walked around the production facility, Jim stopped an employee and asked him what he was doing, and how what he was doing helped the company sell more flowers. After the employee responded, Jim thanked him and told him to get back to work. Jim turned to Jeff and told him that if an employee can't tell him immediately how his actions at any moment helped achieve the goal of selling more flowers, he tells that employee to stop doing what he's doing, and find something to do that actually sells more flowers.

They continued walking, making their way to the garage. Jim stopped a mechanic there who was installing fuel filters on their delivery vans. When Jim asked him how installing fuel filters helped sell more flowers, the mechanic responded that he had done research and found a fuel filter that improved the efficiency of every tank of gas by 11 percent. If he could help the company save 11 percent of the cost of each delivery van's fuel, the company could take some of the savings, and give the rest to the customer in the form of lower prices, which would yield increased flower sales.

As you can imagine, Jeff was floored by how clearly each 1-800-Flowers team member could connect what he or she was doing to the one goal of selling more flowers. He took the idea back to his company and started stopping everyone in the halls to ask what they were doing and how it directly helped the company achieve its main goal.

The core of this technique is crafting your "connection question." What is the single question that you want your team to use internally as a filter to focus them on work that matters and to eliminate work that doesn't?

For 1-800-Flowers, their connection question is, "How does what I'm doing help us sell more flowers?"

For David's business coaching company, Maui Mastermind, their connection question is, "How does what I'm doing help us create and keep a business coaching client?"

For Jeff's innovation company, Colorjar, their connection question is, "How does what I'm doing help us startle and delight our client?"

What is your company's connection question? Of course, coming up with the question is just the first step. You've got to explain the question's importance to your team and give them permission to use it as a benchmark against which to measure the work you're asking them to do at any given moment. This means you've got to also give them the power to call the company on tasks that just don't make sense, and to use their initiative to better direct themselves to create more value for the company. Building a culture where employees feel free to ask piercing questions and challenge the status quo is critical to your ability to have continuous improvement.

## Tapping into Your Team for Ideas to Scale

There is one last practice we want to share with you. It's one that we've used for a while now inside our companies, and we've seen it make a real difference for the companies we coach. We call this practice the "Three Best Ideas Tool," and it helps you enlist your team in developing ideas to scale and improve your company.

Every six months, give your entire team the tool shown in Figure 10.1 (you can also get a full, fancy-formatted two-page PDF version of this tool by going to **www.ScaleYourBusiness ToolKit.com**). Ask each individual to go through the company area by area and write their three best ideas in each section of the tool. Once they've completed this, take their answers and spend several hours going over them to compile the strongest answers. Hold a team meeting to go over the results and involve your team in picking several of the best ideas to immediately implement in the company. Make sure you regularly report back to your team over time how the company is doing on actually *using* their ideas to improve the business. Repeat this process over time and watch not only how your company benefits and improves from these ideas, but how your team responds and grows when they see the company takes their input and ideas seriously.

FIGURE 10.1: THE THREE BEST IDEAS TOOL

| "My Best 3 Ideas to..." | | Reduce Costs | Increase Impact | Accelerate Process | Scale Capacity | Improve Linkages |
|---|---|---|---|---|---|---|
| Sales/Marketing | 1. | | | | | |
| | 2. | | | | | |
| | 3. | | | | | |
| Administration | 1. | | | | | |
| | 2. | | | | | |
| | 3. | | | | | |
| Production/Fulfillment | 1. | | | | | |
| | 2. | | | | | |
| | 3. | | | | | |
| Collection | 1. | | | | | |
| | 2. | | | | | |
| | 3. | | | | | |
| Other Areas | 1. | | | | | |
| | 2. | | | | | |
| | 3. | | | | | |

Copyright © Maui Mastermind®

In the next chapter we'll focus on the final pillar of your company—the Executive Leadership pillar.

# YOUR EXECUTIVE LEADERSHIP PILLAR

## ALIGNMENT, ACCOUNTABILITY, AND LEADING YOUR LEADERSHIP TEAM

The final pillar of your company is the Executive Leadership pillar. This is the pillar that makes the big-picture, strategic decisions and enrolls your entire team in that vision. It is the pillar that sets the tone for your company culture, including establishing a pervading sense of accountability within your business. And finally, this is the pillar that grooms and leads your leadership team, developing your leaders so that the company is radically less reliant on you to make decisions and manage execution.

In this chapter, we'll share our best ideas to help you align your entire team, upgrade the level of accountability inside your company, and lead your leadership team.

## Leaders Clarify the Big Picture

One of your core functions as the leader of your company is to set its big-picture vision. In chapter 5, you began this process by laying out the big-picture view of why you're in business, what your company's Singular Goal is, and how you and your team will pursue that goal. You also uncovered your company's top leverage points (in doing the S-O-O-T and Sweet Spot analyses). You put your seven key strategic decisions on trial, and crafted your big-picture business strategy. This is a great start, but in order to make this vision real inside your business, you need to both communicate it throughout your company and engage your team—quarter by quarter—in taking the small action steps that will, over time, result in you all reaching your goals. Remember, the most effective form of leadership is leading by example. Everyone is watching what you, the business owner, are doing, not just what you are saying. Your responsibility is to effectively communicate your vision, and then live it.

Here are seven concrete suggestions for you to communicate your big-picture vision with your team so that you enlist them in achieving your top business goals:

- **Put your big-picture vision for the company in writing and share it with your team.** We suggest that you edit it down to one page. It will have more impact.
- **Repetition works (so say it again and again).** You need to regularly reinforce your vision with your team. Take every opportunity to bring it up in meetings, in conversation, and in the normal course of your business. When you see an opportunity to highlight how a recent event or action at the company is in direct alignment with that vision, don't miss a chance to point it out.
- **Ask your team to tell you what *they* think the big-picture vision for the company is.** You'll be surprised by what they come up with. This is a great way to check to see if you've been successful in communicating your vision for the company. When David did this a few years ago at a company retreat, he got many different answers, some of which nailed it, others of which were totally different

from the company vision. This became a great coaching moment to clarify the big picture with his team.

- **Use the one-page quarterly planning tool company-wide.** Bring your key leaders together each quarter to create your company's 90-day plan. Share the one-page plan with everyone on your team. Make sure that you give them regular updates on how you as a company are doing on progressing on the steps it outlines. Sharing information is a sign that your company is serious about enlisting your team's best efforts in making the company's vision a reality. And the reverse of that—not sharing company information or progress—is demotivating to your team at any level.

- **Make sure that all team members understand their roles, responsibilities, what success for them in fulfilling those responsibilities looks like, and how they will be measured and given feedback as they go.** As obvious as this seems, in our experience it is a rare company whose entire team understands each of these things, let alone the business that has a formal system to make sure that as they grow, each new team member does too. Publicly reward behavior that directly supports the company's vision.

- **Actions speak louder than words, so make sure your company lives its vision.** Do you regularly use your company values as a filter through which to make your big decisions? Do you put your best resources on projects that are geared to move you closer to your Singular Goal, or do you fritter them away on putting out your brightest momentary fires? Do you regularly assess how your company is progressing on its most important goals, using the feedback to improve the business, or do you just react to things as they hit the business? Your team is watching everything. Make sure what they see reinforces how seriously you take your own big-picture vision for the company.

- **It is your responsibility to make sure you look to the future and ensure that your company invests some of its resources in dreaming up what comes next.** The world is changing so fast; you must keep looking toward tomorrow and thinking about what comes next. You don't have to be the source of the ideas, but as the leader in charge of the big picture, it is ultimately your responsibility to make sure your company asks the right questions so that it stays vibrant and relevant to the world. Complacency in a changing world is fatal.

## Leaders Shape Meaning and Establish Culture

Leaders create the narrative through which their team interprets the business and their relationship to it. As you grow your business, it becomes increasingly more important that you shape the stories and traditions that will become part of your company's culture. Stories and traditions empower employees to make the right decision for the company when no one is around to help and the customer wants an answer immediately. They hold your business on course even when you're no longer present each day to drive it, which is what you want in a Level Three business.

Here are our best tips to shape meaning and establish the company culture you want so that your business thrives long-term:

- **Look for small, symbolic stories that transmit the values of your company and share these stories at every opportunity.** If you see Mark, a client support rep, creatively solve an issue in a way that delights your client, share this story internally with your team again and again. The best of these stories will be absorbed into the mythology of your company and shape the way it sees itself for years to come.

- **Intentionally seize moments to take an action or make a decision that illustrates the best of how you want your team to behave.** Maybe it's always calling your customer by name as they walk back into your store, letting your team see you write out a thank-you card after a sales call, or recapping who owns which action steps after a meeting and by when. Your company's culture is built by the accumulation of thousands of small decisions and examples that happen over and over and over. In your business, there are no throwaway moments; your team watches and absorbs *everything* you do.

- **What you do at stressful moments in the business has a magnified impact on your team and on your company culture.** Think of stress and the heightened emotions that go with it as a magnifying glass that powerfully enhances the impact—good or bad—of your behavior. Use these moments as the golden opportunities they are. Leaders face the hard realities, but do so in a spirit of positive faith that they can find a way through them to the results they want. Whatever you do in these stressful moments will cumulatively impact the tone of how your team will respond to these same circumstances in the future.

- **Help your team see the impact of what they do and what the company does on the lives of one another and your customers.** When a client shares a story of how your product or service impacted their life or business, share that story company-wide. Enroll your team in gathering and sharing these same stories. Make this part of your regular meetings. Archive these stories so that the best of them get told and retold inside your company. Also, make sure that you encourage your team to gather stories of how other team members really helped them out and added to their lives through something they did. Encourage your team to share these stories—publicly and privately—too.

- **Clarify your company's values and make them the filter through which you make all your business's tough decisions.** Encourage your team to use them the same way, and celebrate when they do. From time to time, ask your employees how they used the company's values to make big decisions in the heat of the moment. It's a great barometer of just how deeply your values have been absorbed into the company.

## Leaders Demand Accountability

Great businesses are built on teams that take full ownership of individual responsibilities. Too many businesses let people slide by partially doing things, and accepting excuses for delays and mistakes that could have been avoided. A culture of accountability is one of the most valuable institutional habits that your business can form, and will empower your company to grow and develop.

Accountability starts with you and your leadership team. If you don't move heaven and earth to honor your word and meet all your commitments, your team will learn that they don't have to either. Here are seven time-tested tips on your role in creating accountability in your company:

- **Clarify your commitments in writing at the end of every meeting.** Not only does this make sure that you've captured all your action items, but it is also a powerful way to role-model how you want your team to behave. Wherever possible, try to enumerate all your commitments to make it even clearer what you have agreed you'll do: "So, summing up, I've got three action items here. Item one . . . item two . . . and item three . . ." (while visibly writing each of them down in your notes). Teach your team to employ this same tactic with customers as well. Customers love doing business with companies that follow through.

- **Circle back with the team members who are involved with your action steps and give them feedback on your progress and completion at regular intervals.** This is a great way to model the behavior you want from them, and highlight how important it is inside your company to meet deliverables. "Just wanted to give you a quick update. As I committed to, I did [item one] and [item two] today, and will get [item three] done by close of business Friday." Even when the task isn't complete, don't leave people guessing. Circle back and say, "I haven't solved the problem yet, but I haven't forgotten you and I'm actively working on a solution."

- **Clearly state what you can't commit to so that you don't lower the accountability bar in your company by missing a "phantom deliverable."** Remember back in chapter 8 when we talked about "phantom deliverables"? These are things that the other person *thinks* you committed to but you didn't. As a leader, you need to exhibit great communication by making any phantom deliverables you see come out of a meeting explicit. That way if you can commit to that deliverable, you do so, and if you can't, you clarify that you are not committing to it.

- **Be on time, all the time.** Being on time—all the time—is a simple behavior that your team will generalize to mean that you take your commitments seriously and live with integrity. It is one behavior with a huge return on investment in terms of modeling accountability inside your company. Too many companies implement respect in a hierarchical manner. Your time is *not* more important than an employee's time or a customer's time in their eyes. Being on time shows respect, and it makes a big difference to the receiver.

- **Credibility is a marathon, not a sprint.** It doesn't help if you take off out of the gate gung ho in your desire to model accountability, only to let it slip a few weeks later. If you want accountability to be a real and lasting part of your company culture, you've got to maintain your behavior over time.

- **How you own your failures is as important as how you model your successes.** You're human and you *will* mess up. To think otherwise is just not realistic. How you own your missed deliverables is incredibly important to the culture you are building. Do you make excuses? Sweep them under the rug? Melodramatically beat yourself up? Don't! Instead, show your team how mistakes are a part of being in business, and often can lead to profitable insights. When you make a mistake, publicly take responsibility, share what you learned and how you'll apply it, and implement a better solution going forward.

- **Most breakdowns in accountability come from incomplete or poor handoffs.** At the moment any deliverable is created, it needs to be assigned to someone who will be responsible for seeing that it happens. We call this assignment of a deliverable a "handoff." As a leader, you need to show that every handoff clearly details who is responsible for what, by when, what success in meeting that deliverable looks like, and how he or she will be held accountable for that deliverable. "Sarah, you own this deliverable and it includes doing $x$ and $y$ by Friday close of business. Can you also please make sure to send a quick recap to Tom and me on Monday that shares how client $z$ responded?"

If these are the behaviors that help you and your leadership team model accountability inside your business, here are two additional tools to help your business systematically weave accountability into the fabric of your company culture.

## Accountability Tool #1: Key Performance Indicators

Key performance indicators (KPIs) are the critical metrics that measure how your business is performing in a specific area at any given moment. The right KPIs direct your team's attention to what matters most, and give you and your team the timely feedback you need to make adjustments on the fly.

The best KPIs are "leading indicators." This means that they are numbers that help you predict whether or not you will hit your target and achieve your goals in a specific area. KPIs are critical to track and regularly review because they give you feedback early enough in the game for you to use the information to do something about what they reveal to influence the outcome. For example, if your goal is to increase sales this quarter, potential leading indicators include the number of dials your sales team makes each day, the average dollar per sale, the average number of hours per week your sales team spends on direct sales activities, or your average contact rate per dial. Given that you could measure any of these leading indicators, or in fact dozens more, your choice of the right KPI for a specific area requires you to narrow your selection to the one or two numbers that, more than any other, measure the most important leverage point in helping your company hit its goal in this area.

Don't think of KPIs as absolute numbers, though. Think of them over time as levers you can pull to fine-tune your business. *If I double this number and lower that one, does my business perform better or worse?* It's important to use KPIs as a way not just to measure your current performance, but also to shape and enhance your future performance.

The best KPIs:

- **Measure the most meaningful leading indicator in that area of your business, or in a specific team member's area of responsibility.** KPIs direct attention to what matters most. The very choice of your KPIs helps your company narrow its focus to those fewer, better things where its efforts will have the biggest payoff.

- **Are either automatically tabulated or self-scored so that they give you accurate feedback on a timely basis.** Think about the game of golf—a golfer knows how she is doing at any moment in the round because she is keeping score in real time on a small scorecard. Smart businesses help each team member pick one or two KPIs to individually focus on that give them regular feedback, at least weekly, and ideally daily.

- **Make the score easy to understand.** The best KPIs are concrete and simple such as "percent complete," "visitors to our store per day," or "conversion rate of our main web landing page." In order for the feedback a KPI generates to help direct behavior, the KPI must be obvious and intuitive to understand. Make sure that your team understands what the KPI measures and how increasing or decreasing the number impacts the business.

- **Are leading indicators, as opposed to trailing indicators.** KPIs should measure key leverage points that *predict* your current status and trend in hitting an important goal. In most cases, it is easiest to think of the key goal you are trying to accomplish as the *trailing* indicator. Trailing indicators (also known as results indicators) clarify outcomes that have already happened and as such tell you the score after the game is over. By focusing your KPIs on leading indicators, you give your team feedback in time for them to use that information to influence the eventual outcome in that area.

So how do you best use KPIs to scale your company? In the real world, the two biggest mistakes we watch businesses make with respect to KPIs are either to not have any or to have too many. The businesses that don't use this tool at all lose out on the power that a few carefully chosen metrics can have to direct attention and give timely feedback. Using a KPI doesn't have to be complicated or difficult. It can be as simple as asking the question, "What one variable could we measure that, if we focused on improving that one variable, would have the biggest positive impact on helping us hit our most important goals in this area of our business?"

For example, Sasha, whom we met earlier, owned the dominant dry cleaning business in her area. One of two KPIs she chose for her business was the number of enrollments per week her counter team secured for their "concierge" level of cleaning (a free service that included pickup and delivery and auto billing of all charges to a credit card on account). She knew that her concierge-level clients on average did a much higher volume of business and were more loyal to her company, which meant that increasing the number of enrollments her team signed from walk-in customers sustainably increased sales.

Having too many KPIs is also counterproductive. While it might make sense to measure 15 different variables in your sales and marketing, too much data dilutes the impact that one or two carefully chosen KPIs could have on your sales efforts. By focusing on one or two KPIs in an area, you'll concentrate your efforts on making a few carefully chosen, high-leverage changes to improve performance.

Remember Thomas, who owned the mobile bottling company from chapter 4? One of his company's most important goals was to improve its gross profit margin (the trailing or results indicator). He measured many variables, including his cost of raw materials, his shipping costs, his storage costs, and more. But when he looked closely at all the factors that impacted his gross profit margin, he realized that his top leverage point was controlling overtime worked by his staff, since that overtime added an additional 50 percent per hour to his labor cost. Knowing this, Thomas chose the total number of overtime hours worked per week as one of his KPIs. Tracking this KPI helped his team improve their systems, tighten up on scheduling, and better manage their employees. The bottom-line result was that they reduced overtime hours by *30 percent* within the first six months of implementing this KPI. This wouldn't have been nearly as easy to do if he tried reporting reams of data back to his team. It was the clarity of having that *one* simple KPI for this area that focused attention and helped them get such dramatic results so quickly.

Here are some tips to implement KPIs in your business tomorrow morning:

- **Pick one KPI for each of your three Focus Areas in your quarterly one-page plan of action.** What is your most important result for this Focus Area this quarter? Choose the KPI that is the best leading indicator to help you accomplish this result. For example, if the most important result is to lower your production costs, then a possible KPI could be the percentage of your jobs that require overtime, or the average number of staff hours required to complete a service call. Your goal is to pick a KPI that will help give you feedback on your progress toward your most important result for that Focus Area that quarter.

- **Help each of your team members choose one or two KPIs to focus on each quarter.** For example, you might have your two salespeople focus on the KPI of the number of qualified sales appointments they set each week, or you could have your customer service reps focus on the average number of hours it takes to close out a service ticket. Wherever possible, coach your team members to pick the best KPIs for them to focus on rather than just dictating to them from on high. You'll not only get much deeper buy-in this way, you'll also help your team grow as businesspeople. Your team's KPIs both direct their focus and give them a powerful tool to self-manage their behavior.

- **Create simple *visual* ways that your company and individual team members can see the top KPIs.** Whether you use a graph, a dial, or a thermometer, people understand numbers best when they are put into a simple visual frame.

## Accountability Tool #2: The "Big Rock" Huddle

It's a Monday morning, 9 A.M. Kevin Bassett and the nine members of his tax team gather for a quick team huddle. He briefly shares a recent company victory, then they go around the group with each person succinctly sharing what their top two or three action commitments were for the prior week, and whether they completed them or not. The team then quickly outlines their top two or three action commitments for the coming week, end the huddle, and get back to work.

All totaled, this huddle took less than 15 minutes and ensured that each team member started the week with a clear focus on what mattered most. At the same time Kevin led this meeting for his tax team, his partner, Dane, held the same meeting with the "financial and accounting" group within their CPA firm, Bassett and Byers. We call this structured start to your week the "Big Rock Huddle."

"Big Rocks" are those important and valuable chunks of work that actually help the business make real progress on its most important goals. Every week, we strongly encourage you to ask each team member to identify the two to three Big Rocks they can do that week that will have the greatest positive impact on progressing the business toward accomplishing its most important objectives. Sure, your team is still going to have all the to-dos on their plates to operate the business day to day, but the discipline of identifying and committing to your weekly Big Rocks makes sure that, in the rush of the week, some of your best resources go to doing those key things that actually progress the business.

The best Big Rocks are small enough tasks that they can be completed in 30 minutes to three hours, yet important enough that when accomplished they help your company take a real step forward toward reaching your big business goals. Remember the example of 1-800-Flowers? Make sure the Big Rocks you choose really do help you sell more flowers.

Here are a few other tips to help you use the "Big Rock Huddle" in your company:

- **Keep your Big Rock Huddle short—ideally under 15 minutes.** This may mean you have to break into smaller groups as Kevin and Dane do in their midsize CPA firm.

- **Consider making it a *standing* huddle.** This will force you to keep it short.

- **Teach your team what Big Rocks are, and how to pick the best ones each week.** Don't assume your team will immediately be able to choose the right Big Rocks. For the first 30 to 60 days you implement this idea, don't worry about the Big Rocks they choose. It is more about building the muscle than choosing the perfect Big Rocks. As you progress, make sure you and your management team coach team members to choose better and better Big Rocks. This is a great way to make sure your team understands the real goals of the company and what each team member can do to support those goals.

- **Use your KPIs to help you choose your Big Rocks.** Any Big Rock that has a real impact on a KPI is likely a great choice.

- **Have each team member send a quick summary email at the end of the week.** This Friday email should go out to the entire team or department (depending on how big your company is). In it, your team members should each list what their Big Rocks were and give a bulleted recap of how they did—rock by rock. Your team should also share what their two or three Big Rocks are for the coming week. If you need to up the accountability ante, consider holding a second huddle on Thursday morning to get a quick status check-in on everyone's Big Rocks.

- **Make sure you still have each team member share their Big Rocks and quick update at the huddle.** There is power in people standing before their peers and verbally sharing what they are doing that is most important, and articulating how they are doing on these key commitments.

## Leaders Grow Other Leaders

The final area we want to address in your Executive Leadership pillar is the need to grow and groom your leadership team. For most businesses, directing the leadership team is one of the last responsibilities you the owner will let go of when transitioning to a Level Three business. Prior to that, you're going to need strong leaders heading up each pillar of your business.

Remember, you'll flesh out your leadership team one by one as you progress from Middle Stage Level Two, through Advanced Stage Level Two, and into Level Three. Here are eight important insights to help you grow, integrate, and leverage your leadership team:

- **Generally, your first key management-level hire will be either in the Operations or Sales/Marketing pillar of your company.** If you are more of an operations person yourself, then likely your first management hire will be a sales and/or marketing leader. If you are more sales focused, your first key hire will likely be in operations. You want this first key hire to balance your best abilities and stabilize your company.

- **The right management hire is an investment, not an expense.** For example, David remembers one of his companies that had plateaued at the $1-million-a-year mark. After he brought on a new COO ($100,000 per year) it grew by 600 percent over the next 24 months. That $100,000 annual investment helped the business increase its sales by $5 million per year. You can't play every position on the field. You need talented leaders in your business who are as good as or better than you are in a specific pillar of your company. This frees you up to continue to grow and develop the business.

- **The management team you build today may not be the team you need tomorrow.** As your company grows larger, it is common for it to outgrow the capabilities of its leadership team. Some of your team will continue to grow over time and you'll enjoy their contribution for their entire career. Others on your leadership team stop growing and at some point need to be moved to a different role or replaced. This can be scary and uncomfortable to do, yet ultimately you need to let the needs of the business and the requirements of the position direct these decisions, not your own discomfort with making a tough call.

- **Beware hiring to make yourself feel better about yourself.** Secure business leaders hire better, smarter, more capable people than themselves. They don't fear looking poor in comparison. They realize that the better their team, the more successful their business will be.

- **When you hire smart, talented, experienced people, give them the authority to do what you hired them to do.** We always say hire hard, manage easy. Invest your time up front to get the right people, then let them do their job. Of course, you need to have controls in place that give you regular feedback on your team's results, but when they are performing, let them. Too many business owners undercut their own talent by micromanaging them.

- **Just because you've hired smart, talented, experienced people, don't just abdicate responsibility to them or allow yourself to lose touch with what is happening in the business.** We know this may seem like the opposite of the tip above, but it isn't. Both micromanaging and abdication are recipes for a brutal wake-up call at some point down the line. Your business needs you to make sure that you are using the internal controls you have in place like KPIs, regular progress updates, and spot checks to make sure that problems are discovered early and dealt with while they are small. Since you're the one steering the ship at the highest level, it helps for you to have a sense of what's going on everywhere else on the ship to ensure that you are all moving in the same direction.

- **Make sure each leader in your business has his or her own one-page action plan each quarter.** You can use this plan to help you manage your executive team and hold them accountable. Use the same format you already learned about in chapter 4. Get regular updates (we suggest weekly) to make sure you both stay on track and spot opportunities to coach and mentor your executive team. In order to really set your executive team up to win, you need to invest the time to support them with the direction and feedback to help them win.

- **Invest in your executive team.** Get them together each quarter off-site (even if it is just at a nice location in your city) to take a full day to do your strategic planning. Bring them to industry events or business training programs. Not only will they benefit from the content of the training, but you'll also be able to use the time together outside the business to enhance your relationship. Consider hiring outside coaching for your executive team, especially if mentoring and coaching your leaders is not something that is a personal strength of yours.

Ultimately, your Executive Leadership pillar is the key strategic director that integrates and empowers all the other pillars of your business to work smarter and accomplish more.

# PART IV

# You DO Have the Time

Start by doing what is necessary; then doing what is possible; and suddenly you are doing the impossible.

—**St. Francis of Assisi**

# PRINCIPLE SEVEN

## YOU *DO* HAVE THE TIME TO SCALE YOUR COMPANY

Wearing so many hats in your business and being responsible for so many demands to keep it going, it's hard to imagine scaling your company without working longer hours. As one business owner we talked with put it, "I just don't have any more time. I feel like the only way I can grow my business is by taking away time with my family or time for myself."

This is a false dilemma. You don't have to choose between long hours and growth *or* a lesser business with time. Throughout this book, we've encouraged you to focus on those fewer, better things that make a magnified contribution to your company's growth, knowing that by focusing on less you can accomplish more. Time is one of the most powerful variables you can control in the business success equation. In this chapter, we'll share a revolutionary new time mastery system we developed for business owners like you. This system will help you free up eight hours every week to reinvest in your business in upgraded ways.

Remember the example of Mark from chapter 1? Mark owns

a commercial maintenance company that contracts with homeowner associations. When we first started working with him, he was working 70-hour weeks, including many nights and weekends. After over a decade of these long hours—week after week—Mark was getting burned out. Over a 24-month period, Mark adopted these ideas in his company and grew his business from $750,000 a year in sales to over $1.2 million a year. The best part was that Mark reduced his working hours to 35 a week! Mark's story isn't an anomaly. Remember Tom from that same chapter? Tom reduced his working hours from 80 hours per week to under 20 at the same time he scaled his company from $5 million per year in sales to $23 million.

These stories are powerful reminders that it's not about more, it's about *better*. Scaling your company won't require you to work any more hours—you're already working plenty of hours. Instead, allow us to help you be *smarter* with the hours you are *already* working The more you do for your business, the more you have to keep doing. The more you get the business to do for the business, the more you can step back and grow your company the *right* way.

Many years ago, famed college basketball coach John Wooden said, "It's what you learn after you think you know it all that really matters." You'll get the most out of these time mastery strategies if you keep Coach Wooden's advice in mind and approach this section of the book fresh. You don't have to work nights and weekends to build your business. Working longer hours is rarely the answer. Making better choices with your time and fundamentally changing how you structure your use of time are the best ways to sustainably create the time you need to grow your company. Here are six powerful time mastery strategies to help you do just that.

## Time Mastery Strategy #1

*To upgrade your use of time, first identify what you do that truly creates value for your business.*

As a business owner, you don't get paid for time and effort; you get paid for creating value. So as you build your business, look for ways to create value independent of your personal time. This essentially is what it means to build a business, not a job.

If you've read anything on time management, you've come across Pareto's Principle, inspired by the work of nineteenth-century economist Vilfredo Pareto. Commonly called the 80-20 Rule, Pareto's Principle states that 20 percent of your actions generate 80 percent of your results (high value) and 80 percent of your actions generate the other 20 percent of your results (low value). This useful distinction becomes the basis of a refined model for using your time to create massive value, independent of the hours you put in.

If you take the 20 percent of your actions that generate 80 percent of your results and apply the same distinction a second time, then 20 percent of that 20 percent produces 80 percent of 80 percent of your results. That means 4 percent of your effort (the 20 percent of 20 percent) generates 64 percent of your results (80 percent of 80 percent).

And if you can bear with us for one more math moment, apply this distinction one final time.

Only 1 percent of your effort (20 percent of 20 percent of 20 percent) generates 50 percent of your results! That's right—a tiny fraction of your highest-leverage work produces *half* of all your results.

No, this is not an exact science. Nor does this just work automatically. But Pareto's Principle illustrates a valuable point: All time is not spent equally. Six hours of work on Monday may not produce the same value as six hours of work you did on Tuesday, depending on what you actually did in a given day. A surgeon who answers email on Monday, does a heart surgery on Tuesday, and is a guest on Dr. Oz's television show on Wednesday may have worked the same hours each day, but she did not add the same value to her business each day.

We want to help you focus your time on the most valuable activities. That's why we used this distinction to create the Time Value Matrix—a visual hierarchy of the four types of time: A Time, B Time, C Time, and D Time.[4] (See Figure 12.1.)

> ***D* time** is the 80 percent of unleveraged, wasteful time that produces only 20 percent of your total return. We call this the "80 Percent Mass." We've given it a relative value of 1.

> ***C* time** is the leveraged 20 percent of your time that produces 80 percent of your results. We call this "Leveraged Time." It has a relative value of 16 (¼ less input generating 4 × more output).

> ***B* time** is the highly focused 4 percent that generates 64 percent of your results. We call this time the "4 Percent Sweet Spot." (It has a relative value of 64. That means one hour of B time produces 64 times the value of the same time spent on a D activity.)

> ***A* time** is the top of the pyramid—the "Magic 1 Percent." Fully 50 percent of your results come from these activities. (*A* time has a relative value of 200 times that of *D* time.)

Most business owners have no clue which of their activities fall into these four categories. How in the world can you create more value in the same or less time if you don't know what activities constitute *A* and *B* time for you?

Before we share with you some examples of our *ABCD*-level

---

[4] How you use your time is so critical to your success as a business owner that we've recorded a one-hour online video training to help you get more done in less time. You can access this free video at **ScaleYourBusiness ToolKit.com/videos**.

**FIGURE 12.1:** THE TIME VALUE MATRIX

| | INPUT | OUTPUT | RELATIVE VALUE |
|---|---|---|---|
| **A** time<br>Magic 1% | 1% | 50% | 200 X D |
| **B** time<br>4% Sweet Spot | 4% | 64% | 64 X D |
| **C** time<br>Leveraged 20% | 20% | 80% | 16 X D |
| **D** time<br>80% Mass | 80% | 20% | 1 X D |

activities, understand that one person's *D* activity may be another person's *A*- or *B*-level activity. It's all relative. The examples from our business lives are illustrations that are not to be taken as absolute benchmarks of value. For example, one of David's *D*-level activities is scanning documents. However, people in his company have this activity as one of their *C*- or *B*-level activities. Your *A/B/C/D*-level activities are only comparable to your own value and expertise, not to other people's.

Take action and examine what you do that creates the highest value for *your* business at this moment in time.

• • •

***Identify your A/B/C/D activities and learn what you do that truly creates value for your business. List five of the tasks or activities you currently do at each level.***

***D* Time:** The 80 percent mass of unleveraged, wasteful time that produces only 20 percent of your total return.

Examples of Jeff's *D* activities include: reading emails to route them internally, reviewing bills to spot discrepancies, scheduling meetings and calls, reviewing meeting notes to determine required follow-ups, and writing replies to low-level emails.

***C* Time:** The leveraged 20 percent that produces 80 percent of your results.

Examples of David's *C* activities include: delegating to his assistant, dictating a letter, holding a group meeting versus talking with several people one at a time, updating his master to-do list, and sending out an email update to his executive team.

***B* Time:** The highly focused 4 percent "sweet spot" that generates 64 percent of your results.

Examples of Jeff's *B* activities include: meeting with key clients to solidify the relationship, coaching his management team to be better leaders, sharing company stories/successes/challenges in their biweekly staff meetings, reviewing his company's quarterly progress, instituting a systemic solution to a recurring problem.

***A* Time:** The magic 1 percent that generates more than 50 percent of your total results.

Examples of David's *A* activities include: making executive-level hiring decisions; decision meetings with key joint venture partners to secure high-value, win-win strategic partnerships; making strategic decisions that set the direction of the business; holding the executive team accountable for their deliverables.

Now that you've identified your current *ABCD*-level activities, it's important to understand that what you currently list as an *A*- or *B*-level activity will change. For example, if meeting one-on-one with a prospective client is currently an *A*-level activity for you, make sure that in the next six to twelve months, you've increased the value you create for your business so this activity is pushed down to a *B*- or *C*-level activity. Ideally, working with a joint venture partner who can generate dozens of leads for you every month will become an *A*-level activity, or training your sales team to meet with prospective clients one-on-one, or creating a sales video that generates passive sales. By that point, meeting one-on-one with a prospective client will no longer be important for you to do personally. It will likely still be someone *else's A*- or *B*-level activity, just not yours. This is good; this is growth. And it's how you both grow your business and reduce its reliance on you.

When you get this distinction in your bones and shift your focus from "putting in hours" to *upgrading* the type of work you do (more *A* and *B* time and less *D* time), the results will be amazing.

Take the example of Dr. Gurpreet Padda, a surgeon in St. Louis who also owns more than a dozen other successful businesses. Following the advice in this chapter, Dr. Padda reviewed his *A/B/C/D*-level activities and developed a clear map that delineated those activities he needed to get off his plate, and those he needed to find more time to focus on. By realigning how he spent his time, Dr. Padda added over $1 million of operating profit to his businesses within the first six months! Imagine the potential impact on your business when you do the same.

In order to move from limited Level Two thinking to a smarter Level Three mind-set, you need to stop believing that the solution to growth is working harder and longer, and instead upgrade how you use your time and get rid of the time-sucking *D*-time activities. For example, if you were an attorney who charges $300 an hour, you shouldn't spend your time doing things like fixing a computer glitch, making copies, sorting mail, or little things you can't bill a client for. Instead, you might focus on more useful *C*-time activities, such as any time that's billable, like working on a legal brief, reviewing a contract, or updating a client on legal considerations.

But be careful. While *C* time can provide you with a great income, you'll always have to work exceptionally hard to earn it. This is the trap that catches most high-income professionals. They seek to increase their earnings by cranking out more hours. Mistake! Working more hours will only take you so far. It's just not scalable past a certain point, not to mention that when you get there, you'll be exhausted from so much work, and a stranger to your family too.

The real, scalable solution lies in *A* and *B* time. For an attorney, *B* time might include building relationships with other professionals who can refer valuable business, or putting systems in place so staff can get better results without tapping too much into the attorney's time.

*A* time could be speaking at a large conference where this attorney can generate new client relationships worth hundreds of thousands of dollars in billable services. *A* time might be spent creating an accounts receivable system that increases the collection on all the firm's billings by 10 percent or introducing a new billing model whereby the firm charges a fixed price for a standardized service offering.

See the difference? You want to get *D*-level activities off your plate; *C* time is needed to do your work more efficiently. *A* and *B* time, however, are when you step out of the "job" and do something that improves your capacity to create results, or significantly pushes back your biggest limiting factor.

So here's the big question: *How can you have more* A *and* B *time?* You won't get it by "trying harder" or by sitting down and saying, "OK, let's have an *A* moment right now." It just doesn't work that way. That would be like a parent saying to his three-year-old, "Let's have an hour of quality time right now, Junior." How well do you think that would work?

To get more *A* and *B* time, you have to fundamentally alter the way you structure your day and your week, which is exactly what the next four time mastery strategies will help you do.

# Time Mastery Strategy #2

*To "find" the time, focus first on your D-level activities.*

This one may seem counterintuitive, but the best place to look *first* to upgrade your use of time isn't to your *A*-, *B*-, or *C*-level activities. It's looking at your *D*-level activities. Not only by definition do you spend the most time at this level, but it's the easiest place to make changes because the consequences of dropping *D*-time activities are small.

List all the *D*-level activities you do on a weekly basis. Keep a time log for a week or two to figure out the time spent on low-value *D* activities. Once you've identified them, you can apply the "Four *D*s" to get them off your plate.

### THE FOUR *D*S

1. **Delete it.** Some *D* activities shouldn't be done by anyone. Look at the action item and ask yourself what the consequences would be if no one did it. If it's small, then consider just crossing it off your list altogether. Remember our 1-800-Flowers story? If it doesn't help you sell more flowers, then it's an activity you can possibly delete.

2. **Delegate it.** Maybe it's a task that needs to get done but not necessarily by *you*. Hand it off to your assistant, a staff member, or a vendor. Anytime you can hand off a *D*-level activity to someone, you free up both your time and your focus to do more valuable work for your business. This is the surgeon letting her administrative assistant do email responses, freeing up her time to perform another surgery.

3. **Defer it.** Maybe this task needs to be done and done by you, but that doesn't mean it should happen right now. Sometimes delaying the action is the smartest choice.

4. **Design it out.** If you find yourself handling a recurring *D* activity over and over, improve the process or system to keep the task from coming up in the first place. For example, if you get the same seven customer questions repeatedly, post an FAQ page with the answers on your website. Perhaps you can preempt these questions by giving new clients a "quick start" booklet or instructional video that proactively answers these questions. Designing out a recurring activity is the very essence of building a systems-reliant Level Three business. It simplifies processes and empowers your team to get consistently great results with less and less reliance on you, the business owner.

Look closely at your *D* activities as the place to mine more time. By applying the Four *D*s of Deleting, Delegating, Deferring, and Designing Out, you'll free up eight or more hours each week to reinvest in *A* and *B* activities.

## Time Mastery Strategy #3

*Structure your week to reinvest your "saved" D time in A and B activities.*

It's not enough to free up eight to ten hours each week by clearing the clutter of your *D* activities; you have to fill your freed-up time with *A* and *B* activities. Nature abhors a vacuum, and if you don't fundamentally change how you structure your week, you'll find yourself squandering the time you supposedly saved on more *D*-level "junk."

This brings us to a powerful concept to get more *A* and *B* time and minimize the *D* time that gets in the way: "Focus Days" and "Push Days." A "Focus Day" is a specific day of the week you set aside to primarily work on a few key *A*- or *B*-level projects. "Push Days" are all the other days of the week that you use to just "push" your normal projects another step forward. Focus Days help you create long-term impact on your business; Push Days help you keep your day-to-day operations rolling forward. The key to succeeding with this technique is discipline. When it's your Focus Day, you need to *focus*. Don't get distracted by your Push tasks. We suggest that you set aside a full day each week for your Focus Day and make sure your team supports you in keeping this time clear so you can invest in these high-leverage activities.

On your Focus Day, get outside of your normal environment and work on the highest-leverage, highest-value, highest-return part of your business. This could mean building out a baseline operational process to use with new clients, spending the day creating a hiring system to consistently supply you with quality team members for your sales team, or calling on your two most important prospective customers or joint venture partners to deepen the relationship or close the sale.

Here's an example of how this works in the real world. Mondays and Wednesdays are David's Push Days. These are the days he plows through his project list and takes care of the day-to-day fires that come up in any business and need to be put out. On those days, he is very accessible to his staff and the outside world by phone and email, and gets the bulk of his "job" in his business done.

David sets aside his Tuesdays and Thursdays as his Focus Days. That's when he turns off the phones and email for the majority of the day (usually until 1 or 2 P.M.) and focuses on doing those few, highest-value activities that create the most value for his company. These *A*- and *B*-level activities might include holding a key meeting on a new joint venture, working on a new book, or being in the studio recording a new business-owner video training program.

Three to four hours on his Focus Days can result in more value to his business than *an entire week* living in *C*- or *D*-level activities. Focus Days give David a way to create the space in which to get high-value work done. If a true emergency comes up his staff can reach him, but they've learned to support his Focus Days because they understand how protecting that time produces big results for the company. Plus, David encourages many team members in his company to set aside at least one half day each week for their focus time. This practice has contributed to the triple-digit growth of his company.

Here are a few practical tips to help you implement this strategy:

- Even if you can't set aside two full days a week as Focus Days like David, you *can* find one day or at least *half* a day every week and use it as your Focus Day. If you choose to start with a half day, we strongly suggest you use the first half of the day. You're much less likely to have urgent fires pull you away from your *A* and *B* activities.

- Generally we don't suggest you choose the first or last day of your workweek for your Focus Day. Too many urgencies need your attention on those days.

- Communicate your need for help to your staff so they understand both what you are doing and how it will help the business succeed. Enlist their help. When your team understands how important Focus Days are to the company's ability to achieve its goals, they will rally to support that effort.

- Get out of your office and away from distractions. Work from a quiet conference room, a local café, or the lobby of a nice hotel. Bring only the key project(s) you want to work on for your Focus Day. One component of willpower is controlling your environment to best support you. Leave the other work and distractions behind. That way, you couldn't work on them even if you wanted to.

- Consider prompting your key team members to take their own Focus Days too. You'll quickly see the positive increase in production this will bring.

- Finally, remember that Focus Days aren't about being off by yourself—they are about focusing on your top *A*- or *B*-level activities that truly create value for your company. For many people this can mean meetings, phone calls, or critical email. It's not time off or time away from the hard work; the key distinction is that on your Focus Day you are primarily doing your *A*- or *B*-level activities.

## Time Mastery Strategy #4

*Work first "above the line" and live by the Results Rule.*

Most business owners start each day with high hopes. They take a moment to write down the list of tasks for that day—a list that often grows to 15 or 20 items. Then the day hits and they find themselves pulled off track to deal with customer challenges, operational fires, and sales emergencies.

Here is a better way to organize each day: When you sit down in the morning (or the night before, if you prefer), choose three bottom lines for that day and write them at the top of your to-do list. Draw a line under them to visually mark them as different and special. Make two of them business related and one of them personal. Your bottom lines are the action steps you'll take that day that will create the most value for your business. Generally these are *A*- and *B*-level activities. Here is an example of a time mastery to-do list.

---
**SAMPLE TIME MASTERY TO-DO LIST**

---

- ❏ Draft the marketing calendar for Q1.
- ❏ Call Tom Smith about expanding joint venture.
- ❏ Write my wife a love letter.

---

- ❏ Email Shirley.
- ❏ Check on Collin's project status with Angela.
- ❏ Review web PPC proposal.
- ❏ Call Larry (webinar glitches).
- ❏ Call Jenna (her event questions).
- ❏ Etc.

---

### Live by the Results Rule

The Results Rule says that by 10:30 A.M., you have either completed each of your three bottom lines for the day or have scheduled a definite appointment on your calendar during which you'll complete them. This technique is powerful because it pushes you to do what matters most *first*, and to treat your daily bottom lines with the respect they deserve.

Most business owners put off these bottom lines to deal with the urgent requests that come at them during the day. In doing so, they sacrifice far more than they'll ever know. Avoid this trap by following through on your bottom lines first thing in your day whenever possible. For added benefit, combine Time Mastery Strategy #4 with Time Mastery Strategy #5.

## Time Mastery Strategy #5

*Every "Push Day," schedule a "Prime Time" block to work on A or B activities.*

Everyone has a certain time in the day when they're at their best. A Prime Time block is a 60- to 90-minute appointment that you set for yourself at your peak effectiveness time. That's when you work only on your highest-value items (usually your "bottom lines" for the day). By blocking out this time as an actual appointment on your calendar, you guarantee yourself at least one hour each Push Day to have a focused block of time to create real value for your business.

For example, David schedules his Prime Time in the morning from approximately 9 A.M. until 10:30 A.M. every Monday and Wednesday, his Push Days. He doesn't take inbound phone calls or answer email during that time unless he deems that specific email or phone call to be the highest use of his time. Jeff sets aside every Monday and Thursday morning from 7:30 A.M. to 8:30 A.M. as his Prime Time to do the same.

Don't demand perfection in honoring your Prime Times; you don't need to reach that standard. Even 80 percent consistency here will be enough to create a dramatic increase to your personal productivity. You'll find that setting aside this regular appointment to do your highest-value work for the day allows you to create more value for your business.

## Time Mastery Strategy #6

### Create a "Stop Doing" List and add to it weekly.

Too many people live their lives based on a to-do list to which they keep adding more and more tasks. But they rarely make the hard choices of what to let go of, what to delay, what to delegate, what to delete altogether.

For example, could you delegate vendor issues, or scheduling, or customer-service issues to your staff? Outsource your bookkeeping or computer issues? Hire help to run your personal errands, do yard work, or organize home repairs?

Look at your to-do lists from the past 60 days and identify the activities you can add to your "stop doing" list. How much time will eliminating these tasks save you? Each week, pick a few more activities you deliberately choose to add to your "stop doing" list. You'll find that the items you put on it tend to be tasks you find draining—maybe ones you put on your to-do list out of obligation or inertia. When you get rid of them, you'll not only enjoy a sense of elation and energy but will truly free up your time for more valuable activities.

## The Real Secret to Unshakable Time Discipline

Most people shudder when thinking about the need for greater discipline because they've always associated discipline with pain and effort. It doesn't have to be this way. Instead, we suggest that you link discipline to two very important concepts: Accountability and Environment.

Who holds you accountable for your actions and decisions within your business? Who coaches you to help you develop as a business owner? Who helps keep you on track? It's usually difficult to have this person be someone who works for you (after all, there is a power imbalance to the relationship). If you want to build a Level Three business, it's vital to have an accountability structure and at least one third-party mentor who helps keep you on track.

Discipline also results from working in a structured environment. Take the example of Andrea Butter, owner of Maui By Design, a gift product design and wholesale company. Andrea came to her own business late in her professional life, after a long and successful career in Silicon Valley as a high-level marketing executive. She struggled letting go of things, and found email the irresistible lure that tempted her into personally handling too many of the low-level details of operating her business. This was even harder for her as she worked out of her home and, because she worked with many suppliers in Asia, she found herself responding to work emails in real time during their workday (her nighttime).

Andrea took control of her environment by pulling the cable

out of her Internet modem each day by 6 P.M. to reduce the temptation of checking email one last time. During the first year Andrea did this, not only did she grow her business by over 40 percent, but she got her nights back again.

By controlling your environment, you make healthy, profitable behaviors for your business much easier. Willpower can win a sprint, but rarely a marathon. To win the marathon of building a Level Three business, take control of your environment to ensure it supports your goals each day.

## The Top Ten Best Practices Every Company Should Adopt

Speaking of distractions, we need to address what has grown to be one of the most difficult and addictive time distractions in the business world—*email*! Here are our top ten email best practices we think every company should adopt:

1. **Use powerful subject lines to streamline the time it takes for your team to process and find email.** No more blank subject lines, or "Hello . . ." Instead, you and your team should make your subject line a clear, concise description of the email. This helps you screen messages and it helps you later search for emails you need to find after the fact. If you are forwarding the email, don't be lazy; redo the subject line to make sense to your recipient and ask that your team do that for you too. Also, consider using the "1-2-3" system in your subject line:

    1 = Time sensitive and important. Read and take action ASAP.

    2 = Action required. Read and take noted action in a reasonable time frame.

    3 = FYI. No action required. Scan for content when convenient.

Here's how this might look:

> *2: Notes from Franklin call 2/5/15* (This tells recipient they need to take action on the email.)
> 
> *2 Mark; 3 Sarah: Two follow-up items still needed to complete Sullivan Project* (This tells Mark he needs to take action and Sarah that this is just FYI for her.)

2. **Don't mass "CC" or "BCC."** Only CC or BCC if the person really needs the information. Remember, it's not just that one email, but all the subsequent emails in that chain that you'll likely include that person on.

3. **Turn off your auto send-and-receive function (or at least reduce the frequency it downloads new email).** Contrary to the way it feels, you don't need to see every email the instant it comes in. Also, turn off email alerts (audio and visual). Instead, intentionally check email when you choose versus when someone hits Send to you. Email alerts only promote compulsive behaviors that kill productivity.

4. **To get less email, send less.** The more you send, the more you get.

5. **Consider aging your email before you respond to get less of it.** If something isn't time sensitive or a critical relationship, consider waiting a few days or (gulp!) a few weeks before you reply. We've all had the experience of immediately replying to an email only to get a reply to our reply ninety-four seconds later. (If you like answering right away, consider using the "delayed delivery" option in most email programs to answer now but send the email later.)

6. **If you're involved in a frustrating back-and-forth conversation by email due to hazy understanding on either side, just**

**pick up the phone or speak in person.** Emails are not good as a nuanced conversation tool and shouldn't replace all conversations.

7. **In replying to a long conversation thread, pull up the key information to the top of the email.** Make it easier for your recipient to quickly get what you are communicating. Also, if you are creating a longer email with multiple items, consider numbering your items to make them easier for your reader to follow and respond to your email.

8. **If you think the topic may be a sensitive one, or that the reader may be upset or offended by your email,** *don't* **send it.** Talk with them instead (even if you then send a summary or confirming email after). Also, never say something in an email that you wouldn't be willing to say directly to the person you are speaking to in the email. This goes double for your team. Quickly deal with any inappropriate emails.

9. **Don't use email to manage your "tasks" or to manage your team's tasks.** Use a project list on a spreadsheet, or a shared task management or project management tool instead. Email is a poor place to keep a running list. What comes today is washed away by what comes later today (let alone tomorrow). There are simple, inexpensive project management tools available online and on mobile devices that allow you to list, categorize, prioritize, and share your open action items. It's a worthwhile investment to prevent tasks and follow-ups from falling through the cracks.

10. **Learn your top five email recipients' preferences.** Just sort your "Sent" folder by recipient and pick out the five people you send the most email to. These will likely be internal team members. Ask them if they prefer wide or shallow emails (i.e., one email per subject as it comes up, or a grouped

email that has more items in one single email). When are their email-free times? What do they want to and not want to be CC'd on? What are the three things they like best about how you communicate with them by email? What three things would they like you to do differently about how you communicate by email to make their life better? Then reverse the conversation and share your email preferences with them.

## Accelerate Your Upgrade of Time—Get a Personal Assistant

So far in this chapter, we've asked you to clearly identify the things you do that create the most value for your company and to structure your day and week so that you upgrade eight hours of "*D* time" to *A* and *B* uses.

There is one final element that will help you massively upgrade the value you create for your company—finding, hiring, and leveraging a personal assistant. Whether you bring on a full-time assistant, outsource to a virtual assistant who works remotely, or do something in between, it is our belief that just about any business owner who runs a successful company can leverage a personal assistant to help her radically grow her business.

Figure 12.2 shows a list of 25 things you can ask your assistant to do. While we have a lot more we wanted to share with you about this subject, for the sake of brevity we recorded a full-hour training video on how to find, hire, and leverage your personal assistant and included it free for you to access at **www.Scale YourBusinessToolKit.com**. (See the appendix for full details.)

FIGURE 12.2:   25 THINGS YOU CAN ASK YOUR ASSISTANT
TO DO TO LEVERAGE YOUR TIME

1. Organize your travel (including learning your travel preferences)
2. Handle billing disputes
3. Help set up bills on auto payment on your credit card
4. Address and mail cards, letters, and packages
5. Update your contact manager (or CRM database)
6. Screen your email and handle low-level responses
7. Update your blog and social media accounts
8. Organize and manage your filing system, both paper-based and scanned e-files
9. Take dictation (either live or via recordings)
10. Set up phone appointments
11. Daily cleanup of your office, including refilling items
12. Screen phone and email
13. Take notes at key meetings and follow up with attendees on key deliverables
14. Keep a master chart/list/calendar of your projects and deadlines and set reminders
15. Tickler all birthdays and anniversaries, holidays, or other important dates, and even arrange for gifts, cards, or phone calls that make you look good
16. Update his or her own "Project List" so that all the tasks and deliverables they are responsible for are in one place for you to review
17. Get, open, sort, forward, handle, and if need be shred your mail
18. Coordinate with outsourced vendors when you have an IT issue
19. Order things online for you and handle any product returns or service issues
20. Handle any personal errands or schedule any household repairs
21. Notarize your documents
22. Help you to streamline your office—filing, sorting, and systematizing work flow
23. Perform basic updates to your websites
24. Create and continue to refine the "expert system" for how to be your assistant (this one should be part of their job function right from the start)
25. Take on any parts of your projects that he or she is capable of doing for you

In the end, we all have the same number of hours in a day. The most successful business owners have learned to apply these time mastery strategies to create more value in the same or less time.

> **SCALING PRINCIPLE SEVEN:**
> **YOU DO HAVE THE TIME TO SCALE YOUR BUSINESS AND GET YOUR LIFE BACK.**

# PUTTING IT ALL INTO ACTION

Derek was a mid-twenties college grad who had played linebacker for his college football team. After graduating, he struck out on his own, launching a real estate business. All his life he had achieved his goals by outworking and outhustling everyone else. When he took this same recipe into the world of business ("Put your head down and just outwork everyone else"), however, he soon hit a plateau in his business. Derek had a few team members helping to leverage his time, but he was the critical linchpin that held his company together. Without him, nothing happened. And he did a lot! He listed and sold homes, wholesaled investor deals, and even did a handful of rehab projects each year. But then he hit a wall of what his own personal production could produce, completing the most transactions he could imagine himself person- ally doing in one year—sixty-five. He was financially successful, earning six figures, but he was burnt out and knew that he just couldn't run any faster.

We began working with Derek the very next year after he hit "the wall". He locked on to the ideas you've been learning about in this book and applied them to his business. Within 24 months, his real estate investment company was buying, rehabbing, and profitably re-selling over two hundred houses a year and Derek was the largest player in his city. Three years after that, his real estate brokerage company was doing five hundred transactions a year. He had literally scaled his businesses by over 1,000 percent. This was a guy who used to think that growing required him to work harder and longer than everybody else. It would have been impossible for him to grow to this level if he hadn't let go of the belief that he had to work harder and personally produce more.

Now Derek is the proud father of twin boys and enjoys a strong marriage to an amazing spouse. Each summer, they go out to Southern California for six to eight weeks to enjoy a beachfront house and plenty of family time together. He still contributes great value to his company but is no longer the linchpin who holds everything together. His systems, team, and internal controls have helped him scale well beyond what his old limitations were back in the day when he thought he had to do it all himself.

Jennifer, successful owner of a medical software company in Tuscon, Arizona, was also at a different place in her business life when we first met two years after she had had her "all in" moment when she bought out her business partners and took sole ownership of the company. At that point, not only did she wear most of the hats in the business, but she was the financial backstop for the company with her life savings literally on the line. Though the company was profitable, it was vulnerable because it was almost completely owner-reliant.

Fast forward to today: Jennifer's company has a core leadership team, strong systems, and simple controls that have greatly lessened its reliance on her. She's grown sales by more than 500 percent and the company is worth several million dollars more than it was back when she bought out her partners. Best of all, Jennifer loves her life and her role inside the company, and enjoys watching her company continue to grow by over 35 percent a year.

It *is* possible for you to scale your business and get your life back. You don't have to work harder or longer. You don't have to sacrifice your life to do it. You *can* enjoy rapid growth and greater freedom. And you now have the concrete road map to do it.

Let's walk through a quick recap of the seven principles you'll use to scale your company, and then conclude with five final action steps to apply what you've learned in this book starting tomorrow morning.

## Quick Recap of the Seven Proven Principles to Grow Your Business and Get Your Life Back

*Scaling Principle One: Build a business, not a job.*

The best way to build your business is not by working harder, but rather by reducing your business's reliance on you so that your *business* can produce more. For all the artificial drama implied by the "Hit by a Bus" test, the core lesson is very real: If you ever want to escape the Self-Employment Trap you *must build a business, not a job.*

*Scaling Principle Two: Build on the stable, scalable, three-legged base of systems, team, and internal controls.*

It's not enough to just hire good people. Sustainable growth demands that you support your talented team with the smart business systems and intelligent internal controls that reliably help them produce more and better.

*Scaling Principle Three: Understand why your customers really do business with you.*

This principle boils down to truly knowing your customers—their desires, hopes, fears, aspirations, needs, pain, and perspective—so that you can find a profitable way to create value for them in a niche that you can dominate. This requires clarifying the three dimensions of your business context: your customers, your competitors, and your position and brand.

**Scaling Principle Four: Create the right strategic plan and reduce that plan into a series of rolling, one-page quarterly action plans that help you execute and get results.**

It is only by focusing your company's limited resources on those fewer, better things that you are able to grow your business. Follow our structured five-step process to determine your strategy, and how to best apply it quarter by quarter.

**Scaling Principle Five: Learn to read the world so that you stay relevant and build your business for tomorrow's marketplace, not yesterday's reality.**

In a rapidly changing world, the status quo is never safe. This is why it's crucial that you learn to read the world so that you can innovate and seize opportunities for growth (not to mention avoid being blindsided by a disruptive change and put out of business!).

**Scaling Principle Six: Remove the predictable obstacles to growth—pillar by pillar.**

Every pillar of your business—Sales/Marketing, Operations, Finance, Team, and Executive Leadership—has predictable obstacles that you must move past as you scale your company. Because these obstacles are known, you can proactively chip away at them until they are no longer in the way of your growth.

**Scaling Principle Seven: You do have the time to scale your company and get your life back.**

You don't have to work nights and weekends to grow your company. You are *already* working enough hours to grow your business. You just need to upgrade your use of time to focus on the things that you do that truly create value for your company.

Scaling your company is a process, not a light switch you flip in one moment. While it won't happen overnight, when you stay the course, it will happen faster than you could have imagined.

## Tomorrow Morning

We get asked all the time for the "magic bullet" to immediately make an impact in growing a company. Here, at the end of the book, we want to give you the five highest-leverage action steps you can take starting tomorrow morning to apply what you've learned in this book to make an immediate impact on your company. Each takes less than 30 minutes.

**Action Step #1: Know Your Customers** (pp. 39–45). Write out the one-page summary of your target customers. Who are they? What are their hopes, fears, aspirations, and challenges? The most important place to start is to dive deep into the lives of your customers.

**Action Step #2: Conduct a Sweet Spot Analysis** (pp. 73–79). Determine your business's current Limiting Factor. Then conduct a Sweet Spot Analysis to pick the highest-leverage tactics to push your Limiting Factor back over the next 90 days. Turn your ideas into a mini-plan and get to work.

**Action Step #3: Build Your Own Time Value Matrix** (p. 233). The only way to consistently upgrade your time is to identify what you do that truly creates value for your company. List your *A*-, *B*-, *C*-, and *D*-level tasks so you have a written reminder. Then pick one day each week to be your Focus Day (or at least a half day) and schedule that day to be about *A*- and *B*-level items.

**Action Step #4: Create Your First One-Page Quarterly Action Plan** (pp. 87–92). Don't worry if the process is messy, or if you stumble your way through it. You'll still get great value from doing it and, each quarter going forward, you'll get better and better at the process. Of course you'll still have to take care of the daily operational needs of your business, but your one-page action plan ensures that you consistently invest a portion of your best resources on those things that will actually help you reach your business goals instead of just reacting to the pressing urgencies that will otherwise dominate your day.

**Action Step #5: Register at www.ScaleYourBusinessToolKit.com and Invest Thirty Minutes a Week on the Site.** We've designed this powerful website to help you grow as a business owner and successfully scale your business. Not only will you find all the tools we've shared in this book available for you to download as PDFs, but you'll also be able to access more than two dozen proprietary training videos. Plus you'll be able to connect with Jeff and David via our private LinkedIn business owner mastermind group.

## Worth the Journey

When Jeff was ten years old, he went over to his friend Mike's house, where a few other friends were gathered, fawning over his newest poster of a red Ferrari. Later that day, Jeff asked his mom what the big deal was about the car. He didn't understand why Mike and his friends seemed so impressed by it. Jeff's mom replied that people often find themselves fascinated by things they'll never have. "What do you mean that they'll never have it?" Jeff asked. His mom responded, "Jeff, that car probably costs the same as our house. Very few people will ever be financially successful enough to be able to afford that car."

Jeff clearly remembers saying to her, "But someone must be able to afford that car, why not me?" His mom tried to explain that it just wasn't realistic for him to think he could ever own a car like that. As Jeff walked away, he said one last time, almost as if to himself, "Yeah, but somebody gets that car. . . ."

In retrospect, it was clear that Jeff's mom wanted to protect him from having unrealistic expectations that would lead to disappointment. But Jeff left that conversation thinking that if somebody gets to drive that car, why not him? What if he worked hard enough and smart enough to earn the money to buy that Ferrari? Jeff never forgot that experience, and over time the phrase "Why not me?" became his personal mantra.

Over the years, Jeff never stopped thinking about the car, or the lesson he took from it about the relationship of goals, hard work, focus, and success. Whenever work was hard and he felt like quitting, he thought about that car. The dream of the car gave him the energy to keep going. It wasn't about the money or the material thing. That car become a symbol for him of what he could achieve if he kept working toward his goals, shutting out all the naysayers in his life.

It was a great day for Jeff when he finally bought that car and put on the license plate that read "PCLN," the stock ticker symbol for Priceline.com, the company he'd helped scale whose success had allowed him to own that car. Jeff would often go outside, sit in the car, close his eyes, and just let the sound of the engine drown out the sound of all the nos he had heard in his life. "Somebody drives that car, why not me?"

Many business owners have built thriving Level Three businesses—*why not you?* They successfully scaled their companies and enjoy an incredible lifestyle—*why not you?* They have impacted the world through their businesses, employed people, served their customers, supported their vendors—*why not you?* You now have the road map, your business is the vehicle, and it's just up to you to hit the gas and go.

We believe in you and know you have what it takes to build the company you want to build and create the life you want to enjoy. You are not alone on your journey. Hundreds of thousands of other business owners are committed to the same goals, leveraging the same tools. If you ever doubt yourself, then borrow our faith—we know you can do it. Savor the journey. It truly is worthwhile.

Your friends,<br>Jeff & David

# ACKNOWLEDGMENTS

*Scale* is about building a business that is so much more than just a reflection of the owner. In much the same way, this book is much more than just the direct experiences of the two authors. This book benefited from the enormous skill and experience of a number of people. While the list is too long to thank everyone, we do want to make special mention of several people.

First, thank you to the team at Portfolio. Your passion for the project and editorial insights made the book more than we could have hoped for. A special thank you to Natalie Horbachevsky for all the hours you pored over the manuscript, challenging our assumptions and making key suggestions to radically improve the book, and to the promotional team at Penguin Random House, who helped us get the word out about the book so successfully. Thank you also to our book agent, Jim Levine, who took the mystery out of the publishing equation and helped us pare our message down to its essential core (and to Andrea who introduced us to you). Thank you to Kevin Bassett, CPA, for his keen insights and great suggestions that helped make chapter 9 ("Your Finance Pillar") more concrete and easier to apply.

To make the book flow more smoothly we decided that, rather than laboriously label every story as Jeff's or David's, wherever we felt that the story was one that either of us had had similarly experienced with multiple business owners we've advised, we would use the collective "we." We hope this contrivance enhanced your enjoyment of the book. We would like to thank all the brilliant business owners featured in this book who shared their experiences with us, which resulted in strong examples that any reader could relate to and learn from. Also, we would like to thank the tens of thousands of business owners who've attended our live events over the past ten years and given us such great feedback as to how to best share the *Scale* concepts for fastest implementation.

In addition, Jeff would like to thank: "My parents for always saying 'Why not?' instead of 'You can't.' And to many of you who have worked for me, with me, and next to me over the years, proving that a great team made of people with passion and values can do anything they set their minds to. And finally, to my amazing family, who jumped off so many cliffs with me, knowing I had no parachute, and clung tightly to me anyway because you knew it was the only way I could truly feel alive. Your love and support have always been the wind beneath my wings."

David would like to thank: "My entire team at Maui Mastermind. Your commitment to helping our business coaching clients grow their businesses and reduce their companies' reliance on them, the owners, has directly touched thousands of lives. I am exceptionally proud that as of this printing, your support has helped our clients enjoy an average annual growth rate of 32.4 percent. Also, thank you to all our business coaching clients for being proof positive that any business owner can build a business they love to own again if they are committed and coachable. To my friends and family, thank you for being such a source of joy and support in my life. And finally to Matthew, Adam, and Joshua—you make me so grateful and proud to be your dad; and to Heather—thank you for your love, your friendship, and for sharing your life with me."

# APPENDIX:
# THE SCALE YOUR BUSINESS TOOL KIT
## *Your FREE $1,375 Gift from the Authors*

Dear Reader,

As our way of congratulating you for finishing this book, and supporting you to grow your business, we've created a unique online web tool kit to help you apply the ideas you've learned in this book.

To register, all you need to do is go online to www.ScaleYourBusinessToolKit.com and gain immediate access to this powerful collection of business growth tools. It's designed to help business owners like you apply the "Scale" concepts in the book to grow your business and get your life back.

**Here's What You Get as Part of This Valuable Free Bonus:**

- **Over a dozen video training modules** to help make building your business *easier* and *faster*.
- **Free PDF downloads** of many of the business growth tools David uses with his business coaching clients.
- **Free private 90-minute business coaching session** (if your business qualifies) to customize the strategies from *Scale* to your specific situation so you can grow your company the right way.
- **And much more…**

## You'll also Get 5 Complete Business "Short Courses" to Help You Blow Through Your Biggest Barriers to Growth!

- The "*Grow Your Sales*" Short Course (6 Training Videos and PDF Action Guide)
- The "*Scale Your Operations*" Short Course (3 Training Videos and PDF Action Guide)
- The "*Financial Pillar*" Short Course (6 Training Videos and PDF Action Guide)
- The "*Strategic Planning*" Short Course (4 Training Videos and PDF Action Guide)
- The "*Time Mastery*" Short Course (3 Training Videos and PDF Action Guide)

Best of all, you'll be able to complete all these powerful training mini-courses from the comfort and convenience of your own home or office. You can watch them on your schedule.

### How to Access the Scale Tool Kit Now

Simply go online to **www.ScaleYourBusinessToolKit.com** right now and complete the short enrollment form and you'll get immediate access to this powerful collection of business growth tools. It's literally that easy.

Again, we thank you for reading this book. We wish you a lifetime of success and happiness. Enjoy your "graduation gift" of the *Scale Your Business Tool Kit*!

Sincerely,
Jeff and David

P.S. Because this free tool kit is a limited time offer and may be changed or pulled at any time, we strongly encourage you to go to **www.ScaleYourBusinessToolKit.com** today and register. You'll kick yourself if you miss out.

# ABOUT THE AUTHORS

**JEFF HOFFMAN:**

Jeff is a successful entrepreneur and motivational speaker. In his career, he has been the founder of multiple start-ups and the CEO of both public and private companies, and has served as a senior executive in many capacities. Jeff has been part of a number of well-known companies, including Priceline.com, uBid.com, CTI, and ColorJar.

Today Jeff serves on the boards of companies in the United States, Europe, South America, and Asia. He supports entrepreneurs and small businesses on a worldwide basis, serving on the global advisory boards of Global Entrepreneurship Week (supporting entrepreneurship in more than 130 countries), the U.S. State Department's GIST program (Global Innovation through Science and Technology, working in 49 emerging nations), the APEC Start-up Accelerator Initiative (the Asia Pacific Economic Council's 21-member-nation association), and many more. He supports the White House, the State Department, USAID, and similar organizations internationally on economic growth initiatives and entrepreneurship programs.

Jeff is a frequent keynote speaker, having been invited to speak in more than 50 countries. He speaks on the topics of innovation, entrepreneurship, and business leadership. Jeff also teaches innovation workshops to major corporations on a regular basis.

Jeff is a business expert featured on Fox News, Fox Business, CNN, CNN International, Bloomberg News, CNBC, ABC, and NPR, and in publications including *Forbes, Inc., Time, Fast Company*, and the *Wall Street Journal*.

Jeff received a Lifetime Achievement Award from the national Collegiate Entrepreneurship Organization (CEO) council for his contributions to the field of entrepreneurship, as well as the 2012 Champion of Entrepreneurship Award from JPMorgan Chase, Citibank, and Rising Tide Capital.

Outside the world of technology, Jeff has produced movies in Hollywood; has produced musical events, including concerts, tours, and charity events with such artists as Elton John, Britney Spears, and 'N Sync; and serves on numerous charity and nonprofit boards.

**DAVID FINKEL:**

David Finkel is the *Wall Street Journal* bestselling author of twelve books, including *SCALE* (co-authored with Priceline.com cofounder Jeff Hoffman), *Build a Business Not a Job*, and, *The Freedom Formula: How to Succeed in Business Without Sacrificing Your Family, Health, or Life*. His syndicated business articles on Inc.com, Fastcompany.com, and Forbes.com have garnered millions of readers and his work has been featured in such prestigious media outlets as the

Wall Street Journal, Bloomberg Businessweek, Fox Business, MSNBC, and Inc. Magazine.

David is also the CEO of Maui Mastermind®, the world's premier business coaching company with thousands of clients worldwide. David's clients enjoy an average annual growth rate 5 times higher than the average privately held company in the US, while at the same time increasing their companies' "Owner Independence" by an average of 97.4%. He's helped hundreds of thousands of business leaders grow their companies and get their lives back. To learn more about working with his company to get the structured business coaching you need to take your company to the next level, visit them on the web at www.MauiMastermind.com.

David eats his own cooking which has allowed him the time to start, scale, and sell multiple successful ventures, be on the boards of several other companies, all while holding his working hours to under 40 hours per week while taking five months off each year. He and his wife Heather and their three sons live in Jackson Hole, Wyoming.

# INDEX

Ablitt, Sasha, 46, 47, 48, 219
accountability, 214–23
   Big Rock Huddle and, 221–23
   commitments, enumerating and clarifying, 214–15
   failures, owning, 216
   feedback on progress, providing, 215
   handoffs and, 216
   key performance indicators (KPI) and, 217–21
   phantom deliverables, avoiding, 215
   timeliness, fostering, 215
   time mastery system and, 244–45
accounts payable controls, 195–96
Ackworth, Kimberly, 139
action steps for immediate impact on growing company, 255–56
additional sales, tactics to generate, 131–40
   cross-selling as, 138–39
   formalized referral systems as, 132–33
   reactivation system as, 133–35
   re-selling as, 139–40
   retention system as, 135–36
   up-selling as, 137–38
Amazon, 47, 51, 68
American Express, 202
Apple, 47, 54, 96, 103
Arthur Anderson, 96

Association of Fraud Examiners, 192

base of business, building on, 23–35, 253
   internal controls, building, 28–35
   refining and redesigning systems and controls, as company grows, 34–35
   systems, building, 24–28, 34–35
   team, building, 28
Bassett, Kevin, 221
Bassett and Byers, 221
Bayer Aspirin, 51
best-first search, 43
big-picture planning process, 68–71
   rewards and meaning of reaching Singular Goal, identifying, 70–71
   Singular Goal, identifying, 69–70
   why is company in business, determining, 68–69
big-picture vision, 209–12
   company lives its vision, making sure, 211
   example, leading by, 210
   future, investing in, 212
   planning process for (*See* big-picture planning process)
   quarterly planning tool and, 211
   repetition and, 210
   sharing vision with team, 210
big-picture vision (*cont.*)

# 268 INDEX

team's roles and responsibilities, clarifying, 211
team's thoughts as to, 210–11
written, 210
Big Rock Huddle, 221–23
Black Sky Entertainment, 2–3
bottom line tasks, 241–42
branding, 50, 53–59
   choice of, trial for, 78
   emotions and, 54–59
   inductive perception and, 55–58
   mistakes in, 53–54
   reality checks for, 58–59
   reinforcing, 58–59
business model, choice of, 77
business strategy, 79–83
   questions to help in crafting, 79–81
   Sittercity.com case study, 81–82
business systems. *See* systems
business to business, common elements of best buyers for, 41
business to consumer, common elements of best buyers for, 41
business versus job, building, 9–22, 253
   freedom, paradox of, 15–17
   "hit by a bus" test and, 13–14
   Level Three Road Map and (*See* Level Three Road Map)
   loss of control, fear of, 12
   self-employment trap, escaping, 14–15
   specialness of business belief, as trap for owners, 11–12
   working harder as part of problem, 16–17
Butter, Andrea, 244–45
Byers, Dane, 221

capabilities company will need in future, 85–87
capital investments, 188
cash controls, 194–95
cash flow, 172–88
   collecting more of what is owed, 173–75
   expenses, management of, 181–82
   faster collections, 175–78
   income/expenses, predictability and consistency of, 179–81
   margins, managing, 183–85

   pricing and purchasing decisions, 186–88
   timely and accurate financials, maintaining, 178–79
CertifiedTaxCoach.com, 119–20
change, and strategic plan, 65–67
chief financial officer (CFO), 172
Circuit City, 96
Cleveland Clinic, 153
collecting more of what is owed, 173–75
   frontloading of collection efforts, 175
   invoicing, frequency of, 174–75
   parties responsible for collections, assigning, 175
   paying attention to A/R reporting, 175
   tracking what is owed, 174
collection practices
   collecting more of what is owed (*See* collecting more of what is owed)
   collections cycle, accelerating (*See* collections cycle, accelerating)
   controls for, 195
collections cycle, accelerating, 175–78
   advance payments, 176–77
   financing charge for accruing bills, use of, 177
   incentivizing advance payments, 177
   making payments, ease and convenience of, 178
   production and delivery cycles, accelerating, 177
   service or delivery, collecting at time of, 177
ColorJar
   big-picture planning process at, 68–69
   connection question for, 206
   innovation sessions at, 104–5
company culture, 212–14
   action/decision moments that illustrate way team should behave, seizing, 213
   impact on client's life or business, sharing stories illustrating, 213
   leader's establishing and shaping of, 212–14
   stressful moments, handling of, 213
   symbolic stories that transmit company values, sharing, 212
   team and, 28

values of company, clarifying, 214
compensation, 203–5
Competitive Matrix, 48–49
competitors, 45–49
   Competitive Matrix, building, 48–49
   direct, 46
   disruptive, 47–48
   indirect, 46–47
   strengths and weaknesses, identifying, 45–46
connection question, 205–7
consistency, controlling for, 156–57
control for consistency, 156–57
controller, 171–72
controls
   financial controls (*See* financial controls)
   internal (*See* internal controls)
   marketing (*See* marketing controls)
converting leads into sales, 140–45
   baseline sales system, building, 142–45
   checklist for evaluating lead-conversion challenges, 141–42
   conversion rates, calculation of, 143–44
   leveraged improvements, identifying, 144
   mapping out sales process, 143
   mini-action plan to implement leveraged improvements, creating, 144
   quarterly implementation, tracking and refining, 144–45
   scorecard for conversion points, development of, 143–44
cost per lead, 129
cost per sale, 129
cross-selling, 138–39
   margins and, 184
   stabilizing income and expense and, 181
CTI, 131, 202
culture. *See* company culture
customer relationship management (CRM) solution, 130
customers
   as funding source, 189
   real reason for doing business with you (*See* customer's real reason for doing business with you)
   retention of, and margins, 185
customer's real reason for doing business with you, 37–60, 253–54, 255
   competitors, analysis of, 45–49
   context of business, understanding, 39
   knowing customer's businesses, 38
   positioning and, 50–60
   target market, identifying, 39–45

delegating versus controlling dilemma, 29–31
deliverables, 150–52
   external, 150
   internal, 150–51
   phantom, 151, 215
   reverse phantom, 151
direct competitors, 46
discipline, and time mastery system, 244–45
disruptive competitors, 47–48
dollar sold per dollar spent on lead cost, 129–30
drive-up teller, 97
Drucker, Peter, 61

eBay, 63, 64
80-20 Rule, 231
email best practices, 245–48
   aging email before responding, 246
   auto-send-and-receive function, turning off, 246
   conversation in lieu of email, 246–47
   inappropriate emails, dealing with, 247
   mass CC or BCC, avoiding, 246
   preferences of most commonly emailed recipients, learning, 247–48
   send less email, 246
   subject lines for emails and, 245–46
   task management via email, avoiding, 247
embedded controls, 32–33
emotions, brand, 54–59
eToys.com, 111

Evernote app, 99
Executive Leadership, 113–14, 209–25
 accountability and, 214–23
 big-picture vision of company set by, 209–12
 company culture, establishing and shaping, 212–14
 Five-Pillar Audit tool to map baseline of, 114–17
 key responsibilities of, 114
 leadership team, growing and grooming, 223–25
expenses
 better pricing, negotiating for, 181
 discounts, asking for, 182
 fiscal discipline as core company value, cultivating, 182
 management of, 181–82
 stabilizing (*See* stabilizing income and expenses)
 strategic versus nonstrategic, 188
 variable versus fixed, 182
 vendors, review of and competition by, 181–82
Expert Systems, 148–60
 control for consistency, 156–57
 deliverables, defining, 150–52
 key component to refine first, mapping out, 157–59
 optimal level of expertise for each step in, determining, 153–55
 process used to create deliverables, laying out, 152–53
 quarterly reevaluation to prioritize next block of system to refine, 159–60
external deliverables, 150

FedEx, 47
Finance, 112, 171–96
 cash flow, managing, 172–88
 Chief Financial Officer (CFO), role of, 172
 components of, 171
 controller, duties of, 171–72
 financial controls to safeguard against fraud and theft, 192–96
 Five-Pillar Audit tool to map baseline of, 114–17
 funding rapid growth, sources of capital for, 188–92

 key responsibilities of, 112
 financial controls, 192–96
 accounts payable controls, 195–96
 cash controls, 194–95
 collections controls, 195
 financial records, reviews of, 194
 footprints in financial system, creating, 193–94
 money flows, having two unrelated parties involved in, 192–93
Finkel, David, 1–2, 57, 99, 127, 223–24, 234, 239–40
The Fireplace Place, 179–80
Five-Pillar Audit tool, 114–17
fixed expenses, 182
focus areas for quarterly action plans, 89–91
 criteria defining success for, 90–91
 key performance indicator (KPI), tracking, 91, 220
 Limiting Factor, pushing back, 89–90
 mitigating gravest threat as, 90
 opportunities, seizing, 90
 selecting, 89–90
focus days, 238–41
focusing on fewer, better things, 61–105
 learning to read world to build for tomorrow's marketplace, 95–105, 254
 strategic plan, creating, 63–93, 254
formalized referral systems, 132–33
formal reactivation system, 133–35
formal retention system, 135–36
format layer, of business systems, 25–27
foundation for business, building, 7–60
 base of business, building on, 23–35, 253
 business versus job, building, 9–22, 253
 customer's real reason for doing business with you, understanding, 37–60, 253–54
Fowler, Pete, 157
fraud, financial controls to safeguard against. *See* financial controls
freedom, paradox of, 15–17
frequent flyer mileage programs, 136

funding rapid growth, sources of capital for, 188–92
  customers, 189
  internal, 190–91
  investors, 191–92
  lenders, 190
  vendors, 189

Grand National Bank, 97
*Grease* (movie), 95
gross profit margins, 183–84

handoffs
  accountability and, 216
  linkages and, 168–70
Harkness, Stephanie, 86
"hit by a bus" test, 13–14
Hoffman, Jeff, 2–3, 42–44, 57, 59, 63, 95–96, 131, 133, 153, 198–99, 202–6, 234, 256–57
Hollywood Video, 96
Home Run filter, for identifying sweet spot tactics, 74–75

income, stabilizing. *See* stabilizing income and expenses
indirect competitors, 46–47
inductive perception, 55–58
In-N-Out Burger, 97
innovation sessions, 100–105
internal controls, 28–35
  control and controls distinguished, 30–31
  delegating versus controlling dilemma, 29–31
  embedded, 32–33
  examples of, 29, 33–34
  procedural, 32
  refining and redesigning of, as company grows, 34–35
  visual, 31–32
internal deliverables, 150–51
internal funding, 190–91
investors, 191–92
iPhone, 103
iPod, 96, 103
iTunes, 47, 96

Jackson, Phil, 201
Jordan, Michael, 201
Jordan, Thomas, 78–81, 219–20

Kerr, Steve, 201
key performance indicators (KPI), 217–21
  accurate feedback on regular basis, providing, 218
  easy to understand, selecting indicators that are, 218
  focus areas, tracking KPI for, 91, 220
  leading indicators, 180–81, 217–18
  mistakes companies make with respect to, 218–19
  selection of, 217–18
  visuals for, 220–21
Kim, Dr., 134–35
KPI. *See* key performance indicators (KPI)

L. H. Thompson Inc., 149–50
leadership
  executive (*See* Executive Leadership)
  supporting team as role of, 202–3
  team for, growing (*See* leadership team)
leadership team, 221–23
  authority, delegation of, 224
  company growth, and changes to, 224
  first key management hires for, 223
  as investment, 223–24, 225
  oversight of, 224–25
  quarterly action plans for, 225
lead-generation and conversion. *See* Sales/Marketing
leading indicators, 180–81, 217–18
learning to read world to build for tomorrow's marketplace, 95–105, 254
  innovation sessions, 100–105
  music industry's failure to, 95–96
  new inputs, exposure to, 98–100
  trends, cross-industry/geographic boundaries movement of, 96
lenders, 190
Level One business (start-ups), 4, 14, 18
Level Three business (rapid growth/exit stage company), 4, 14–15
Level Three Road Map, 4, 17–22
  determining where your are in business lifecycle, quiz for, 21–22
  Five-Pillar Audit tool and, 114–17

## INDEX

Level One, 18
Level Three, 21
Level Two, 18–20
Level Two business (owner-reliant company), 4, 14, 15, 18–20
   owner-reliant business phase of, 19–20
   post-launch start-up phase, 18–19
   rapid-growth phase of, 20
leverage points of business, 71–79
   Limiting Factor, identifying and pushing back, 73–75, 89–90, 255
   S-O-O-T Review of, 71–73
   strategic decisions, examination of, 75–79
   Sweet Spot Analysis Tool and, 74–75, 76, 255
Lexus, 55, 56
Limiting Factor, 73–75, 89–90, 255
linkages, 168–70
   boundaries for handoffs, establishing, 169
   explicit handoffs, 169
   moving start, getting, 169
   needs of both halves of handoff, determining, 169–70
   processing out steps in handoff, 170
loss of control, fear of, 12
Low-Hanging Fruit filter, for identifying sweet spot tactics, 74–75
loyalty programs, 136
Lyle, Jennifer, 47

margins, 183–85
   gross profit, 183–84
   low-margin clients, products or services, cutting, 185
   operating profit, 183
   retention of customers and, 185
   scrap, spoilage and waste, avoiding, 185
   upgrading of customers to higher-value products or services, 184
   up-selling and cross-selling to increase average unit of sale, 184
   velocity (turnaround time) and, 184
marketing calendar, 126–27
marketing channel, choice of, 78
marketing collateral, standardization of, 127–28
marketing controls, 126–30
   customer relationship management (CRM) solution, 130
   marketing calendar, 126–27
   marketing collateral, standardization of, 127–28
   scoreboard for marketing efforts, 128–30
Marketing Markers, 41–42, 43
market position. *See* positioning
Maui By Design, 244
Maui Mastermind
   branding and, 57
   connection question for, 206
   target market needs, mapping out, 44
   why company is in business, determining, 68
McAnn, Jim, 205–6
Microsoft Dynamics, 130
Molina, Dominique, 119–20
momentum, and strategic plan, 65–67
music industry, 95–96

new inputs, exposure to, 98–100
'N Sync, 95

obstacles
   to scaling (*See* obstacles to scaling)
   S-O-O-T Review and, 72
obstacles to scaling, 107–225, 254
   Executive Leadership pillar and, 113–14, 209–25
   Finance pillar and, 112, 171–96
   Operations pillar and, 111–12, 147–70
   Sales/Marketing pillar and, 109–11, 119–45
   Team pillar and, 113, 197–208
1-800-Flowers, 205–6, 222
operating profit margins, 183
Operations, 111–12, 147–70
   Expert Systems, building, 148–60
   Five-Pillar Audit tool to map baseline of, 114–17
   key responsibilities of, 112
   linkages, reinforcing, 168–70
   Ultimate Business System (UBS), building, 160–67
opportunities, 72
opportunity cost, 67, 75

# INDEX    273

Oracle, 130

Pacific Plastics and Engineering, 86
Padda, Gurpreet, 235
Pareto, Vilfredo, 231
Pareto's Principle, 231
parking space theory of positioning, 50–53
   examples of, 51
   factors relevant to determining, 50
   questions to help pick best parking space for business, 52
   as single thing you want to be known for, 51
Peachtree, 193
Peregrine Mobile Bottling, 78–79
personal assistant, 248–49
phantom deliverables, 151, 215
Pippen, Scottie, 201
policies and procedures manuals, 27–28, 160
positioning, 50–60
   branding and, 50, 53–59
   choice of, trial for, 78
   parking space theory of, 50–53
Prego Spaghetti Sauce, 51
Priceline.com, 2, 257
   branding and, 57
   cross-selling at, 138–39
   parking space of, 51
   profiling of target customers at, 43–44
   why company is in business, determining, 68
Priceline Yard Sale, 57
pricing, choice of, 77
pricing decisions, 186–88
   changing how you charge, 187
   clues pricing may be too low, 187
   review of, 186–87
Prime Time block, scheduling, 242–43
procedural controls, 32
process layer, of business systems, 25
product, choice of, 77
product pathway, choice of, 78
profile of target customer, building, 42–43
purchasing decisions, 186–88
push days, 238–41

qualitative goals of future business, 69–70
quantitative goals of future business, 69–70
quarterly action plans, 66–67, 87–93, 255–56
   criteria defining success for focus areas, 90–91
   example of, 88
   focus areas, selecting and tracking, 89–91
   innovation sessions, 100–105
   key action steps and milestones, laying out, 91–93
   key performance indicator (KPI)
      for focus areas, tracking, 91, 220
      for leadership team, 225
   responsibility for action steps, assigning, 92
QuickBooks, 193

reactivation system, 133–35
RedTag.com, 2
referral systems, 132–33
reinforcing brands, 58–59
re-selling, 139–40
Results Rule, 242
retention system, 135–36
reverse leverage, 83–85
reverse phantom deliverables, 151

St. Francis of Assisi, 227
sales database, 130
salesforce.com, 130
Sales/Marketing, 109–11, 119–45
   additional sales, tactics to generate, 131–40
   baseline lead-generation system, building, 124–26
   checklist for evaluating lead-generation challenges, 121–22
   converting leads into sales, 140–45
   Five-Pillar Audit tool to map baseline of, 114–17
   key responsibilities of, 110–11
   marketing controls and, 126–30
Sales/Marketing (cont.)
   weaknesses in lead generation, evaluating, 120–23
sales model, choice of, 78
scaling principles

base of business, building on, 23–35, 253
business versus job, building, 9–22, 253
customer's real reason for doing business with you, understanding, 37–60, 253–54
learning to read world to build for tomorrow's marketplace, 95–105, 254
obstacles to growth, removing, 109–18, 254
strategic plan, creating and executing on, 63–93, 254
time to scale business, 229–50, 254
scoreboard for marketing efforts, 128–30
  cost per lead, 129
  cost per sale, 129
  dollar sold per dollar spent on lead cost, 129–30
scrap, 185
self-employment trap, escaping, 14–15
service, choice of, 77
Singular Goal, 69–70
Sittercity.com, 81–82
Snyder, Harry, 97
S-O-O-T (Strengths-Obstacles-Opportunities-Threats) Review, 71–73
specialness of business belief, as trap for owners, 11–12
spoilage, 185
stabilizing income and expenses, 179–81
  cross-selling or up-selling opportunities, look for, 181
  external events, monitoring of, 180
  leading indicators, monitoring, 180–81
  long-term contracts, use of, 180
Stop Doing list, 85, 243–44
storage technology for UBS, selection of, 164–67
strategic decisions, examination of, 75–79
  branding, choice of, 78
  business model, choice of, 77
  marketing channel, choice of, 78
  positioning, choice of, 78
  pricing, choice of, 77
  product, choice of, 77
  product pathway, choice of, 78
  sales model, choice of, 78
  service, choice of, 77
  target market, choice of, 76–77
strategic plan, 63–93, 254
  big-picture planning process, 68–71
  business strategy, choosing, 79–83
  capabilities company will need in future and, 85–87
  change and momentum, balancing, 65–67
  innovation sessions, 100–105
  investment of key resources defines actual strategy, 83–84
  iterative model of, 65
  leverage points of business, determining, 71–79
  long-term plan, annual review of, 66
  opportunity cost and, 67, 75
  purpose of, 64
  quarterly action plans, 66–67, 87–93, 255–56
  as recurring activity, 64–65
  reverse leverage and, 83–85
  Stop Doing list, creating, 85
strengths, 72
SugarCRM, 130
Sweet Spot Analysis Tool, 74–75, 76, 255
Swissair, 96
switching costs, 187
systems, 24–28
  Expert Systems (*See* Expert Systems)
  format layer of, 25–27
  internal controls (*See* internal controls)
  list of potential formats for packaging of, 26–27
  policies and procedures manual, creation of, 27–28
  process layer of, 25
  purpose and components of, 24
  refining and redesigning of, as company grows, 34–35
  team members interaction with, as feedback on, 25–26

# INDEX

Ultimate Business System (UBS). *See* Ultimate Business System (UBS)

Tapley, Klayton, 179–80
target market, 39–45
 business to business, common elements of best buyers for, 41
 business to consumer, common elements of best buyers for, 41
 fastest to close customers, identifying, 40
 Marketing Markers, 41–42, 43
 Maui Mastermind case study, 44
 non-target market, identifying, 42
 profile of target customer, building, 42–43
 prompts for identifying, 40–42
 tool for mapping out psychological and emotional needs of, 44–45
target market, choice of, 76–77
Team, 28, 113, 197–208
 achievements, immediacy and authenticity in rewarding, 201–2
 common sense, and employee manual, 198–99
 company culture and, 28
 company where talent wants to work, creating, 200–202
 compensation of, 203–5
 connecting team with company goals, 205–7
 Five-Pillar Audit tool to map baseline of, 114–17
 ideal team member, defining and profiling of, 200
 key responsibilities of, 113
 leadership and, 202–3
 managing team members individually, 200–201
 poor performers, removing, 201
 selectivity in hiring talent, 200
 sharing information with, 201
 standards for, 201
 Three Best Ideas Tool and, 207–8
theft, financial controls to safeguard against. *See* financial controls
*This Old House* (TV show), 34
Thomson, Brian, 176
threats, 73

Three Best Ideas Tool, 207–8
time mastery system, 229–50, 254
 *A/B/C/D* activities, identifying, 234–36
 accountability and, 244–45
 bottom line task to-do list, 241–42
 discipline and, 244–45
 *D*-level activities, focusing on and eliminating, 237–38
 email best practices and, 245–48
 focus days, 238–41
 Pareto's Principle and, 231
 personal assistant, hiring, 248–49
 Prime Time block, scheduling, 242–43
 push days, 238–41
 reinvesting saved *D* time in *A* and *B* activities, 238–41
 Results Rule and, 242
 Stop Doing list, creating, 243–44
 Time Value Matrix and, 232–33, 255
 value you create for business, identifying, 231–36
Time Value Matrix, 232–33, 255
Toyota Prius, 51
trailing indicators, 218

uBid.com, 2
 formal reactivation system at, 133
 profiling of target customers at, 42–43
 strategic plan of, 63–64
Ultimate Business System (UBS), 160–67
 company culture of creating and using, 167
 existing systems and tools, renaming and storing, 163–64
 organizational hierarchy for UBS file folders, creating, 161–63
 policies and procedures manuals distinguished, 160
Ultimate Business System (UBS) (*cont.*)
 prioritized list of systems to build in current quarter, creating, 163–64
 sample outline for, 162–63

## 276 INDEX

storage technology for, 164–67
team training and involvement in, 167
up-selling, 137–38
   margins and, 184
   stabilizing income and expense and, 181
U.S. Postal Service, 47

value you create for business, identifying, 231–36
variable expenses, 182
vendors
   expenses, review of and competition by vendors to reduce, 181–82
   as funding source, 189

Virgin, 55
visual controls, 31–32

Walmart, 51
waste, 185
Wooden, John, 230
www.ScaleYourBusinessToolKit.com, 6, 256, 261–64

Zappos.com, 45–46, 51, 59
Zoho, 130

# A FINAL MESSAGE FOR BUSINESS OWNERS WHO WANT TO GET THEIR LIVES BACK FASTER

Dear Reader,

Most business owners want growth, but they hold themselves back because they fear that to get that growth they'll have to sacrifice their lives.

They point to statistics like the Wells Fargo/Gallup Small Business Index which says the average small business owner works 52 hours a week, with over 57 percent of them working six days a week, and more than 20 percent of them working *seven* days a week.

But it doesn't have to be that way. You don't have to brute force your way to business growth through more hours and effort.

You've been introduced to a more elegant way to grow your business in *Scale*.

As you've learned in the pages of this book, the only way to *sustainably* grow your company is to reduce its reliance on you, the owner. Done right, you get growth *and* you get your life back.

For going on 20 years now we've helped our business coaching clients around the world build thriving owner-independent companies. On average, our clients enjoy an annual growth rate *five times higher* than the average privately held company in the United States while at the same time increasing their owner independence by 97.4 percent. And I wanted to invite you to explore the possibility of working together to help you scale your company and get your life back.

I do want to caution you: If you're looking for a magic bullet, the Business Coaching Program is not for you. It's for serious business owners who want to legitimately break through to the next level and build a thriving, owner-independent company.

Imagine tapping into this proven program. No more guessing; no more struggling; no more doubting yourself or your decisions. Just consistent growth and greater time freedom.

For years this is exactly what we've been doing—helping business owners just like you build a business, not a job.

And the most important thing of all is that we helped them do it by working *fewer hours.*

How can we be so confident that we can help you get great results? That's a fair question. And my answer is simple: We've done it ourselves—again and again.

Remember, our coaching team has built dozens of multimillion-dollar companies from the ground up. We've faced the same challenges you're facing: creating a winning business strategy, dealing with employee and vendor issues, controlling costs, and growing sales.

In fact, over the past 25 years, **the Maui coaches and advisors have personally scaled companies with an aggregate value of $63** *billion.*

But more important than the fact that we've done it in our own business lives is the impact our ideas and program have had on the lives of other business owners like you.

In the pages of this book you've already met *dozens* of our successful clients and learned about the dramatic difference working together has had on their businesses and their lives. What they all have in common is that they've recognized that being part of a *structured,* proven program is the fastest and surest way to succeed. And now it's your turn.

If you're serious about intelligently scaling and building an owner-independent company, and want a structured, proven program to help you do it the best way possible, I urge you to go online to see if your business qualifies for a *free* one-to-one business coaching session. I'm not sure whether your business is a fit for the program, but I do know that there is only one way to find out—go to **www.MauiMastermind.com/scalecoaching** right now.

If your business qualifies, we'll schedule a FREE 90-minute business coaching session focused on how to sustainably grow your company and get your life back. This private, one-to-one call is an actual *working session* on your business. We'll do a deep dive into your business and map out the best way to grow it. In fact, we'll do this session as if you were already one of our business coaching clients so that you can get a real sense of what it would be like to work with us, and we can get a real feel for what it would be like to work with you as a client if we invited you into the program.

There is no cost or obligation on either of our parts. Past experience has shown us that this is the most accurate way to try out the fit.

Either way, you'll leave the session with a greater sense of clarity about the best strategy to grow your company, including the precise leverage points and concrete action steps to take.

Don't miss out on this opportunity. The Business Coaching Program was designed to give you the structure *and* the accountability, the map *and* the upgraded peer group, the direction *and* the feedback that you need to take your business to the next level.

You don't have to go it alone out there. Together, we will make certain that you'll succeed and reach your business goals.

Sincerely,

*David Finkel*

David Finkel
CEO
Maui Mastermind

P.S. Stop building your business in isolation and let our team coach and guide you. Go to **MauiMastermind.com/scalecoaching** right *now*.

# LISTEN TO WHAT OUR CLIENTS SAY...

### Tom Santilli
*xByte, Inc.*

"Before Maui I was successful (financially) with a business doing $5 million a year in sales with over $1 million in profit per year. But I was working myself to death to do it. I was working 80 hours a week and the stress was killing my health, my family, and just about everything else. Here I am seven years later and **my company has grown fourfold to over $20 million a year in sales, and over $3 million in profits**— and best of all, I'm literally not needed to do anything for the business anymore."

### Jennifer Lyle
*STS, Inc.*

"The results speak for themselves: Last year **my business generated 9 times the operating profit**... I have more time off, am more relaxed, and have a much better quality of life. It's really hard to beat that return on my investment."

### Paul Robinson
*Ensunet*

"Before Maui I was the typical lone-wolf business owner carrying everything on my shoulders. Now I have a peer group to challenge my thinking and push me to think bigger. **Since joining the program we've literally grown 1,100%!**"

### Ron McVety
*Facts Engineering*

"I knew I wanted to step back to a more passive role in the business. I'd been leading the company for over 35 years and wanted to make sure the next generation of leaders was ready to lead FACTS Engineering into the future. We've been using the Maui business coaching system for five years now and during that time **we've doubled our profits and increased our growth rate by 300%**. I'm a believer in the program because I have seen the direct impact on my company. So when they launched the leadership program we immediately signed up our key leaders. Over the last two years it has been one of my biggest joys to see our top leaders grow into bigger roles, taking on many of the responsibilities that for years I had been the only one capable of doing."

### Dr. Shekhar Challa, MD
*Kansas Medical Clinic*

"**Our medical practice has been working with the Maui team now for roughly 36 months. Our top of line revenue increased by $4.1 million and our profits have grown too**. But the biggest impact from the program has been the growth in our leadership team as we've reduced our reliance on me and our practice COO. We have plans to continue to scale our multi-disciplinary, state-wide practice further, and the business coaching program has been a valuable resource helping us to do it. I encourage any other medical group to get their help, both to grow your practice and to increase your personal time freedom."

## See If Your Business Qualifies for a FREE Business Coaching Session:
MauiMastermind.com/ScaleCoaching

Made in the USA
Las Vegas, NV
15 August 2025

26405614R00164